PORTFOLIO THEORY, 25 YEARS AFTER

STUDIES IN THE
MANAGEMENT SCIENCES

Editor in Chief

ROBERT E. MACHOL

Volume 11

NORTH-HOLLAND PUBLISHING COMPANY – AMSTERDAM · NEW YORK · OXFORD

PORTFOLIO THEORY, 25 YEARS AFTER

Edited by

E. J. ELTON
M. J. GRUBER

Essays in Honor of Harry Markowitz

1979

NORTH-HOLLAND PUBLISHING COMPANY – AMSTERDAM · NEW YORK · OXFORD

This North-Holland/TIMS series is a continuation of the Professional Series in the Management Sciences, edited by Martin K. Starr

North-Holland ISBN for this volume: 0 444 85279 4

Reprinted from TIMS Studies in the Management Sciences, Volume 11

Published by:
NORTH-HOLLAND PUBLISHING COMPANY
AMSTERDAM • NEW YORK • OXFORD

Sole distributors for the U.S.A. and Canada:
ELSEVIER NORTH-HOLLAND, INC.
52 VANDERBILT AVENUE
NEW YORK, NY 10017

Printed in The Netherlands

PREFACE

Twenty five years have elapsed since the initial appearance of Markowitz's pioneering work on portfolio theory. Few articles have had as much impact. His initial article and subsequent book:

(a) revolutionized the theory and teaching of investments,
(b) created the central model in the economics of uncertainty,
(c) provided the basis for the development of general equilibrium models which have restructed corporate financial theory.

Markowitz not only developed the essence of modern portfolio theory, he developed one of the first algorithms for solving the problem and discussed many of the extensions that were subsequently developed. Some of these suggestions were the use of the single index model, the use of dynamic programming for solving the multi-period problem, the geometric mean as an objective function and approximation theorems for differing utility functions.

It is impossible in a single volume to cover of the areas of research which have been an outgrowth of Markowitz's pioneering work. We have had to pick and choose in an attempt to find articles which are both significant in contribution and diverse in subject matter. We have included articles dealing with such different subjects as the implementation of portfolio selection and multi-period general equilibrium models. In addition, the articles included utilize methodologies covering a wide range of both theory and empirical applications

We, the editors, dedicate this book to Harry Markowitz, for his contribution to finance and economics, and for creating a new field in which we have enjoyed teaching and doing research.

TABLE OF CONTENTS

TIMS Studies in the Management Sciences 11 (1979) 1–6
©North-Holland Publishing Company

INTRODUCTION

In this volume we have compiled a series of articles that are at the frontier of the fields of portfolio analysis and general equilibrium theory. Almost all of the articles have implications for optimum investment decisions and the pricing of risky assets. That these implications are not always consistent with each other should not be surprising in what is still a relatively new and evolving area of research. Part one of this book deals primarily with the design of optimal portfolios. Part two deals with general equilibrium models. To the extent that general equilibrium implies that prices are not predictable, many of the techniques described in part one are un-necessary. On the other hand, to the extent that participants in the market possess any predictive ability or want to ascertain whether they have economically relevant predictive ability, the techniques of part one become relevant and promise a real return.

While parts one and two deal with problems over a single time horizon, part three re-examines these problems in a multi-period framework. The multi-period formulation of the problem is relevant for many situations. However, there is a cost in moving to a multi-period framework. In particular there is a need to make stronger simplifying assumptions, a great increase in the complexity of the analysis, and a diminished ability to arrive at tractable solutions.

Research continues in each of the areas discussed in parts one, two, and three. At this time we can't predict which set of models will eventually become the dominant set, if any, but we do know that important implications for the behavior of investors and capital markets will continue to be produced by researchers in all three areas. Hopefully, this volume will give the reader sufficient knowledge of the types of research being undertaken in all three areas that he can continue to follow the evolving structure of portfolio and capital market theory and perhaps contribute to it. In the rest of this introduction we shall briefly discuss each of the three parts of this book.

Part one of this volume deals with the design of optimal portfolios. All of these papers utilize the mean variance framework of Markowitz or extensions of it. In very practical terms, if the investor believes that he possesses information about the behavior of the returns of individual securities, how can he optimally design a portfolio of securities given his information about each security? Part one has two sections. The first deals with techniques for the selection of optimal portfolios. The second deals with some empirical evidence bearing on the characteristics of optimal portfolios.

The first section of part one contains three papers. The first two papers deal with the selection of optimal portfolios when outcomes can meaningfully be analyzed in terms of means and variances. The first paper by Elton, Gruber and Padberg demonstrates that when the correlation structure of returns can be meaningfully characterized by a reasonably general form of a multi-index model, the portfolio problem can be solved quite simply, without resorting to quadratic programming (or a linear approximation to the quadratic programming solution). Perhaps of more importance than the saving in computation time is the fact that the solution technique reveals that a unique metric exists which can be used to rank all securities. This metric should have wide appeal because it has an intuitively appealing explanation and its existence means that all securities can be ranked (by desirability for inclusion in the optimal portfolio) before the job of designing the optimal portfolio is begun. This paper is one of a series of papers by the authors (see Bibliography at the end of article) which develops simple rules for determining optimal portfolios under alternative assumptions about the nature of the correlation structure of security returns.

The second paper in this section by Rudd and Rosenberg discusses an alternative framework for the solution of another version of the portfolio problem. This paper is interesting for it reviews previous algorithms for the solution to portfolio problems. It then examines alternative formulations of the problem placing emphasis on the role of market and nonmarket risk, transaction costs, limits on the size of the holdings of any security, and goals as to the dividend yield on the portfolio. The authors show how Von Hohenbalken's mathematical programming algorithm can be used to reach solutions to the optimal portfolio problem even in the presence of institutional factors and preferences such as those listed above.

The last paper in this part by Bawa and Chakrin examines the portfolio problem under an alternative assumption about the relevant "space" in which portfolio analysis should be performed. The authors show that if returns are lognormally distributed (as some of the empirical evidence indicate) a meaningful formulation and solution to the portfolio problem exists. The relevant space for this analysis is defined in terms of mean and logarithmic variance rather than mean and variance. However, the authors show how existing algorithms can be used to define the frontier of all efficient portfolios. The final part of this paper deals with topics of general equilibrium which are treated more extensively in part two. The authors show that even in the case of multivariate lognormal returns, a two-fund separation theorem holds and a form of the capital asset pricing model exists, though it is different from the form proposed when mean variance analysis is deemed appropriate.

Part two of the first section contains three papers which deal with important empirical issues in portfolio theory. The first paper by Levy examines the question of whether "diversification pays." The impact of diversification on the *variance* of portfolio returns has been examined on both a theoretical and empirical level. Levy studies the question on a much broader basis by examining total distributions and their economic properties. More specifically, he employs the well-known theorems on second order stochastic dominance to see if larger portfolios will be preferred by all risk averse investors. His results, while in the main consistent with past studies do point out that the payoff from diversification are in part a property of the investor's time horizon and that for long time horizons, larger portfolios do not necessarily dominate smaller portfolios.

The second paper by Frankfurter and Phillips also has implications for the effect of size on portfolio risk. The authors are treating a special case of a general problem: what is the effect of employing estimated rather than true parameters for the selection of portfolios? The authors study portfolio selection with the context of a model that assumes the only source of interaction between securities comes about because of a common response to market movements. They recognize that errors exist in the estimates of the parameters of this model. The authors perform simulations based on realistic parameters (estimated from historical data) and find that errors in predicting (measuring) the true parameters of the model lead to an overestimate of return, an underestimate of risk, and a change in the perceived size of optimal portfolios. These results are consistent with suggestions in the theoretical literature and they highlight the fact that these influences are of an economically significant order of magnitude.

While the theory of portfolio choice can equally easily be applied to nominal or real returns, almost all applications of the theory and tests of the theory have been conducted on nominal returns. This is true despite the fact that some economic theory would suggest real returns as the relevant variable. Brenner and Sarnat examine the differences in optimal portfolios when returns are measured in real and nominal terms. After examining factors affecting the relationship between real and nominal returns, they generate efficient portfolios in terms of both real and nominal returns and compare their performance.

One of the major outgrowths of the mean variance portfolio theory of Markowitz has been the development of a theory of the pricing of risky assets. No area in finance has evolved as rapidly in the last decade. An examination of the categories used to classify articles in the *Journal of Finance* shows that ten years ago capital asset pricing models were not considered important enough to be separately identified. By 1977, over 100 articles categorized under the heading of Capital Asset Pricing Models were submitted to the *Journal of Finance*. These represented about 20% of all submissions. Capital asset pricing models are prominently discussed in most new texts, are being used by business firms in investment decisions, and are frequently discussed in regulatory proceedings.

Since the capital asset pricing theory has evolved from the pioneering work of Harry Markowitz, and since it receives so much attention from researchers and practitioners, it seems appropriate to include it in this volume. This part of the book is divided into two sections: one dealing with theory, and one dealing with empirical research. The first section discusses two questions that are important in the development of CAPM models.

The paper by Litzenberger and Ramaswamy derives the necessary assumptions about the return generation process for the two fund separation theorem to hold.

Two fund separation exists when all investors can select a portfolio from two funds (groups of assets) that are at least as desirable as any portfolio selected from the full population of assets. The existence of two fund separation is important for investors and mutual fund managers. It also has important implications for CAPM theory because if two fund separation holds, then one of the standard versions of the capital asset pricing models holds (the Zero Beta Version). Litzenberger and Ramaswamy conclude their article with a discussion of the conditions for two fund separation to be generalized to k fund separation where $k > 2$.

The second paper in this section is by Eric Lindenberg. He presents a derivation of a new capital asset pricing model. Standard capital asset pricing models assume that the security transactions of all investors are small enough that each investor can act as if he can buy and sell all the securities he desires at the market price. Lindenberg argues that for large mutual or pension fund this assumption may be invalid. Lindenberg derives a capital asset pricing model under the assumption that some investors may be large enough to affect security prices by their actions. He compares the implications of this model with the standard model for both the pricing of risky assets and the investment behavior of large institutions.

The second part of this section deals with the empirical testing and use of capital asset pricing models. The paper by Carleton discusses the use of the capital asset pricing model for estimating the required rate of return in regulating proceedings. Carleton argues that obtaining reasonable estimates of the parameters of the CAPM model is so difficult and the errors associated with even the best estimates are so large that the CAPM model is of limited use in regulating proceedings.

The paper by Dick Roll is concerned with procedures for testing whether a portfolio is *ex ante* mean variance efficient. No investor would deliberately choose a portfolio that was dominated by a second. However, after the fact most *ex ante* efficient portfolios are likely to turn out to be dominated. It is important to an investor whose portfolio is *ex post* dominated to know whether this occurred by chance or because his portfolio was poorly chosen. There is another reason why the *ex ante* efficiency of a portfolio is important. It has been shown that if the market portfolio is *ex ante* efficient, then security prices must be determined by a capital asset pricing model. Roll presents a number of procedures for the very difficult econometric problem of testing a portfolio's *ex ante* efficiency. In addition, he discusses the reasonableness of several empirical tests contained in the literature.

The final paper in this section shows why the cross-correlation in security price return series reported by some authors is not inconsistent with the existence of a capital asset pricing model. Cohen, Maier, Schwartz and Whitcomb assume that shifts in bids and asks are independent through time but show how a common change of information can result in serially cross-correlated security returns. A number of authors testing CAPM models have reported serial correlation in indexes and deterioration in R^2 as data from short-time intervals are used. This paper provides an explanation for these findings.

The last part of this book deals with multi-period analysis. Most investors' portfolio problems are multi-period. Almost all individuals invest and save over a number of periods. Institutions also have a multi-period horizon. However, most portfolio theory and capital asset pricing theory assumes an investor has a single time horizon. The important question is under what conditions is the single period decision equivalent to the first decision of more realistic multi-period problem and when it is not equivalent, how must the analysis by modified. This section is especially appropriate for this volume both because of its importance in recent research and because much of this research follows Markowitz's suggestions in his pioneering book.

In the first paper in this section Hakansson shows that as the number of periods grows, the set of investment policies that is optimum in the first period narrows drastically. Investors with very different utility functions will tend to follow the same policies. It is tempting to suggest that the policy they should follow is one with little probability of ruin. Unfortunately, as Hakansson shows, this is incorrect, and many investors who maximize expected utility will follow policies with high probability of ruin. Hakansson also discusses the time path of capital accumulation over time, the behavior of expected utility, and the special role played by the growth optimal model (a policy with low probability of ruin).

The second paper, by Brodt, uses the Markowtiz mean variance model to analyze the asset and liability choices of commercial banks. He incorporates a multi-period framework and a rich post-optionality analysis. The model is very flexible and can be easily applied by bankers.

The next paper by Sethi, Gordon and Inghan considers the portfolio problem in a multi-period welfare state. If welfare programs exist, then an investor has a floor below which his investments cannot fall. The existence of welfare programs influences the optimal investment and consumption behavior. As shown in this paper, the effect of welfare on the investor's optimal investment program depends critically on the number of periods until the investor's horizon and the investor's wealth level.

The last two papers in this section deal with the capital asset pricing model in a multi-period context. The first paper by Richard presents a multi-period CAPM model. In a seminal paper in 1973, Merton pointed out that the investment opportunity set changed through time due to the stochastic nature of the short term interest rate. He showed that the standard one-period CAPM must be modified to accommodate this uncertainty and derived an alternative model. Richard extends the Merton model to include any source of uncertainty in the investor's opportunity set. In addition, he extends the model to incorporate stochastic earnings, progressive taxation, and state dependent utility functions.

The final paper, by Stapleton and Subrahmanyan, uses a multi-period CAPM model to analyze the optimal investment decisions of the firm. Previous work utilizing the CAPM as a framework for investment decisions either utilized the single period model or made an assumption that the single period model holds sequentially over time. Subrahmanyan and Stapleton show that this latter is inconsistent with multiperiod theory and derive a model that is consistent with this theory.

We hope that this volume will serve to point out some of the important areas of research that have followed from Markowitz's pioneering work. We know that the different areas, methodologies, and assumptions contained in these articles will be a source of puzzlement to some readers, but we hope they well be a source of inspiration to others.

TIMS Studies in the Management Sciences 11 (1979) 7–19
© North-Holland Publishing Company

SIMPLE CRITERIA FOR OPTIMAL PORTFOLIO SELECTION:
THE MULTI-INDEX CASE

Edwin J. ELTON, Martin J. GRUBER and Manfred W. PADBERG
New York University

Modern portfolio theory dates from Markowitz's poioneering article [10] and subsequent book |9]. Since that time a major effort has been expended on simplifying the amount and type of input, as well as computational procedures, needed to perform portfolio analysis. Perhaps the major breakthrough in simplifying inputs came with Sharpe's development of the single index model. For the first time input data was reduced to a manageable size. However, a complex quadratic programming (or linear programming approximation (Sharpe [12]) still had to be solved in order to select optimum portfolios. In addition, the reasons why a stock entered or did not enter into an optimal portfolio was extremely difficult to relate to portfolio managers.

Recently a series of papers have shown, under alternative sets of assumptions, that extremely simple techniques exist for solving the portfolio calculation problem without resorting to mathematical programming and that these techniques result in the development of criteria for the inclusion of stocks in a portfolio which are easily understood and accepted by portfolio managers. Most of these papers have assumed that the assumptions of the Sharpe single index model are an accurate description of reality. [1] Elton, Gruber and Padberg [3] discuss the case where unlimited lending and borrowing are allowed at a riskless rate of interest and the case where lending and borrowing are disallowed both with and without shortselling. Treynor and Black [15] discuss the case where lending and borrowing are allowed at the riskless rate of interest, unlimited short selling is allowed, and a market security exists.

In recent years increased attention has been paid to modifications of the Sharpe single index model. In particular, the fact that residuals from the single index model are not uncorrelated but rather follow a correlation structure that can be explained by industry influences or other broad economic influences has led to the develop-

---

[1] In addition, Elton, Gruber and Padberg [4] have also explored simple portfolio algorithms with alternative simplifications of the covariance structure. One particular model analyzed was Cohen and Pogue's multi-index model. The Cohen and Pogue model assumes that the coefficient associated with the market index is a constant times the coefficient associated with the industry index and the constant is constrained to be the same for all members of the same industry. This leads to results which are simpler but less general than those in this paper.

ment of multi-index models. [2] In this paper we will show that optimal portfolios can be constructed quite simply (without the use of mathematical programming) when a particular type of multi-index model is used to describe the return characteristics of stocks and portfolios. We shall examine three cases. First we shall examine portfolio selection among individual securities when unlimited short selling is allowed. Then we shall continue the assumption of short selling but shall introduce a security called the market which has zero residual risk. Finally, we shall disallow short selling. Throughout the paper we shall assume unlimited borrowing and lending at a riskless rate of interest. Elsewhere [5] we have shown how a method of analysis developed under riskless borrowing and lending can be extended to the case where these transactions are disallowed. The same procedure could easily be applied here.

1. The multi-index model

In this section we shall assume that the return on any stock can be related to a market index plus a second index which characterizes its industry or economic sector. Furthermore, we shall treat the market index and economic indices as orthogonal to one another. Sharpe [13, p. 127] shows how a set of nonorthogonal indices can always be reduced to a set of orthogonal indices. Thus the orthogonality assumption should not trouble the reader. Let us assume that we wish to select portfolios from among N stocks which are members of H industries. Then the multi-index model can be presented as:

1. $R_i = \alpha_i + \beta_i I_m + b_{ih} I_h + \epsilon_i,$
2. $I_m = A_m + \epsilon_m$
   $I_h = A_h + \epsilon_{N+h},$
3. $E(\epsilon_i \epsilon_j) = 0, \quad i = 1, ..., N, \quad j = 1, ..., N, \quad i \neq j,$
4. $E(\epsilon_i \epsilon_m) = 0, \quad i = 1, ..., N,$
5. $E(\epsilon_i \epsilon_{N+h}) = 0, \quad i = 1, ..., N, \quad h = 1, ..., H,$
6. $E(\epsilon_{N+h} \epsilon_m) = 0, \quad h = 1, ..., H,$
7. $E(\epsilon_{N+i} \epsilon_{N+h}) = 0, \quad i = 1, ..., H, \quad h = 1, ..., H,$

where

R_i = the return on security i (a random variable),
I_m = a market index,
I_h = an index for industry h,
α_i = the return on security i which is independent of the market and industry indices,

---

[2] See King [8] for an early documentation of the presence of residual correlation.

β_i = a measure of the responsiveness of security i to changes in the market index,

b_{ih} = a measure of the responsiveness of security i to changes in the index for industry h (where firm i is a member of industry h),

ϵ_i = a variable with a mean of zero and a variance of $\sigma^2_{\epsilon_i}$,

ϵ_m = a variable with a mean of zero and a variance of σ^2_m,

ϵ_{N+h} = a variable with a mean of zero and a variance of $\sigma^2_{I_h}$.

(3)–(7) characterize the approximation of our multi-index model to the variance covariance structure. These equations result from (a) the assumption of the model that the only joint movement between securities comes about because of joint movement with a market index and an industry index, and (b) the design of the industry and market indices so that they are orthogonal.

We shall show that under these assumptions we can solve for optimal portfolios with relatively simple decision criteria without resorting to mathematical programming. The solutions we present are not approximations to a quadratic programming solution; they are exact solutions.

2. Case I: Short selling allowed among all individual securities

If unlimited lending and borrowing is allowed at a riskless rate of interest (R_f) then as Lintner [7] has shown, the optimal portfolio to hold is that portfolio which has the highest ratio of excess return to standard deviation. The problem can be stated as [3]

$$\text{Maximize } \theta = \frac{\bar{R}_p - R_f}{\sigma_p}$$

where

$\bar{R}_p$ = expected return on the portfolio,

σ_p = the standard deviation of the return on the portfolio.

---

[3] Since the denominator appearing in θ is defined with respect to a positive-definite quadratic form, θ is continuously differentiable everywhere except for the point X with all coordinates $X_i = 0$ for $i = 1, ..., N$. It is not difficult, however, to verify that θ is bounded in zero. For $X \neq 0$, it follows from the Cauchy-Schwartz inequality that θ is bounded from above and that the maximum is unique up to a multiplicative factor. Consequently, the calculation outlined above produces a maximum. See also Lintner [7]. Note furthermore, that the maximum value of θ and thus the transformation of X to Z below involves a positive factor. This follows since the standard deviation and excess return of the optimal portfolio are both positive since otherwise the investor holds the riskless asset.

From the definition of the multi-index model

$$\theta = \sum_{j=1}^{N} X_i(\bar{R}_i - R_f)/[\sum_{i=1}^{N}\sum_{j=1}^{N} X_iX_j\beta_i\beta_j\sigma_m^2 + \sum_{i\in 1}\sum_{j\in 1} X_iX_jb_{i1}b_{j1}\sigma_{I_1}^2 + ...$$

$$+ \sum_{i\in H}\sum_{j\in H} X_iX_jb_{iH}\sigma_{I_H}^2 + \sum_{i=1}^{N} X_i^2\sigma_{\epsilon_i}^2]^{1/2}$$

where 1 defines the set of stocks which are members of group 1 and H defines the set of stocks which are members of group H. X_i = the fraction of funds invested in security i. [4]

To find the set of X_i's which maximize θ we take the derivative of θ with respect to each X_i and set it equal to zero. Taking the derivative, substituting in the expression $Z_i = [(\bar{R}_p - R_f)/\sigma_p^2]X_i$ and solving for Z_i yields [5]

$$Z_i = \frac{\bar{R}_i - R_f}{\sigma_{\epsilon_i}^2} - \frac{\beta_i}{\sigma_{\epsilon_i}^2}\sigma_m^2\sum_{j=1}^{N} Z_j\beta_j - \frac{b_{i1}}{\sigma_{\epsilon_i}^2}\sigma_{I_1}^2\sum_{j\in 1} Z_jb_{j1}$$

$$... - \frac{b_{iH}}{\sigma_{\epsilon_i}^2}\sigma_{I_H}^2\sum_{j\in H} Z_jb_{jH} \qquad (1)$$

We can solve for the summations in (1) quite simply. By multiplying (1) by β_i, summing over all securities and rearranging we get

$$0 = \sum_{j=1}^{N}\left(\frac{\bar{R}_j - R_f}{\sigma_{\epsilon_j}^2}\beta_j\right) - \left(1 + \sigma_m^2\sum_{j=1}^{N}\frac{\beta_j^2}{\sigma_{\epsilon_j}^2}\right)\sum_{j=1}^{N} Z_j\beta_j$$

$$- \sigma_{I_1}^2\left(\sum_{j\in 1}\frac{\beta_jb_{j1}}{\sigma_{\epsilon_j}^2}\right)\sum_{j\in 1} Z_jb_{j1} - ... - \sigma_{I_H}^2\sum_{j\in H}\frac{\beta_jb_{jH}}{\sigma_{\epsilon_j}^2}\sum_{j\in H} Z_jb_{jH}.$$

If we now multiply (1) by b_{ih}, sum over all members of group h and recognize that

---

[4] X_i can be negative for short sales. We are following Lintner's [7] suggestion in treating short sales. That is, the short seller pays any dividends which accrue to the person who lends him the stock and gets a capital gain (or loss) which is the negative of any price appreciation. In addition, the short seller is assumed to receive interest at the riskless rate on both the money loaned to the owner of the borrowed stock and the money placed in escrow when the short sale is made. See Lintner [7] for a full discussion of these assumptions. If the reader prefers the assumption that $\Sigma X_i = 1$, the analysis follows with appropriate changes in the definition of X_i.

[5] We have not constrained the sum of the X_i to equal 1. Because the equation is linear homogeneous of degree 0 we can solve for an unconstrained vector of weights and scale these weights at a latter point in the analysis in order to insure that we are fully invested.

$b_{ik} = 0$ if $k \neq h$, repeat for all possible values of h (1, ..., H) then we get H additional equations of the form

$$0 = \sum_{j \in h} \left(\frac{\bar{R}_j - R_f}{\sigma_{\epsilon_j}^2} \, b_{jh} \right) - \sigma_m^2 \sum_{j \in h} \frac{\beta_j b_{jh}}{\sigma_{\epsilon_j}^2} \sum_{j=1}^{N} Z_j \beta_j -$$

$$- \left(1 + \sum_{j \in h} \frac{b_{jh}^2}{\sigma_{\epsilon_j}^2} \sigma_{I_h}^2 \right) \sum_{j \in h} Z_j b_{jh}.$$

Note that we have a system of $H + 1$ simultaneous equations and $H + 1$ terms containing the summation of $\Sigma Z_j \beta_j$ over different limits. We can solve for these summations employing the following matrix notation.

Let

$$\gamma = \begin{bmatrix} \sum_{j=1}^{N} Z_j \beta_j \\ \sum_{j \in 1} Z_j b_{j1} \\ \vdots \\ \sum_{j \in H} Z_j b_{jH} \end{bmatrix}, \qquad K = \begin{bmatrix} \sum_{j=1}^{N} \frac{\beta_j (\bar{R}_j - R_f)}{\sigma_{\epsilon_j}^2} \\ \sum_{j \in 1} \frac{b_{j1}(\bar{R}_j - R_f)}{\sigma_{\epsilon_j}^2} \\ \vdots \\ \sum_{j \in H} \frac{b_{jH}(\bar{R}_j - R_f)}{\sigma_{\epsilon_j}^2} \end{bmatrix}$$

$$A = \begin{bmatrix} 1 + \sum_{j=1}^{H} \frac{\beta_j^2 \sigma_m^2}{\sigma_{\epsilon_j}^2} & \sum_{j \in 1} \frac{b_{j1} \beta_j \sigma_{I_1}^2}{\sigma_{\epsilon_j}^2} & \cdots & \sum_{j \in H} \frac{b_{jH} \beta_j \sigma_{I_H}^2}{\sigma_{\epsilon_j}^2} \\ \sum_{j \in 1} \frac{b_{j1} \beta_j \sigma_m^2}{\sigma_{\epsilon_j}^2} & 1 + \sum_{j \in 1} \frac{b_{j1}^2 \sigma_{I_1}^2}{\sigma_{\epsilon_j}^2} & \cdots & 0 \\ \vdots & \vdots & & \\ \sum_{j \in H} \frac{b_{jH} \beta_j \sigma_m^2}{\sigma_{\epsilon_j}^2} & 0 & \cdots & 1 + \sum_{j \in H} \frac{b_{jH}^2 \sigma_{I_H}^2}{\sigma_{\epsilon_j}^2} \end{bmatrix}.$$

Then

$$A\gamma = K$$

or

$$\gamma = A^{-1} K.$$

This system of equations can be solved explicitly. In solving a conventional port-folio problem via Lintner's [7] technique one must invert a matrix whose dimen-sion is equal to the number of securities under consideration. Here we need only invert a matrix with dimensions equal to 1 plus the number of industries under con-sideration. Here we can write (1) for a member of group h as

$$Z_i = \frac{\bar{R}_i - R_f}{\sigma_{\epsilon_i}^2} - \frac{\beta_i}{\sigma_{\epsilon_i}^2}\gamma_1 - \frac{b_{ih}}{\sigma_{\epsilon_i}^2}\gamma_{h+1}. \tag{2}$$

The formulae for each element in γ are displayed in Appendix A, where γ_h are the elements in the vector γ. Since each element in γ is independent of the optimal portfolio and all other terms in the above expression are independent of the com-position of the optimal portfolio, an optimum value of Z_i can be found for all stocks under consideration. Any stock which has a positive value for Z_i should be bought long, any which has a negative value sold short. All that remains is to scale the individual Z_i so that we are fully invested. Defining X_i^o as the proportion to invest in security i in the optimal portfolio

$$X_i^o = \frac{Z_i}{\sum\limits_{i=1}^{N} |Z_i|}.$$

Note that we have now arrived at the optimal portfolio without solving a quadratic programming problem. (2) allowed us to determine the unscaled amounts to place in each security in terms of the characteristics which were unique to that security plus a series of coefficients that were only dependent on the population of stocks being considered. The formulae for determining these coefficients is given in Appendix A.

3. The introduction of a market security

If we follow the Treynor—Black procedure of introducing a market portfolio, the results in the last section can be considerably simplified and the results of the multi-index model contrasted with the Treynor—Black results for a single index model. However before proceeding with the analysis the reader should be warned that the use of index models with a market portfolio and general equilibrium expressions contains an internal inconsistency that makes the final result at best an approximation to the exact solution given in the last section. In particular Fama (6) has shown that the use of a single index model based on a market index can not produce residuals which are independent and which have a weighted sum (residual for the market portfolio) equal to zero. If a special index is computed so that the sum of the residuals from the index is zero, the coefficients of the index model (the Beta) will be inconsistent with the capital asset pricing model and the true market portfolio will not have zero residual risk. Since the Treynor–Black analysis continues to receive attention, and since it leads to a real simplification in this case it is worthwhile to explore a multi-index model under the Treynor–Black assumptions with this appropriate warning of the approximate nature of the solution. [6]

Introducing a market portfolio with zero residual risk and calling it security N we have

$$b_{N1} = b_{N2} = \dots = b_{NH} = \sigma^2_{\epsilon_N} = 0.$$

Thus from (1) we have (before dividing through by $\sigma^2_{\epsilon_i}$)

$$\beta_N \sigma^2_m \sum_{j=1}^{N} \beta_j Z_j = \bar{R}_m - R_f$$

or since $\beta_N = 1$ we have [7]

$$\sum_{j=1}^{N} \beta_j Z_j = \frac{\bar{R}_m - R_f}{\sigma^2_m} .$$

Substituting this equation into equation (1) yields for members of group h

$$Z_i = \frac{\bar{R}_i - R_f}{\sigma^2_{\epsilon_i}} - \frac{\beta_i (\bar{R}_m - R_f)}{\sigma^2_{\epsilon_i}} - \frac{b_{ih}}{\sigma^2_{\epsilon_i}} \sigma^2_{I_h} \sum_{j \in h} b_{jh} Z_j .$$

The capital asset pricing model implies that $\bar{R}_i - R_f = \beta_i(\bar{R}_m - R_f)$. If we let α_i equal deviations from the capital asset pricing model then $\alpha_i = \bar{R}_i - R_f - \beta_i(\bar{R}_m - R_f)$. Substituting this into the above, we have [8]

$$Z_i = \frac{\alpha_i}{\sigma^2_{\epsilon_i}} - \frac{b_{ih}}{\sigma^2_{\epsilon_i}} \sigma^2_{I_h} \sum_{j \in h} b_{jh} Z_j = \frac{b_{ih}}{\sigma^2_{\epsilon_i}} \left[\frac{\alpha_i}{b_{ih}} - \sigma^2_{I_h} \sum_{j \in h} b_{jh} Z_j \right] . \tag{3}$$

We can get an expression for $\Sigma_{j \in h} Z_j b_{jh}$ by multiplying both sides of this equation by b_{ih} and summing over all members of group h. Solving this expression for

---

[6] The original problem solved by Treynor and Black has been solved without this approximation in (3).

[7] This expression can be used to solve for the amount in the market portfolio. It is

$$Z_N = \frac{\bar{R}_m - R_f}{\sigma^2_m} - \sum_{j=1}^{N-1} \beta_j Z_j.$$

[8] The first term in the right-hand side of this expression is the result found in Treynor and Black [15].

$\Sigma_{j \in h} Z_j b_{jh}$ yields

$$\sum_{j \in h} Z_j b_{jh} = \frac{\displaystyle\sum_{j \in h} \frac{b_{jh}\alpha_j}{\sigma_{\epsilon_j}^2}}{1 + \sigma_{I_h}^2 \displaystyle\sum_{j \in h} \frac{b_{jh}^2}{\sigma_{\epsilon_j}^2}}.$$

Substituting this expression in equation (3) yields

$$Z_i = \left[\frac{\alpha_i}{b_{ih}} - \frac{\sigma_{I_h}^2 \displaystyle\sum_{j \in h} \frac{b_{jh}\alpha_j}{\sigma_{\epsilon_j}^2}}{1 + \sigma_{I_h}^2 \displaystyle\sum_{j \in h} \frac{b_{jh}^2}{\sigma_{\epsilon_j}^2}} \right] \frac{b_{ih}}{\sigma_{\epsilon_i}^2}.$$

Notice that for any security i in group h the last term in brackets is a constant. Denoting the constant for any group h as θ_h this equation can be written as

$$Z_i = \frac{b_{ih}}{\sigma_{\epsilon_i}^2} \left(\frac{\alpha_i}{b_{ih}} - \theta_h \right). \qquad (4)$$

If all $b_{ih} = 0$, then examining (4) shows that the solution is identical to the solution in the single index case ([3] and [14]). In the single index case the sign of Z_i is the same as the sign of α_i. Thus in the single index case all securities with positive α_i are purchased in positive amounts above the amount already contained in the market portfolio, all securities with $\alpha_i = 0$ are purchased only as part of the market portfolio, and all securities with $\alpha_i < 0$ are sold short. [9]

From (4) if b_{ih} is greater than zero Z_i is positive only if (α_i/b_{ih}) is greater than θ_h. Thus θ_h serves the role of a cut-off rate for group h in the same way that zero served as a cut-off rate with the single index model. If $b_{ih} > 0$ then securities with (α_i/b_{ih}) greater than the cut-off rate have positive Z_i, those with (α_i/b_{ih}) equal to the cut-off rate have zero Z_i and those with (α_i/b_{ih}) less than the cut-off rate have negative Z_i. If b_{ih} is negative the reverse is true. In any case the use of the multi-index model leads to results which are different from thos produced by the use of a market portfolio in a single index model.

---

[9] It might well disturb the reader that securities will be purchased long and sold short in the same portfolio. This event is due to an internal inconsistency in the Treynor–Black model. The market portfolio is assumed to have zero residual risk while composing a portfolio by buying the stocks contained in the market portfolio would produce a portfolio with a positive residual risk. This biases the Treynor–Black result in favor of the market portfolio and thus makes it appear optimum for stocks to be bought long and solid short at the same time.

4. Short sales not allowed

If we assume that a market security exists with zero residual risk and that it is optimum for an investor to hold part of his wealth in that security, then we can derive an algorithm for solving the portfolio selection problem when short sales are not allowed. As discussed earlier, such a security cannot really exist so that at best this section should be considered an approximation to the true solution. If we restrict management by disallowing short sales we must modify the solution presented in the last section. In particular, if short selling is disallowed then we must introduce the constraints that all $X_i \geqslant 0$. This requires employing the Kuhn–Tucker conditions. Since the variance–covariance matrix is positive definite the Kuhn–Tucker conditions are both necessary and sufficient for an optimum. (See (3).) Applying the Kuhn–Tucker conditions yields for $i \in h$: [10]

$$Z_i \sigma_{\epsilon_i}^2 + \beta_i \sigma_m^2 \sum_{j=1}^{N} \beta_j Z_j + b_{ih} \sigma_{I_h}^2 \sum_{j \in h} b_{jh} Z_j + \mu_i = \bar{R}_i - R_f, \tag{5}$$

$$\mu_i Z_i = 0, \tag{6}$$

$$Z_i \geqslant 0, \quad \mu_i \geqslant 0. \tag{7}$$

Assume that the investor places some fraction of his funds in the market portfolio and that security N is the market portfolio. Then for security N, $\sigma_{\epsilon_N}^2 = 0$, $b_{Nh} = 0$ for all h, and $\mu_N = 0$. Substituting these values into (5) yields

$$\sum_{j=1}^{N} \beta_j Z_j = \frac{(\bar{R}_m - R_f)}{\beta_N \sigma_m^2}.$$

Substituting this into (5), recognizing that $b_{ih} = 0$ for $i \in h$ and $\beta_N = 1$ we have for a member of group h

$$Z_i = \frac{(\bar{R}_i - R_f) - \beta_i (\bar{R}_m - R_f)}{\sigma_{\epsilon_i}^2} - \frac{b_{ih}}{\sigma_{\epsilon_i}^2} \sigma_{I_h}^2 \sum_{j \in h} b_{jh} Z_j + \mu_i \tag{5'}$$

$$= \frac{\alpha_i}{\sigma_{\epsilon_i}^2} - \sigma_{I_h}^2 \frac{b_{ih}}{\sigma_{\epsilon_i}^2} \sum_{j \in h} b_{jh} Z_j + \mu_i.$$

Without loss of generality we can assume that we can identify all securities in group h which are included in the optimum portfolio and can call this set N_h.

---

[10] Obviously, for a member of group h, $b_{ih} = 0$ if $i \in h$. Therefore the last summation in (1) could have been radically simplified.

Multiplying equation $(5')$ by b_{ih}, recognizing that $\mu_i = 0$ for securities in the optimum portfolio, and summing over all members of the set N_h, we have

$$\sum_{j \in N_h} b_{jh} Z_j = \sum_{j \in N_h} \frac{\alpha_j b_{jh}}{\sigma_{\epsilon_j}^2} - \sigma_{I_h}^2 \sum_{j \in N_h} \frac{b_{jh}^2}{\sigma_{\epsilon_j}^2} \sum_{j \in h} b_{jh} Z_j .$$

Since $Z_j = 0$ for all securities not in the optimum portfolio $\sum_{j \in N_h} b_{jh} Z_j = \sum_{j \in h} b_{jh} Z_j$ and we have

$$\sum_{j \in h} b_{jh} Z_j = \frac{\displaystyle\sum_{j \in N_h} (\alpha_j b_{jh}/\sigma_{\epsilon_j}^2)}{1 + \sigma_{I_h}^2 \displaystyle\sum_{j \in N_h} (b_{jh}^2/\sigma_{\epsilon_j}^2)} .$$

Substituting this into equation $(5')$ yields

$$Z_i = \frac{b_{ih}}{\sigma_{\epsilon_i}^2} \left[\frac{\alpha_i}{b_{ih}} - \frac{\sigma_{I_h}^2 \displaystyle\sum_{j \in N_h} (\alpha_j b_{jh}/\sigma_{\epsilon_j}^2)}{1 + \sigma_{I_h}^2 \displaystyle\sum_{j \in N_h} (b_{jh}^2/\sigma_{\epsilon_j}^2)} \right] + \mu_i. \tag{5''}$$

The term containing the μ_i can only increase Z_i. Hence if Z_i is positive with μ_i zero a positive value of μ_i cannot make $Z_i = 0$. Thus any security with positive Z_i when $\mu_i = 0$ must be included. Correspondingly, any security with negative Z_i when $\mu_i = 0$ must be excluded.

Assume now that $b_{ih} > 0$. If $b_{ih} < 0$ or $b_{ih} = 0$, the analysis follows in an analogous way. If a security with a particular (α_i/b_{ih}) is included in the optimal portfolio all securities with higher values of (α_i/b_{ih}) must also be included in the optimal portfolio. This holds because with $b_{ih} > 0$ the sign of Z_i depends on the sign of the term in the brackets. The term in the brackets is (α_i/b_{ih}) minus a constant. Thus, if a stock with a particular (α_i/b_{ih}) has a positive Z_i all stocks with higher (α_i/b_{ih}) ratios will also have a positive Z_i. Thus all we have to do to find the securities in group h included in the optimal portfolio is rank from 1 upwards all securities in group h by (α_i/b_{ih}). Then compute a value for $(5'')$ as if the included set only contained the first security. Next we calculate $(5'')$ setting $i = 2$ and letting the included set contain the first two securities. We proceed for $i = 3, 4, \ldots$ until Z_i computed from $(5'')$ with $\mu_i = 0$ turns negative. If it turns negative for the $j + 1$st security then the included set contains the first j securities. This procedure guarantees that the Kuhn–Tucker equations pertaining to set h are met. Once the securities contained in the optimum portfolio are determined the Z_i value for all securities in the set can be found simply by calculating the Z_i for each security from $(5'')$ recognizing that the μ_i for each of these securities equals zero.

Notice that the ranking of the securities in any group h are completely independent of the securities in any other group. Furthermore, the cut-off rate for group h

and the value of Z_i for any stock in group h is completely independent of the characteristics of stocks in all other groups. In other words the selection of the stocks from any group and the relative weights that will be placed on alternative stocks within a group can be decided before the stocks from any other group are examined. This has the convenient property of allowing security analysis to be organized by groups (or industries).

The fraction of our funds which should be placed in each security can be found by recognizing that the sum of the fractions placed in all securities must equal 1 or by dividing the Z_i found for each security by the sum of the Z_i across all stocks in all groups (including the market). Once again a simple and very quick procedure has been found for designing an optimal portfolio. [11]

5. Conclusion

In this paper we have developed simple decision rules for the construction of optimal portfolios when a multi-index model is assumed to describe the variance covariance structure between securities. We have shown that both for the case where short sales are allowed and the case where they are disallowed stocks can be ranked according to their unique characteristics and simple cut-off rates found which determine both the make up and percentage composition of the optimal portfolio. The procedure described is so simple it can easily be done without the aid of a computer and it produces results which are identical to the results that would be found by solving a fully quadratic programming problem.

Appendix A

Noting that the matrix A defined in § 2 is "almost" diagonal we can solve for the expression $\Sigma_{j \in h} Z_j b_{jh}$ for group h:

$$\sum_{j \in h} Z_j b_{jh} = A_h \{ \sum_{j \in h} [b_{jh}(\bar{R}_j - R_f)/\sigma^2_{\epsilon_j}] - \sigma^2_m \sum_{j \in h} [b_{jh}\beta_j/\sigma^2_{\epsilon_j}] \sum_{j=1}^{N} Z_j\beta_j \}$$

(A-1)

---

[11] We would like once again to caution the reader that this section is based upon assumptions that cannot all hold and is therefore an approximation. The case of no short sales allowed has been solved in (3) for the case of the single index model. The manner selecting from among these models must determine whether the improvement in predicting the correlation structure which might come about from adding industry indexes to the single index model is sufficient to compensate for the approximate nature of the multi index solution. We have only included this section because a number of readers of an earlier draft believed that the solution is a useful approximation. This is not a view we necessarily share.

where

$$A_h = [1 + \sum_{j \in h} (b_{jh}^2 \sigma_{I_h}^2 / \sigma_{\epsilon_j}^2)]^{-1}. \tag{A-2}$$

Using the first equation of the system of equations we obtain the expression for $\Sigma_{j=1}^{N} Z_j \beta_j$:

$$\sum_{j=1}^{N} Z_j \beta_j = C \{ \sum_{j=1}^{N} [\beta_j (\bar{R}_j - R_f)/\sigma_{\epsilon_j}^2] - \sum_{h=1}^{H} A_h^* \sum_{j \in h} [b_{jh}(\bar{R}_j - R_f)/\sigma_{\epsilon_j}^2] \} \tag{A-3}$$

where we have set

$$A_h^* = A_h \sigma_{I_h}^2 \sum_{j \in h} [b_{jh} \beta_j / \sigma_{\epsilon_j}^2], \tag{A-4}$$

$$C = \{ 1 + \sigma_m^2 \sum_{j=1}^{N} (\beta_j^2 / \sigma_{\epsilon_j}^2) - \sigma_m^2 \sum_{h=1}^{H} A_h \sigma_{I_h}^2 (\sum_{j \in h} [b_{jh} \beta_j / \sigma_{\epsilon_j}^2])^2 \}^{-1}. \tag{A-5}$$

Substituting (A-3) into the expression (A-1) obtained for $\Sigma_{j \in h} Z_j b_{jh}$ permits one to calculate the coefficients of the vector γ explicitly.

References

[1] Edwin J. Elton and Martin J. Gruber, Estimating the dependence structure of share prices – implications for portfolio selection, Journal of Finance XXVII, No. 5 (December 1973), pp. 1203–1233.

[2] Edwin J. Elton and Martin J. Gruber, Finance As A Dynamic Process (Prentice Hall, Englewood Cliffs, New Jersey, 1975).

[3] Edwin J. Elton, Martin J. Gruber and Manfred W. Padberg, Simple criteria for optimal portfolio selection, Journal of Finance (December 1976).

[4] Edwin J. Elton, Martin J. Gruber and Manfred W. Padberg, Simple criteria for optimal portfolio selection: the multi-group case, Journal of Financial and Quantitative Analysis (September, 1977).

[5] Edwin, J. Elton, Martin J. Gruber and Manfred W. Padberg, Simple criteria for optimal portfolio selection: obtaining the full efficient frontier, Operations Research (November–December, 1977).

[6] Eugene F. Fama, Risk Return and Equilibrium: Some Clarifying Comments, Journal of Finance 23 (March, 1968), pp. 29–40.

[7] John Lintner, The valuation of risk assets on the selection of risky investments in stock portfolios and capital budgets, The Review of Economics and Statistics (February 1965), pp. 13–37.

[8] Benjamin King, Market and industry factors in stock price behavior, Journal of Business (January 1966), pp. 139–190.
[9] Harry Markowitz, Portfolio Selection (John T. Wiley and Sons, Inc., New York, 1959).
[10] Harry Markowitz, Portfolio selection, Journal of Finance (March 1952), pp. 77–91.
[11] William Sharpe, A simplified model for portfolio analysis, Management Science (January 1963), pp. 277–293.
[12] William Sharpe, A linear programming algorithm for mutual fund portfolio selection, Management Science (March 1967), pp. 499–510.
[13] William Sharpe, A linear programming approximation for the general portfolio selection problem, Journal of Financial and Quantitative Analysis (December 1971), pp. 1263–76.
[14] William Sharpe, Portfolio Theory and Capital Markets (McGraw–Hill, New York, 1970).
[15] Jack L. Treynor and Fischer Black, How to use security analysis to improve portfolio selection, Journal of Business, pp. 66–86.

TIMS Studies in the Management Sciences 11 (1979) 21–46
© North-Holland Publishing Company

REALISTIC PORTFOLIO OPTIMIZATION *

Andrew RUDD
Cornell University
and
Barr ROSENBERG
University of California, Berkeley

The paper first surveys some algorithms and approaches to portfolio management. After reviewing the goals of portfolio management and desiderata for algorithms to achieve these goals, we report extremely encouraging results with a new mathematical programming algorithm, developed by Von Hohenbalken.

We have programmed the algorithm to solve a realistic version of the optimal portfolio revision problem, taking into account bounds and targets for portfolio yield and beta, upper limits on holdings, transactions costs, and a penalty for variance of total return implemented through a realistic model of the covariances among security returns. The algorithm seems to be ideally suited for this kind of problem; it approaches the optimum utility value with unprecedented rapidity and apparent robustness, and operates in small workspace.

1. Introduction

An algorithm may be thought of as an explicitly defined procedure, which, when followed, leads to the resolution of a well defined problem. Thus a portfolio optimization algorithm obtains, through a sequence of steps, an optimal portfolio. The input is a set of goals (the utility function and constraints on permissible solutions); an investment opportunity set (the universe of available assets and their relevant characteristics); a formalization of the portfolio revision process (possibly taking into account transaction costs incurred in modifying the portfolio); and a mathematical specification of the solution sought (a desired optimum defined by a convergence criterion or possibly a search of the range of optima for alternative goals).

In § 2, the history of computerized portfolio optimization algorithms is touched upon, with special concern for the limitations that have restrained their use. The

* Support from the American National Bank and from National Science Foundation Grant GS 3306a has contributed to this research. We are indebted to the Dean Witter Foundation grant and the Institute of Business and Economic Research for assistance in preparing this paper. An earlier version of this paper was presented at the Spring Seminar of the Institute for Quantitative Research in Finance, Cambelback Inn, Scottsdale, Arizona, May 2–5, 1976.

majority of limitations have arisen in three areas: difficulty in obtaining reasonable problem specifications, excessive expense in computations, and increasingly unreasonable problem specifications stemming from a compromise intended to further reduce computation cost.

Then, in § 3, we introduce a fresh approach to the problem. Little that is new is added to the problem formulation; rather, certain simplifying assumptions that might be regarded as counterproductive have been removed. But two innovations allow the general problem to be approached in a fashion that appears, at this writing, to promise useful application. These innovations are: (1) a "multiple-factor" model of security returns, resulting in an appealing and computationally convenient model of security covariances, and (2) the use of a highly innovative mathematical programming algorithm, conceived by Balder Von Hohenbalken [11]. With these innovations, convergence to within a satisfactory tolerance of optimality can be achieved for a realistic portfolio revision problem (46 stocks in the portfolio, 106 in the universe; realistic objectives with regard to portfolio beta, portfolio cash yield, portfolio residual risk (or equivalently, total risk); and upper and lower bounds on holdings of individual securities) in 2.5 seconds of CPU time on the CDC 7600 at Berkeley (at a cost of 50 c).

The last section of the paper is more technical; in § 4, we offer a rigorous presentation of the problem formulation and an introduction to the Von Hohenbalken algorithm.

2. A brief review of the history of portfolio optimization algorithms

The central theme of the development of portfolio optimization algorithms has been selective simplification of the problem, and even approximations to the problem. This has been done chiefly for three reasons: ease of exposition, reduction of computational cost, and simplification of use through a reduction in the complexity of inputs. A history of algorithms is thus a record of simplifications and their explanation. These simplifications have occurred in three forms. First, the problem has been simplified by deleting some of its salient features; as a leading instance of this, transaction costs have been assumed away. Second, the utility function has been simplified. Third, the realistic model of variances and covariances of security returns, allowing a "full covariance" matrix, has been simplified to the "diagonal" or "single-index" model.

2.1. Linearization of the utility function

Because quadratic programming algorithms are much more expensive than linear programming algorithms, a substantial savings in cost can be achieved if the objective function is linearized. The price of linearization is oversimplification of the utility function and inaccurate treatment of the portfolio variance. Consider, for example, a target for beta, β_T, which is shown later to be induced from a mean-variance utility function in the quadratic form $(\beta_p - \beta_T)^2$, where β_p denotes portfolio beta. At the cost of oversimplifying the tradeoff among alternative portfolio attributes, these quadratic penalties can be replaced by upper and lower bounds that are centered about the optimal values on the variables in question. This results in any point within the intervals being treated as equally desirable. This simplification may result in an overly inaccurate utility function. Sharpe [10] has explained that the quadratic function can be approximated by a piecewise linear function.

Next, consider the problem of introducing portfolio residual risk into the objective function: Portfolio residual variance is inescapably a quadratic function of the holdings. There is no computationally appealing way to approximate this by a piecewise linear function. However, a crude upper bound on total portfolio residual variance can be obtained by imposing bounds on holdings in each of a number of categories making up a "framework." For example, assets can be classified into categories along each of four axes: economic sector, growth orientation, risk level, and size. Each axis might be partitioned into five quintiles. Then the total portfolio investment in each of the twenty categories could be held within bounds of $(x + 5)$ percent and $(x - 5)$ percent, where x is the capitalization of the market portfolio in that category. Also, the holdings of individual stocks could each be held within bounds of, say, $(x_n + 4)$ percent and $(x_n - 4)$ percent, where x_n is the percentage of market capitalization in that asset.

This approach does offer the advantage of direct control of investment allocation through a linear program, but it has the grave disadvantage of coarsely reflecting the sources of residual risk or poor diversification. The approach cannot accurately implement the risk/return tradeoff: if the bounds are tight enough to ensure a given level of diversification, they will inevitably overstate the restrictions, in the sense that there will be many portfolios far outside the bounds with risk levels that are below the desired minimum.

These approaches have all of the disadvantages of approximations. Since no descriptive model suggests their use, there is no guidance as to how to apply these constraints most effectively, so they must be manipulated by trial and error to achieve realistic solutions. Nonetheless, when quadratic optimization was precluded, due to the expense of appropriate algorithms, they were worth trying. In most instances, the rigorous quadratic programming solution may actually be less expensive than the approximated linear programming approach, for the reason that the LP approximation entails the addition of otherwise unnecessary activities and constraints, which increase the LP far beyond the minimal size necessary in the exact formulation.

2.2. The diagonal model or the multiple-factor model of residual variance

The bulk of the literature on portfolio optimization has included an assumption, which has been called the "diagonal model." To understand this assumption, it is important first to explain that residual risk in a portfolio arises from two sources: "specific risk" and "extra-market covariance."

Specific risk is the uncertainty in the return of an asset that arises from events that are specific to that firm. It is that part of risk that is due to events in the firm that are unrelated – or, at most, distantly related – to events that impact other firms. A leading example of this kind of risk was provided by the sudden announcement of Penn Central's financial troubles. The news had a disastrous effect on the prices of its common stock and other liabilities. Of course, the announcement also conveyed, by implication, some fresh news about the state of the economy, about railroads in general, and about potentially illiquid firms that led to small changes in other firms' values. But the interrelationship was negligible in comparison to the change in the values of Penn Central's own liabilities.

Extra-market covariance is the remaining component of risk. It is manifested as a tendency for the prices of related assets to move together in a way that is independent of the market as a whole. An illustration is the tendency for airline stocks to move together as the prospects of the industry change, at times when the market may be moving in the other direction. The adjective "extra-market" rules out that part of asset covariance that is related to the market as a whole. Covariance within an industry group is intermediate between systematic and specific risk: systematic risk impacts all firms in some way; specific risk impacts only one firm; industry-group covariance impacts a group of firms. Other forms of extra-market covariance may impact a very large number of firms; for example, a contractionary monetary policy may reduce the values of firms that have assumed much financial risk, at the same time that the market as a whole is rising because of favorable economic news. In this example, a large group of firms, which cuts across industries, will be exposed to the change in monetary policy and will covary.

If we were assuming away all extra-market covariance then the only contribution to residual risk from the stock would be from its specific risk. When the portfolio investment weight is identical to the market proportion of the stock, the portfolio has zero exposure to the specific risk of that stock. [1] In this case, the specific risk of the stock makes a contribution of zero to the residual risk of the portfolio. The contribution of the firm's specific risk to portfolio residual risk increases as the holding differs from the market proportion in either direction.

When the diagonal model is assumed, the portfolio optimization problem is enormously simplified. Markowitz [3] first suggested the model, and much of Sharpe's [9] pioneering expository work, including the first widely circulated portfolio optimization algorithm, exploited this assumption. It was also employed in

[1] When the beta of the equity portfolio is not equal to unity, the point of zero residual risk becomes the proportion in the "equal-beta levered market portfolio," or $\beta_p W_{Mn}$. The discussion below then goes through with $\beta_p W_{Mn}$ replacing W_{Mn} at all points.

the popular literature explaining the risk/return tradeoff. [2]

The crucial question is whether the assumption of zero extra-market covariance is sufficiently realistic to be justified, and whether a viable alternative exists. King's [2] important study showed that an important proportion of residual variance could be associated with common factors of return, which took the form of industry indexes. Cohen and Poque [1] pointed out that such a model, if implemented, would allow great computational savings over the full covariance model.

Rosenberg, Houglet, Marathe, and McKibben [6] first applied a straightforward procedure developed by Rosenberg [4] that yields accurate estimates of a portion of the extra-market covariance among security returns. The portion that is estimated is that part due to common factors in security returns whose effects are determined by observable "descriptors" of the firms. Included in this category are industry factors and factors associated with fundamental characteristics. Recent research by Rosenberg and Marathe [7] has shown that such factors account for a large portion of the covariance among security returns, and that this portion can be accurately established.

The availability of a model for extra-market covariance allows an experiment to be carried out. For any portfolio, the partial derivative of residual risk with respect to each holding, as implied by the diagonal model, can be computed and compared by the model, including both specific risk and extra-market covariance. Table 1 reports the results for an interesting "portfolio," the thirty Dow Jones Industrial Stocks, as weighted by their proportions in the Dow Jones Index on January 22, 1976. The contributions of these holdings to portfolio residual risk, relative to a market portfolio defined as S&P 500, are computed for each of the two models. Table 1 reports the partial derivatives for the thirty stocks in the portfolio. It is apparent that the effects on residual risk implied by the diagonal model grossly understate and incorrectly order the effects on residual risk. Since the estimation procedure for extra-market covariance that was used to develop this computation tends, if anything, to understate the magnitude of extra-market covariance, this result shows the defects of the diagonal model rather convincingly.

This pattern appears in every institutional portfolio that we have analyzed. For institutional portfolios, the changes are strikingly large, and it is apparent in almost

---

[2] It should also be noted that the literature uses an inferior form of the diagonal model, so that important improvements can be made without any increase in computational difficulty. The articles weight the specific risk of the asset by its total portfolio investment weight w_n, rather than by the correct weight, which equals the difference between the portfolio investment and the market proportion ($w_n - w_{Mn}$). The use of w_n is formally correct, so there is no error in logic here. The problem is that, with a capitalization-weighted market portfolio, the diagonal model with weight w_n leads to ridiculous results for well-diversified portfolios, whereas the diagonal model with correct weighting provides a fair approximation, failing only in the omission of extra-market covariance.

Table 1
Partial derivatives of residual risk of the Dow Jones 30 industrial index

	Company	Partial derivatives	
		Multiple-factor model	Diagonal model
1	EXXON Corp.	−0.8	0.2
2	American Tel. and Teleg. Co.	−0.5	−0.1
3	Procter and Gamble Co.	−0.4	1.1
4	Eastman Kodak Co.	−0.4	0.8
5	Standard Oil Co. of Calif.	0.1	0.3
6	Texaco Inc.	0.1	0.1
7	Sears Roebuck and Co.	0.5	0.6
8	General Electric Co.	0.8	0.4
9	General Foods Corp.	1.0	0.6
10	Esmark, Inc.	1.2	1.0
11	Westinghouse Electric Corp.	1.4	0.6
12	Goodyear Tire and Rubber	1.4	0.6
13	Johns Manville Corp.	1.6	0.8
14	General Motors Corp.	1.7	0.1
15	American Brands, Inc.	1.7	0.6
16	International Nickel	1.8	0.6
17	Aluminum Company of America	2.0	1.3
18	Woolworth, F.W. Co.	2.0	0.8
19	Union Carbide Corp.	2.1	1.1
20	American Can Company	2.2	0.4
21	United Technologies CP	2.2	1.7
22	International Paper Co.	2.5	1.5
23	Bethlehem Steel Corp.	2.6	0.7
24	Owens Illinois, Inc.	2.6	1.2
25	Allied Chemical Corp.	2.7	1.0
26	International Harvester	2.8	0.7
27	United States Steel Corp.	3.2	1.3
28	Anaconda Company	3.3	0.7
29	Du Pont E.I. De Nemours	3.6	2.2
30	Chrysler Corp.	3.8	0.6

Source: Fundamental Risk Measurement Service. We are grateful to Walt McKibben for preparing this analysis.

Note: This analysis shows the Dow Jones 30 Industrial Index, viewed as a portfolio, compared with the S&P 500 Index, viewed as the market portfolio: partial derivatives of the standard deviation of monthly Dow Jones residual return (in percent) with respect to the holdings of the 30 Dow Jones Industrials. Comparison of the partial derivatives is based on the multiple-factor model with those based on the diagonal model.

every institutional portfolio that the "diagonal" assumption is a very bad assumption indeed. It is such a faulty assumption because investment management generally leads to a portfolio whose fundamental characteristics and industry group investments differ from the market portfolio. In a randomly chosen portfolio, exposure to extra-market covariance would average out to be nearly zero. But portfolios chosen by institutional managers are far from random: They reflect the deliberate choice of a kind of company that is expected to do unusually well; those choices lead, in our experience, to portfolios that are exposed to extra-market covariance as a result. The diagonal model, which might be adequate for a random policy, is seriously invalid for institutional portfolios.

2.3. Treatment of the revision problem

To include transaction costs properly in the portfolio-revision problem, it is necessary to include a set of purchase activities and a set of sales activities in place of the original set of holdings. This increases the number of activities in the mathematical program. The short-selling exclusion must now be implemented by upper bounds on sales, which results in the addition of a number of constraints. The end result is a very large mathematical program, with a large number of activities (columns) and constraints (rows). For a general quadratic programming algorithm, unable to take advantage of the special structure of this problem, the computational costs are impossibly high.

The problem has been computationally feasible for a quadratic program that could take advantage of the special structure by using the "implicit bounded variables" version of linear programming. Some quadratic programming algorithms, such as Lemke's, simply do not lend themselves to this variant, so that their use is precluded for the revision problem. Others, such as Wolfe's, can apparently be adapted, but computational cost remains high.

Thus, there has been a strong tendency to overlook transactions costs in favor of a simplified treatment of the revision problem. In our view, all of these simplifications have been less than satisfactory.

2.4. Minimum bounds on investments

One important feature of portfolio management is that very small holdings and transactions are inconvenient and tend to be impractical. Realistic reflection of this feature of the problem requires a constraint of the following sort: either hold a zero amount of each asset, or hold more than some minimum amount, such as 1 percent of the portfolio. Unfortunately, this constraint increases the complexity of the problem importantly, for the optimization problem no longer has simple linear constraints. For this reason, all algorithms have overlooked this constraint, and as a result have tended to produce small positive holdings of some assets. In practice, the solution has been to exclude the stocks which turned out, at the end of an initial run, to have small holdings, and to rerun the analysis with a reduced investment opportunity set.

3. A fresh approach to the portfolio optimization problem

Stated simply, the portfolio management goal is to achieve high return, after subtraction of taxes and transactions costs incurred in managing the portfolio, and to achieve this return at a low level of risk. In some cases, the goal of total return must be refined to reflect a distinction between cash yield (dividends and coupons), on the one hand, and capital gains on the other.

3.1. The risk/return tradeoff

It is widely accepted that a reduction in risk can be achieved but at a sacrifice in expected return. The investor or the investment manager must establish the relative importance of reduced risk and increased return, or the "risk/return tradeoff." The function that weights return and risk against one another, resulting in a measure of the overall desirability of the combination of risk and return, is the utility function.

The utility function is a means by which various portfolio attributes are made commensurate, and their desirability is combined into a single objective. There are two natural measures: the utility of the portfolio expressed as an equivalent riskless return, and the utility of the portfolio expressed as the present value to the investor of the investment returns that are promised. The former, which corresponds to a risk-adjusted return, will be used in this paper.

3.2. Two aspects of risk

The central premise of the modern theory of capital asset pricing is that there are two essentially distinct forms of investment risk: first, systematic or undiversifiable risk; second, residual or diversifiable risk.

Systematic risk is unavoidable to the society and, indeed, is intrinsic to the uncertainties in the growth and change in the economy. Since it is unavoidable, it is appropriate that there be a reward for investors who bear systematic risk. The reward takes the form of an average "risk premium" or "excess return" that is earned by risky assets, over the return of risk-free assets. Asset prices tend to be set so that the "market portfolio," made up of each stock in proportion to its outstanding value, earns the risk premium with minimal risk. Thus, in holding the market portfolio, one assumes only socially necessary risk or systematic risk. Any portfolio's exposure to such risk is described by its systematic risk coefficient, or "beta." Knowledge of this coefficient is the first essential step in determining the risk of the portfolio.

Moreover, beta determines the exposure of the portfolio to market movements. For instance, if an optimistic forecast of the market exists, the beta may be increased in expectation of profit from a rising market. Thus, beta is, at the same time, the determinant of exposure to systematic risk and the determinant of exposure to the market return.

The second aspect of portfolio risk is residual risk or diversifiable risk. Such risk is assumed whenever the portfolio differs from the market portfolio. Whenever the investor takes such a position, some other investors elsewhere in the economy must be taking the reverse position, since the aggregate of their holdings is the market portfolio. As such, this is "diversifiable" risk, which could be removed if the investors were to move to the market portfolio. Since diversifiable risk is avoidable for society as a whole, the capital markets can provide no reward, in aggregate, for those who assume it. Some may profit, but others must lose equally. Nevertheless, the market's efficiency requires that investors do take positions in response to their beliefs.

To the degree that a manager believes the market valuation of an asset to be erroneous, the opportunity exists for extraordinary return by taking an active position with respect to that asset. If the stock is believed to be overvalued, a smaller holding than the market proportion allows the opportunity to outperform the market portfolio and vice versa. However, any deviant position carries with it a consequent risk: To the degree that the portfolio differs from the market portfolio, there is exposure to the uncertain events that might cause the selected asset not to perform as expected.

3.3. Determining the risk/return tradeoff

In practice, the choice of a risk/return tradeoff is tantamount to the choice of the appropriate long-term average level of beta for the portfolio. [3] The reason for this, quite simply, is that in a strategy that includes long-term bonds and corporate equities, the largest component of risk in diversified portfolios — even modestly diversified ones — arises from market or systematic risk, and beta determines the exposure of the portfolio to that risk. Hence, the choice of the appropriate value for beta fixes the largest component of risk. Studies of mutual funds and individually managed portfolios within trust departments have confirmed that there is a good relationship between the risk tolerance implicit in the stated investment goals and the beta the portfolio chooses to meet those goals.

In any one period, the goal for portfolio beta is set by weighing the desirability of the expected market return against the undesirability of the exposure to systematic risk. It is reasonable to consider a utility function of the "mean-variance" form, which is an increasing function of the mean portfolio return and a decreasing function of the variance of portfolio return, and to assume, for simplicity, that the function is linear, of the form:

$$\text{utility} = \text{expected portfolio return} + \Lambda \text{ (variance of portfolio return)},$$

[3] This situation is complicated by the presence of differential taxation on capital gains and yield from bonds and stocks, but the spirit of the argument can be preserved in that context.

where Λ is the (negative) coefficient of aversion to total risk.

Since expected portfolio return is linear in beta and variance of portfolio return is quadratic in beta this results in a quadratic function of beta with a unique maximum corresponding to the target beta. This can be represented by:

$$\lambda_\beta \text{ (portfolio beta} - \text{target portfolio beta)}^2,$$

where λ_β is a negative coefficient.

Thus far, the distinction between systematic and residual risk has been emphasized. This distinction is certainly useful, for the two sources of risk enter very differently into the portfolio management process. However from the point of view of the investor and investment manager it is the level of total variance of the portfolio (the sum of residual variance and systematic variance) that is the source of disutility.

The investment manager determines the investor's aversion to total variance, Λ. This parameter then determines the attitude toward beta through the process already described. It also determines the attitude toward portfolio residual variance. Under reasonable assumptions the aversion parameter for residual variance λ_V, equals that for total variance, Λ.[4] The investment manager will choose to deviate from the market portfolio in the hope of earning extraordinary return. The expectation of extraordinary return for the portfolio, called the "portfolio appraisal premium," is denoted by α_p. This expectation is achieved at the cost of residual variance, which will be denoted by ω_p^2. The contribution to the utility function from these two sources, because of the previously determined risk/return tradeoff, is $\alpha_p + \lambda_V \omega_p^2$

3.4. The portfolio–revision problem

The vast majority of portfolio management decisions takes place in the context of the revision of an existing portfolio. If transactions costs (commisions + taxes incurred as a result of sale + losses due to adverse price movements caused by the act of trading) were zero, and if there were no institutional consequences from realizing an asset whose market value differs from the book value (cost basis), then the existing holdings would be immaterial, for the simple reason that it would cost nothing to liquidate the entire portfolio and start over from scratch. However, transactions costs do exist and, for many institutions, there are accounting conventions rooted in basis costs. As a consequence, the portfolio-revision problem is crucially influenced by present holdings.

The portfolio management goal is to improve the utility of portfolio risk and return attributes, but to do this in such a way that only an appropriate amount of transactions costs and book adjustments are made. This is accomplished by an aug-

[4] See Rosenberg [5] for a more complete discussion of this point.

mented utility function, in which the effects of transactions on utility are included. In general, there may be a different utility coefficient attached to the purchase and sale of each individual stock.

When these effects are included in the utility function, it assumes the form:

Utility = constant term

$$+ \alpha_p + \lambda_V \omega_p^2 + \lambda_\beta \text{ (portfolio beta} - \text{target beta)}^2$$

$$+ \sum_{\substack{\text{assets available} \\ \text{for sale} \\ l=1,\dots,L}} \text{(sale penalty on asset } l)$$

$$* \text{ (amount of asset } l \text{ that is sold)}$$

$$+ \sum_{\substack{\text{assets available} \\ \text{for purchase} \\ k=1,\dots,K}} \text{(purchase penalty on asset } k)$$

$$* \text{ (amount of asset } k \text{ that is purchased)}.$$

3.5. The portfolio yield goal [5]

In ideal circumstances, there is no important distinction between the dividend component of portfolio return and the capital gain component, and as a result, the portfolio cash yield is a matter of indifference. However, in many cases these two components are differentially taxed, so that the distinction becomes a matter of importance. Further, in many institutional contexts, the portfolio yield has symbolic importance (viz., endowment funds) or legal status (viz., the distinction between income beneficiary and remainderment in a trust portfolio). For these reasons, there may be (1) either a general desire to maximize portfolio yield or achieve a tradeoff with some other portfolio attribute, or (2) an important portfolio goal with respect to cash yield. This latter goal can be implemented through a target yield, and a disutility penalty that is incurred when that yield is not achieved. These are accomplished by adding to the utility function terms:

$$\lambda_c \text{ (portfolio yield} - \text{target yield)}^2 + \lambda_y \text{ (portfolio yield)},$$

where λ_c and λ_y are negative and positive coefficients, respectively.

---

[5] See Rosenberg and Rudd [8] for further discussion of this topic.

3.7. Bounds on asset holdings

For diverse reasons, holdings on some assets may be required to be greater than some minimum or below an allowable maximum. Sometimes these bounds exist for economic reasons, as when a portfolio holding must be maintained above a minimum to preserve a controlling interest in some firm. Sometimes the bounds reflect preferences, as when companies in questionable businesses, such as liquor, tobacco, or weapons, are prohibited. Most often, the bounds reflect legal restrictions designed to enforce diversification or to otherwise ensure prudence. A striking example is the virtually universal exclusion 'of short selling, which results in the lower bound of zero for almost all portfolio investment problems.

These goals, with regard to asset holdings, are best implemented by means of constraints, and an absolute restriction on acceptable portfolios is expressed by upper and lower bounds on holdings of individual securities or groups of securities.

3.8. The model for residual variance [6]

For each asset n, $n = 1, ..., N$, let $x_{1n}, ..., x_{6n}$ be six "risk-index" continuous variables, characterizing six aspects of the firm's condition: respectively, "market variability," "earnings variability," "immaturity and smallness," "low valuation and unsuccess," "growth orientation," and "financial risk." Also, let $j_{1n}, ..., j_{39n}$ be the weights of the firm's activity in each of thirty-nine industry groups, summing to 1. (In practice, these weights are currently assigned so that the weight in the principal industry group is one, and in all other industry groups, zero.) Let $x_n = (x_{1n}:...:x_{6n}: j_{1n}:...:j_{39n})'$ be the 45-element column vector that characterizes firm n.

Let σ_n^2 denote the specific risk of asset n and β_n the systematic risk coefficient of asset n. For any portfolio, let $w_{E1}, ..., w_{EN}$ denote investment weights on the N assets, summing to one. Similarly, let $w_{M1}, ..., w_{MN}$ denote weights of the N assets in the market portfolio.

Then the residual variance of the portfolio is predicted as

$$\omega_E^2 = \sum_{n=1}^{N} (w_{En} - \beta_E w_{Mn})^2 \sigma_n^2 + x_E' F x_E$$

where $x_E = \Sigma_{n=1}^{N} w_{En} x_n$ is the portfolio characterization vector, and where F is a 45×45 variance-covariance matrix of factors associated with the forty-five characteristics.

In practice, F is further decomposed as:

$$F = ECE' + \text{diag}(f_i),$$

---

[6] This model, explained in detail in Rosenberg and Marathe [7], is estimated by the approach developed in Rosenberg [4].

where E is a 45×9 matrix, C is a 9×9 variance-covariance matrix, and $\text{diag}(f_i)$ is a diagonal matrix, whose forty-five diagonal entries are variances associated with the characteristics and industries. The use of a multiple-factor model with a factor matrix of small dimension (9 in this case) preserves much of the computational economy of the diagonal model, while permitting the important gain in accuracy from more efficient use of information.

3.9. Sources of inputs for the optimization

The inputs for the utility function are specified according to judgment of the user. There are fewer than ten utility parameters, and the upper and lower bounds on holdings can be designated as constant ranges about market proportions, thereby simplifying their input.

The predictions for yield, beta, and specific risk of each asset and the multiple-factor model are presumed to be drawn from a risk measurement service, so that these would not ordinarily be provided by the user.

Forecasts of appraisal premiums on individual stocks are judgmental inputs provided by the user.

Transactions costs estimates are provided by the user, obeying an algorithm that assumes different costs in different markets and at different levels of trading activity. Capital gains and tax or book value effects can be taken into account, provided that basis cost is available.

3.10. Some applications

We have programmed the approach to portfolio optimization that has been discussed in this section. For the last two years it has been used by several investment managers in a variety of interesting applications, some of which are described below.

Index and index-like portfolios

Portfolios that closely track visible indexes have recently become very popular in the investment industry. The selection of an "index" portfolio is easily performed using the approach described here; all that is required is to set (i) a beta target of unity, (ii) all judgmental alphas and transactions costs to zero, and (iii) minimize residual risk. It is perfectly feasible to create index portfolios from large universes (up to 1000 assets); annual residual standard deviation is usually reduced to less than 0.5% in 15–25 cycles of the Von Hohenbalken algorithm (§ 4.6).

A similar project is to determine, for instance, the most diversified 60–stock portfolio with a beta of one from the S&P 500. An approximation to this "integer" selection problem (restricting the number of stocks in this manner is an integer constraint) can be easily found by first finding the most index-like portfolio, then discarding all but the most diversifying 60 stocks, and finally re-optimizing over this restricted list of assets.

Revision, market timing, and diversification with yield goals

A good approximation to the true portfolio revision problem is obtained when using the assumption of linear transactions costs. Inserting nonzero transactions costs frequently changes the nature of the optimal portfolio, and increases the convergence rate dramatically.

One common task is to modify an initial portfolio, which may have been obtained when a client changed investment managers, to display different attributes. Frequently this revision must take place by investing cash flow and without any sales. The solution to this problem can be determined by declaring upper bounds of zero on all the sale transactions, and forcing the investment of the cash by setting the upper and lower bounds of the cash holding also to zero. The portfolio attributes can then be satisfied by using the required goals.

Virtually the opposite procedure is followed when the manager desires, perhaps because of a market timing strategy, to decrease the value of the equity portfolio and place the proceeds in cash or equivalents. In this case (i) maintaining the same beta target, (ii) forcing the sale of some securities by using the investment holding bounds, and (iii) minimizing residual risk, performs the required task with maximum diversification.

For some funds, particularly endowment funds, achieving a high portfolio yield is of prime importance. In this case the criterion is to obtain the best diversified portfolio with a large yield target, the target on portfolio beta perhaps being disregarded since this could be met by controlling the bond/stock mix. Including portfolio yield in the objective function is also important, in the case of nontaxable investors, if it is believed that differential taxation on cash dividends and capital gains induces higher total return to high-yielding securities.

Including judgmental information

The compensation for portfolio residual risk is the expected appraisal premium. If it is believed that security analysis can detect over- and undervalued securities, the optimal portfolio appraisal return is easily determined. Further, the information content of the analysis can be readily adjusted by varying the relative weight of the security appraisal returns if the analysts appear either unduly optimistic or pessimistic. The optimization also provides a feedback loop to the security analysts; for instance, if the optimal portfolios, given the perceived levels for appraisal return, are consistently highly concentrated in the securities researched by a particular group of analysts, this may indicate a need for more "quality control" of the investment research function.

4. Portfolio optimization

4.1. Glossary of notation

Conventions

Subscripts m and n refer to individual assets; the subscript E refers to an equity portfolio; the subscript M refers to the market. A tilde beneath a character denotes a column vector or matrix; lower case characters are column vectors, upper case characters are matrices; characters without tildes indicate scalars. A prime denotes transposition, e.g., $c = (c_1:...:c_N)'$ is a column vector, and $D = (d_1:...:d_N)$ is a matrix.

Yield, systematic risk, and appraisal premia

y_E the expected proportional cash yield on the portfolio,

y_M the expected proportional cash yield on the market portfolio,

y_n the expected proportional cash yield on individual stock n,

y_T the target expected proportional cash yield, i.e., the value toward which the revised portfolio should aim,

y_{max} maximum acceptable expected proportional cash yield of portfolio,

y_{min} minimum acceptable expected proportional cash yield of portfolio.

Similarly,

β_E, β_n, β_T, β_{max}, and β_{min} are, respectively, the portfolio, individual stock n, target portfolio, maximum acceptable portfolio, and minimum acceptable portfolio systematic risk coefficients

and

α_E and α_n are, respectively, the portfolio and individual stock n expected appraisal premia.

Finally,

E_M is the expected excess return on the market portfolio.

Residual variance

V the full variance-covariance matrix of residual risk;

F the factor variance matrix;

γ_n the loadings of stock n onto the factors;

γ_E the loadings of portfolio E onto the factors;

Γ stock loading matrix; $\Gamma = \{\gamma_1, \gamma_2, ..., \gamma_N\}$;

ω_E^2 the portfolio residual risk, expressed as the variance of annual residual return;

Δ_σ the diagonal matrix of specific variances, i.e., the nth term on the diagonal is the specific variance of the nth asset, σ_n^2;

V_M variance of excess return on market portfolio.

Asset and cash holdings

w_n the portfolio investment weight in stock n, expressed as the ratio of the portfolio value in that stock to the total portfolio value;

w_n^0 initial portfolio investment weight in stock n;

w_E portfolio investment weights for portfolio E;

w_{Mn} the weight of stock n in the market portfolio, equal to the percent of the aggregate market value of all common stocks in the market index which is in this stock;

w_M vector of market weights w_{Mn};

z_E vector of portfolio investment weights for portfolio E less the investment weights in an equal-beta, levered, market portfolio = $w_E - \beta_E w_M$;

$wmax_n$ maximum acceptable holding in stock n;

$wmin_n$ minimum acceptable holding in stock n;

c_{max} maximum acceptable cash holding in portfolio;

c_{min} minimum acceptable cash holding in portfolio;

c_E cash holding in portfolio E;

c_E^0 initial cash holding in portfolio;

p_k purchase adjustments in portfolio revision, $k = 1, ..., K$;

$pmax_k$ maximum purchase adjustments in portfolio revision, $k = 1, ..., K$;

q_l sale adjustment in portfolio revision, $l = 1, ..., L$;

$qmax_l$ maximum sale adjustment in portfolio revision, $l = 1, ..., L$;

d_n feasibility adjustment in stock n relative to initial asset holding, w_n^0.

Transaction costs

t_p proportional transactions costs for a purchase;

t_q proportional transactions costs for a sale;

t_E total transactions costs incurred in revision from portfolio with asset holdings w^0 to portfolio with asset holdings w_E where purchases incur proportional costs t_p and sales proportional costs t_q.

Objective function

U objective function used in optimization,

Λ penalty to risk-adjusted return for portfolio variance,

λ_α coefficient of expected appraisal premium in utility function,

λ_y coefficient of cash yield in utility function,

λ_v coefficient of residual variance in utility function,

λ_t coefficient of transactions costs in utility function,

λ_β coefficient of systematic risk target in utility function,

λ_c coefficient of cash yield target in utility function.

4.2. Objective function

The objective function determines the utility of the revised portfolio and is defined in terms of various portfolio constructs. These are designed for two purposes:

(1) to quantify the desirability or attractiveness of the portfolio, and

(2) to allow the optimization algorithm to implement portfolio management goals.

Clearly, all aspects of the portfolio that give rise to desirability or undesirability should be considered. The following constructs are included in the objective function for any given portfolio E revised from initial asset holdings w^0:

(1) the expected portfolio appraisal premium α_E,

(2) the portfolio cash yield y_E,

(3) the portfolio residual variance ω_E^2,

(4) the portfolio beta β_E,

(5) the transactions costs necessary to achieve E t_E.

This list could be extended to include any portfolio construct or function of portfolio constructs that has, at most, squared terms in the portfolio asset holdings. The utility of the portfolio can be expressed in terms of present value (dollars) or in terms of risk-adjusted expected return. We express it in terms of expected return, so that the objective function coefficient of α_E, the portfolio appraisal premium, is $\lambda_\alpha = +1$ by definition.

The portfolio systematic risk coefficient, β_E, contributes to the portfolio utility positively, through its contribution to portfolio expected return and, negatively, through its contribution to portfolio risk. When these two contributions are summed, the result takes the form of a quadratic function of beta, with the maximum point at that value of beta where the optimum tradeoff between systematic risk and expected market return is obtained. This quadratic function may be written as:

$$\lambda_\beta(\beta_E - \beta_T)^2,$$

where β_T is the optimal or target beta. [7]

Including the remaining terms as defined in § 3, it is seen that for any equity portfolio E revised from a portfolio with asset holdings w^0, the utility (or objective

---

[7] For this purpose, portfolio utility may be written as:

$$U^* = \beta_E E_M + \Lambda\beta_E^2 V_M$$

$$= \Lambda V_M\left[\beta_E + \frac{E_M}{2\Lambda V_M}\right]^2 - \frac{E_M^2}{4\Lambda V_M},$$

whence

$$\lambda_\beta = \Lambda V_M \text{ and } \beta_T = -\frac{E_M}{2\Lambda V_M}.$$

function value) can be written as:

$$U(w_E) = \lambda_\alpha \alpha_E + \lambda_y y_E + \lambda_t t_E + \lambda_v \omega_E^2 + \lambda_\beta (\beta_E - \beta_T)^2 + \lambda_c (y_E - y_T)^2.$$

Note that each term in the objective function is independent in the sense that each is weighted individually. This enables great flexibility with regard to specifying any tradeoffs among portfolio attributes.

All the constructs are simple functions of the assets holdings w_E. In particular, $\alpha_E = \alpha' w_E, \beta_E = \beta' w_E$, and $y_E = y' w_E$.

The residual variance can be written in two forms: either as a straightforward quadratic term involving the full variance-covariance matrix V, or as the sum of two terms – extra-market covariance and specific risk. In the latter decomposition, extra-market covariance is computed through a multiple-factor model. The two representations are:

$$\omega_E^2 = w_E' V w_E,$$

or

$$\omega_E^2 = \beta_E' F \beta_E + z_E' \Delta_\sigma z_E.$$

In either case, the residual variance can be expressed as a quadratic term in the asset holdings; for the full variance-covariance matrix V, the utility can be written:

$$U(w_E) = \lambda_\alpha \alpha' w_E + \lambda_y y' w_E + \lambda_t t_E + \lambda_v w_E' V w_E + \lambda_\beta (\beta' w_E - \beta_T)^2$$
$$+ \lambda_c (y' w_E - y_t)^2.$$

Under the assumption of proportional transactions costs (which is made throughout this paper), t_E, the total transactions costs in revision, can be written:

$$t_E = \sum_{\{n : w_n > w_n^0\}} t_p(w_n - w_n^0) + \sum_{\{n : w_n < w_n^0\}} t_q(w_n^0 - w_n).$$

4.3. Portfolio restrictions

To make the problem realistic, various attributes of the revised portfolio may need to be restricted, either to a given value or to a given range. For instance, it may be desired to maintain the portfolio cash yield to more than five percent per annum. These restrictions are handled by means of linear constraints on the asset holdings.

The problem formulation will allow any restriction that can be expressed as such an equality or inequality constraint. Realistic constraints include:

(1) bounds on the asset holdings, for each asset n $wmin_n$, $wmax_n$,

(2) bounds on the portfolio systematic risk coefficient β_{min}, β_{max},

(3) bounds on the portfolio cash yield y_{min}, y_{max},

(4) bounds on the portfolio cash holding c_{min}, c_{max}.

Bounds on holdings in asset classes (such as industry groups) could also be easily introduced.

4.4. Problem transformation

One approach to the optimization problem would be to operate at all times on the initial portfolio and universe. The constraints and bounds in tableau form for this approach are shown in table 2. This formulation is the natural one for the traditional portfolio-selection problem and, in a sense, supposes that all transactions are purchases.

Table 2
Tableau of untransformed portfolio

Constraint number	Activities						Right-hand side
	Asset Holdings			Slack Variables			
	w_1	w_2 ...	w_N	a_1	a_2	a_3	
1. Budget/cash constraint	1	1	1	1			$= 1$
2. Systematic risk coefficient constraint	β_1	β_2	β_N		1		$= \beta_{max}$
3. Cash yield constraint	y_1	y_2	y_N			1	$= y_{max}$
4. Lower bounds	w_{min_1}	w_{min_2}	w_{min_N}	c_{min}	0	0	
5. Upper bounds	w_{max_1}	w_{max_2}	w_{max_N}	c_{max}	β_{max} $-\beta_{min}$	y_{max} $-y_{min}$	
6. Linear terms in objective function	$\lambda_\alpha \alpha_1$ $+\lambda_y y_1$	$\lambda_\alpha \alpha_2$ $+\lambda_y y_2$	$\lambda_\alpha \alpha_N$ $+\lambda_y y_N$	0	0	0	

Note: Objective function also includes nonlinear terms:

$$\lambda_t \sum_j t_j + \lambda_v w' V w + \lambda_\beta [\sum_j \beta_j w_j - \beta_T]^2 + \lambda_c [\sum_j y_j w_j - y_T]^2,$$

$$\text{where } t_j = \begin{cases} t_p \cdot (w_n - w_n^0) & \text{if } w_n > w_n^0 \\ t_q \cdot (w_n^0 - w_n) & \text{if } w_n^0 > w_n \end{cases}.$$

When we consider the problem of revising an existing portfolio, the quantities that are of primary importance are not the optimal asset holdings themselves, but the purchases and sales that transform the initial portfolio to the optimal revised portfolio. For this reason, it is necessary that the optimization be performed in a transformed environment where the activities are not the asset holdings, but purchases and sales. The transformation, then, for any initial holding w_n in asset n with minimum and maximum acceptable bounds $wmin_n$ and $wmax_n$, is to introduce two new variables, p_k and q_l, with minimum and maximum acceptable bounds for both variables, zero, $pmax_k$ and zero, $qmax_l$, respectively; p_k and q_l represent the purchase and sale of asset n, respectively. The change in indexing from n to k and l is necessitated by the fact that there is not a purchase and sale activity associated with every original asset. The number of purchases, K, is the number of assets in the portfolio and universe not at their maximum bounds, while the number of sales, L, is the number of assets in the portfolio and universe not at their lower bounds. In general, K will be much greater than L.

The transformed problem is thus composed of more activities or variables than the original untransformed tableau. All, however, are bounded by zero below and by some finite number above. Such a tableau is displayed in table 3.

A further aspect of the transformation is that it is necessary, at all steps in the optimization, that the portfolio be feasible — that is, that it obey all the restrictions. This is achieved in two stages. First, prior to the portfolio—transformation stage outlined above, the portfolio is made feasible with respect to the asset-holding bounds by "selling off" or "buying into" assets as necessary. There are three possible cases:

(1) $w_n^0 > wmax_n$: initial holding is greater than bound. $w_n^0 - wmax_n$ is "sold off," cash account is credited, and transactions cost penalty is noted. Write $d_n = wmax_n - w_n^0$.

(2) $wmin_n \leqslant w_n^0 \leqslant wmax_n$: initial holding is within bounds. No feasibility adjustment is necessary. Write $d_n = 0$.

(3) $wmin_n > w_n^0$: initial holding is smaller than bound. $wmin_n - w_n^0$ is "bought in" asset n, cash account is debited and transaction cost penalty is noted. Write $d_n = wmin_n - w_n^0$.

At this stage, the portfolio is feasible with respect to the asset holdings; that is, $wmin_n \leqslant w_n^0 + d_n \leqslant wmax_n$ $n = 1, ..., N$; it may not be feasible with respect to the portfolio beta constraint, the cash-yield constraint, or the budget/portfolio cash constraint.

The portfolio is now transformed as described above. Variables p_k and q_l are introduced, such that:

$$0 \leqslant q_l \leqslant qmax_l = (w_n^0 + d_n) - wmin_n; \qquad \text{if } qmax_l > 0;$$

$$0 \leqslant p_k \leqslant pmax_k = wmax_n - (w_n^0 + d_n); \qquad \text{if } pmax_k > 0.$$

Second, the transformed tableau is processed to make it feasible with respect to

Table 3

Tableau of transformed portfolio

Constraint number	Activities						Slack Variables			Right-hand side
	Purchases			Sales						
	p_1	$p_2 \dots$	p_K	q_1	$q_2 \dots$	q_L	a_1	a_2	a_3	
1. Budget/cash constraint	-1	-1	-1	1	1	1	1			$= c_{max} - c_E$
2. Systematic risk coefficient constraint	β_{p_1}	β_{p_2}	β_{p_K}	β_{q_1}	β_{q_2}	β_{q_L}		1		$= \beta_{max} - \beta_E$
3. Cash yield	y_{p_1}	y_{p_2}	y_{p_K}	y_{q_1}	y_{q_2}	y_{q_L}			1	$= y_{max} - y_E$
4. Lower bounds	0	0	0	0	0	0	0	0	0	0
5. Upper bounds	$pmax_1$	$pmax_2$	$pmax_K$	$qmax_1$	$qmax_2$	$qmax_L$	$c_{max} - c_{min}$	$\beta_{max} - \beta_{min}$	$y_{max} - y_{min}$	0
6. Linear terms in objective function	$\lambda_\alpha \alpha_{p_1}$ $+\lambda_y y_{p_1}$ $+\lambda_t p_{p_1}$	$\lambda_\alpha \alpha_{p_2}$ $+\lambda_y y_{p_2}$ $+\lambda_t p_{p_2}$	$\lambda_\alpha \alpha_{p_K}$ $+\lambda_y y_{p_K}$ $+\lambda_t p_{p_K}$	$\lambda_\alpha \alpha_{q_1}$ $+\lambda_y y_{q_1}$ $+\lambda_t q_{q_1}$	$\lambda_\alpha \alpha_{q_2}$ $+\lambda_y y_{q_2}$ $+\lambda_t q_{q_2}$	$\lambda_\alpha \alpha_{q_L}$ $+\lambda_y y_{q_L}$ $+\lambda_t q_{q_L}$	0	0	0	

Note: Objective function also includes nonlinear terms:

$$\lambda_v w' V w + \lambda_\beta [\beta_E + \sum_k p_k \beta_k - \sum_l q_l \beta_l - \beta_T]^2 + \lambda_c [y_E + \sum_k p_k y_k - \sum_l q_l y_l - y_T]^2 .$$

where

$$w_n = w_n^0 + p_k - q_l .$$

the remaining constraints. For this purpose we use the same constraints as in table 3 but modify the objective function as follows: Corresponding to variable p_k is cost element t_p; corresponding to q_l is t_q. This is a simple linear program that determines the minimum transaction costs required to insure feasibility.

The transactions required in these two stages correspond to the preliminary transactions of the revision process and produce the initial feasible portfolio. Before optimization, the tableau is updated by redetermining the bounds of all the activities that were used in the second stage of the feasibility adjustment and by recalculating the quantities shown in table 3 as c_E, β_E, and y_E; that is, the cash, beta, and yield of the initial feasible portfolio.

This process can be described more succinctly as follows. Let the objective function be $U(w, w^0)$, the constraint matrix be A, and the right-hand side be b (these latter two are displayed in table 3). Then, the initial problem can be expressed:

$$\max_{w} U(w, w^0),$$

subject to:

$$wmin_n \leqslant w_n \leqslant wmax_n; \quad n = 1, ..., N,$$

$$c_{min} \leqslant 1 - \sum_n w_n \leqslant c_{max};$$

$$Aw = b.$$

The transformed problem can then be written as:

$$\max_{\Delta w} U(w + d + \Delta w, w^0)$$

subject to:

$$0 \leqslant p_k \leqslant pmax_k; \quad k = 1, ..., K;$$

$$0 \leqslant q_l \leqslant qmax_l; \quad l = 1, ..., L;$$

$$c^0 + \sum_n d_n + c_{min} \leqslant \sum_n \Delta w_n \leqslant c^0 + \sum_n d_n + c_{max};$$

$$A(\Delta w) = b - A(w^0 + d),$$

where Δw is compounded from p and q by reassociating each purchase index k and cash sale index l with the natural ordering of asset holdings, n; that is, $\Delta w_n = p_k - q_l$.

4.5. Evaluation of objective function and partial derivatives

If the objective function, U, is defined in terms of the full variance-covariance matrix, V, then for any portfolio E,

$$U(w_E) = \lambda_\alpha \alpha_E + \lambda_y y_E + \lambda_t t_E + \lambda_v w_E' V w_E + \lambda_\beta (\beta_E - \beta_T)^2$$

$$+ \lambda_c (y_E - y_T)^2.$$

Whence,

$$\frac{\partial U(w_E)}{\partial w_E} = \lambda_\alpha \boldsymbol{\alpha} + \lambda_y y + \lambda_t t + 2\lambda_v V w_E + 2\lambda_\beta (\beta_E - \beta_T) \boldsymbol{\beta}$$

$$+ 2\lambda_c (y_E - y_T) y,$$

where: $t = \partial t_E / \partial w_E$ and is given by

$$t_n = \begin{cases} t_p & \text{if } w_n > w_n^0 \\ t_q & w_n^0 > w_n \end{cases}; \quad n = 1, ..., N.$$

The formulation is more complex if the residual variance is decomposed into factors. In this case:

$$\omega_E^2 = \gamma_E' F \gamma_E + z_E' \Delta_\sigma z_E,$$

where $\gamma_E = \Sigma_{n \in E} \, w_n \gamma_n$, the summation being over all stocks n in portfolio E. Hence,

$$\frac{\partial \omega_E^2}{\partial w_E} = 2\Gamma' F \gamma_E + 2\Delta_\sigma z_E - 2\beta z_E' \Delta_\sigma w_M,$$

where $\Gamma = \{\gamma_1 : ... : \gamma_N\}$.

The advantage of using the decomposed form of the matrix is now clear. Using the full variance matrix, each evaluation of the partial derivative requires, for the residual variance term alone, the calculation of the matrix product $V w_E$; V is an $N \times N$ matrix and w_E an $N \times 1$ column vector. This is a calculation with at least $2N^2$ multiplications and additions. However, it is seen that the decomposed form of the partial derivative calculation comprises the matrix multiplication $\Gamma' F \gamma_E$ plus two vector multiplications each of order N operations. $\Gamma' F$, an $N \times J$ matrix, where J is the number of factors, is constant over the universe. Hence, ignoring the formation of portfolio factor loadings, the calculation at each stage is only of order $NJ +$

N multiplications and additions. For large N, this saving is highly significant.

The computational advantage of the decomposed form is even more significant when evaluating the objective function. In the full-variance case, the number of computations to calculate the residual variance is of order $N^2 + N$, while in the decomposed form, ignoring the formation of portfolio factor loadings, it is only of order $J^2 + J$.

4.6. Optimization

The transformed problem is a quadratic programming problem having linear constraints with all variables bounded. This latter fact renders most quadratic programming codes unusable, as they are unable to handle upper-bounded variables implicitly; explicit treatment of bounded variables requires the addition of an extra constraint and an extra slack variable.

This diminishes the dimension of the problem that can be handled, as the size of the tableau increases rapidly. For instance, a problem with 100 variables all upper bounded and three constraints expands to 200 variables, and 103 constraints if the upper-bounded variables are enforced by constraints.

The algorithm proposed here is a very elegant method conceived by Von Hohenbalken [11]. It differs from other quadratic programs in being straightforward to implement, requiring comparatively small work space, and approaching the optimum from the interior of the feasible region. Essentially, the algorithm requires internal representation in order to select simplexes contained within the feasible set.

The algorithm cycle can be divided in two: a major cycle and a minor cycle. These cycles govern the manner in which the algorithm proceeds from w^k, the maximizer of U over simplex S^k, to w^{k+1}, the maximizer of U over the next simplex S^{k+1}. The major cycle determines whether w^k, the current "optimum" at step k, is the global optimum. If not using linear programming, a simplex $S, S^k \subset S$ is found which contains points of greater functional value than w^k. The minor cycle then follows, which determines the simplex $S^{k+1} \subset S$, such that the maximizer, w^{k+1}, of U over it satisfies

$$U(w^{k+1}) > U(w^k).$$

The simplex S^k at each stage k is defined by the affine basis B^k, whose elements are previous solutions to the linear program and vertexes of the feasible set. Thus, only the basis B^k and the current optimum w^k need to be updated at each stage.

The initial step of the algorithm is to find a zero-dimensional simplex, that is, a single point corresponding to an extreme point of the feasible region. For the transformed problem, this is trivial; the starting simplex is the origin that is equivalent to the initial feasible portfolio.

If the origin (initial feasible portfolio) is not optimal, linear programming

Table 4
Flowchart of portfolio optimization algorithm

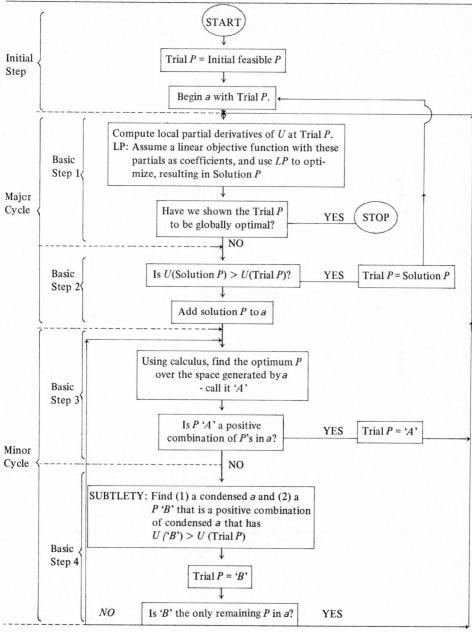

P = Portfolio
a = List of adjustment portfolios
U = function

guides the algorithm to another extreme point of the feasible region. This is the first major cycle. The first minor cycle then finds a point on the one-dimensional simplex (that is, the straight line between the origin and the extreme point found from the linear program) which corresponds to the first adjustments required to transform the initial feasible portfolio into a "better" portfolio.

The algorithm continues in the same sequence. First, test to find if the current position is optimal. Then, determine a new simplex in which points of greater functional value lie. Finally, the minor cycle entails searching for one of these points. A flow chart of the algorithm is shown in table 4.

References

[1] Kalman J. Cohen, and Jerry A. Pogue An empirical evaluation of alternative portfolio-selection models, Journal of Business 40 (1967).

[2] B.F. King, Market and industry factors in stock price behavior, Journal of Business 39 (1966).

[3] Harry M. Markowitz, Portfolio Selection: Efficient Diversification of Investment. Cowles Foundation Monograph No. 16. (John Wiley and Sons, New York, 1959).

[4] Barr Rosenberg, Extra-market components of covariance among security prices – I. Journal of Financial and Quantitative Analysis 9 (1974).

[5] Barr Rosenberg, Security appraisal and unsystematic risk in institutional investment, Proceedings of the Seminar for Research in Security Prices. (University of Chicago, November, 1976).

[6] Barr Rosenberg, Michel Houglet, Vinay Marathe and Walt McKibben, Components of covariance in security returns, working Paper No. 13, Research Program in Finance. Institute of Business and Economic Research, University of California, Berkeley (1973, revised 1975).

[7] Barr Rosenberg and Vinay Marathe, Common factors in security returns: microeconomic determinants and macroeconomic correlates. Proceedings of the Seminar for Research in Security Prices. University of Chicago (May 1976).

[8] Barr Rosenberg and Andrew Rudd, The yield/beta/residual risk tradeoff, working paper no. 66, Research Program in Finance. Institute of Business and Economic Research, University of California, Berkeley (1977).

[9] William F. Sharpe, A simplified model for portfolio analysis, Management Science 9 (1963).

[10] William F. Sharpe, A linear programming approximation for the general portfolio analysis problem, Journal of Financial and Quantitative Analysis (December 1971).

[11] Balder Von Hohenbalken, A finite algorithm to maximize certain pseudoconcave functions on polytopes, Mathematical Programming (1975).

TIMS Studies in the Management Sciences 11 (1979) 47–62
© North-Holland Publishing Company

OPTIMAL PORTFOLIO CHOICE AND EQUILIBRIUM IN A LOGNORMAL SECURITIES MARKET

Vijay S. BAWA and Lewis M. CHAKRIN

Bell Laboratories

1. Introduction

The Markowitz–Tobin ([14],[15],[26]) mean–variance selection rule has enjoyed a great deal of popularity in portfolio theory and in its applications in financial economics. The selection rule is used to generate the admissible subset of investments for risk averse individuals by eliminating any investment which has a lower mean and higher variance than a member of the given set of investment alternatives. But even though the mean-variance approach has spawned a considerable body of literature, including most notably the Sharpe–Lintner–Mossin Capital Asset Pricing Model (CAPM) [Sharpe [24], Lintner [12] and Mossin [19]] that is used extensively in modern finance theory. It has been well known for some time that the approach is of limited generality since it is the optimal selection rule only if investors have quadratic utility functions or investment returns are normally distributed. Arrow [1] and Hicks [10] have pointed out that the assumption of quadratic utility is highly implausible in that it implies increasing absolute risk-aversion. Also, the assumption of normally distributed investment returns carries with it the unrealistic implication of unlimited liability and rules out asymmetry or skewness in the probability distribution of returns. [1] In addition, several authors, e.g., Cootner [6], Lintner [13], Rosenberg [21], Blattberg and Gonedes [5], have found that actual security price data are well approximated by the lognormal (and not normal) distribution. Furthermore, empirical tests of the aforementioned CAPM produced rather disappointing results, e.g., Lintner [12], Douglas [8], Miller and Scholes [18].

Despite all of these objections, the mean-variance approach has maintained its popularity because it provides a tractable theoretical basis for portfolio selection and evaluation, and because the theory is not computationally difficult to implement. It may be viewed as a tractable approximation to the investors expected utility maximization problem. Ross [22] has shown that under certain conditions,

---

[1] Progressive taxation and limited liability of corporations imply that the probability distribution of net returns is quite likely to be skewed.

the approximation is good in an asymptotic sense as the number of securities approaches infinity. Samuelson [23] has provided a weighty defense of mean-variance analysis when the probabilities are "small risk" (see Samuelson [23] for details).

In this paper, we develop the optimal portfolio selection rule and asset valuation model under the more plausible assumption of lognormally distributed investment returns. More specifically we assume that the distribution of one plus the rate of return on individual investments can be approximated as multivariate lognormal. [2] The basic approximation that we utilize is that the return on any portfolio of risky investments is also lognormal. [3] Since linear combinations of lognormally distributed variables are not lognormal, one needs to evaluate the appropriateness of the approximation. An exact measure of the goodness of this approximation will naturally depend upon the specific problem being considered, i.e., on the parameters of the joint lognormal distribution and the utility function employed. [4] However, it must be realized that in fact, security returns are not truly normal, lognormal or distributed according to any well-known probability density. Thus, the true test of the relative merits of any of these approximations in a model of security valuation depends upon how well the results conform to empirical evidence.

While the normal approximation requires no further approximation to treat linear combinations of securities, extensive empirical analysis by Lintner [12] suggests that not only individual security returns but also portfolios (of the basic securities) are more closely lognormal than normal. [5] In light of this evidence, it would seem important to derive the correct form of the valuation model under the lognormality approximation and to rerun some of the more well-accepted empirical procedures used to test the validity of the traditional CAPM, using this alternative specification. In this paper, we derive the new valuation model and make some preliminary comments with respect to the validation procedures. The actual empirical tests will be reported in a future paper.

In § 2, we use the lognormal approximation and use Stochastic Dominance results in Bawa [2] to obtain the admissible set of portfolios for all risk-averse

---

[2] We shall refer to one plus the rate of return of an investment as the "return" throughout this paper.

[3] Merton [16] utilized the lognormal assumption in his analysis of portfolio choice in a dynamic framework and with continuous trading showed that portfolios also have lognormal distribution. This does not hold in a static single period model.

[4] In some empirical tests for the case of isoelastic utility functions, Dexter, Yu and Ziemba [7] found virtually negligible differences between the efficiencies of the true optimal portfolios and those obtained using the lognormal approximation.

[5] Intuitively, if the security and portfolio returns over certain holding periods are products of independent random variables, (the geometric random walk hypothesis), then these empirical results are to be expected.

investors with concave utility functions monotonically increasing in wealth. The results are derived under two alternative specifications of the feasible set of portfolios. We show that for both cases the admissible portfolios are obtained by the use of mean-logarithmic variance rules. We note the extreme similarity and subtle differences between the admissible sets and the computational methods associated with the mean-variance and mean-logarithmic variance rules. In a manner similar to Merton [17], we analytically derive the mean-logarithmic variance efficient portfolio frontier when short sales are allowed. In § 3, we show that the well-known mutual fund separation results also hold in this case and explicitly derive the equilibrium value of assets. We note the difference between the traditional Capital Asset Pricing Model and the CAPM under the lognormality assumption and provide a testable specification of the new CAPM in § 4. Some concluding remarks are provided in § 5.

2. Optimal portfolio choice

We are interested in obtaining the optimal portfolio choice for the case where there are n risky securities and the return on these securities is a random variable which has a multivariate lognormal distribution. For $i = 1, 2, ..., n$, we let R_i denote the random return on security i and X_i denote the fraction of an investor's wealth invested in security i. We let R and X, with $R' = (R_1, R_2, ..., R_n)$ and $X' = (X_1, X_2, ..., X_n)$, denote the vector of security returns and the vector representing investor's portfolio choices respectively. Thus, under our assumptions, R has a multivariate lognormal distribution with logarithmic mean vector M and logarithmic variance-covariance matrix S, i.e., $M' = (M_1, M_2, ..., M_n)$ and $S = (S_{ij})$ where $M_j = E(\ln R_j)$ and $S_{ij} = \text{cov}(\ln R_i, \ln R_j)$. We assume that S is positive definite.

The return on a particular portfolio X, R_X, equals $X'R$. We employ the approximation that R_X is lognormally distributed with logarithmic mean M_X and logarithmic variance S_X^2. To obtain M_X and S_X^2 as functions of the basic parameters (M, S), we use the properties of lognormal distributions. Let, for $j = 1, 2, ..., n$, E_j denote $E(R_j)$ and let E, with $E' = (E_1, E_2, ..., E_n)$, denote the vector of mean returns. Then we have

$$E(R_X) = E(X'R) = X'E, \tag{1}$$

and

$$\text{var}(R_X) \equiv E(\{X'R - E(X'R)\}^2) \tag{2}$$

$$= X'\epsilon'\Omega\epsilon X,$$

where

$$\epsilon = \begin{bmatrix} E_1 & & & & \\ & & & 0 & \\ & E_2 & & & \\ 0 & & & \ddots & \\ & & & & E_n \end{bmatrix} \tag{3}$$

and Ω is an $n \times n$ matrix with (i, j) element $(\exp(S_{ij}) - 1)$.[6] Using the afore-mentioned approximation, it follows that M_X and S_X^2 are given by the solution to the following equations:

$$E(R_X) = \exp(M_X + \tfrac{1}{2} S_X^2), \tag{4}$$

$$\mathrm{var}(R_X) = (E(R_X))^2 \{\exp(S_X^2) - 1\}. \tag{5}$$

The specification of M_X and S_X^2 identifies the lognormal distribution of portfolio X completely and the portfolio choice problem involves the selection of the portfolio, from among the set of all feasible portfolios, which maximizes an individual's expected utility of $X'R$. The set of feasible portfolios is either the complete set of convex combinations of securities $C(X) = \{X | \Sigma_{i=1}^n X_i = 1\}$ or the subset of $C(X)$ which excludes negative holdings or "short sales" of securities, i.e., $C_{NS}(X) = \{X | \Sigma_{i=1}^n X_i = 1, X_i \geqslant 0, i = 1, 2, ..., n\}$. The admissible set of portfolios for all risk-averse investors with concave utility functions monotonically increasing in wealth is given by the use of the following result on the comparison of lognormal distributions:

Theorem 1. For any two lognormal distributions, one is preferred to another for all risk-averse individuals if and only if it has at least as large a mean (in natural units) and at least as small a logarithmic variance.

The proof follows directly from Theorem 11 in [2] and is omitted.[7]

Theorem 1 enables us to obtain the admissible set of portfolios for all risk-averse individuals as the parametric solution, over all feasible values of μ, to the following optimization problem:[8]

[6] $\exp(X)$ denotes e^X.
[7] Elton and Gruber [9] provide a different proof of the theorem for the special case of equal logarithmic variances.
[8] For $C_{NS}(X)$, the feasible range of μ is from the minimum of the means of the individual securities to the maximum of the means of the individual securities. For $C(X)$, the feasible range is $-\infty \leqslant \mu \leqslant \infty$.

$$\min_X S_X^2$$

subject to $\quad X'E = \mu \qquad\qquad\qquad$ (I)

$$X \in C(X) \quad \text{or} \quad X \in C_{NS}(X).$$

We let $S^2(\mu)$ be the minimum objective function value of (I) when the portfolio mean equals μ. We note that, in view of (4) and (5), the admissible set of portfolios is also obtained as the parametric solution, over all feasible values of μ, to the following alternative quadratic programming problem:

$$\min_X X' \epsilon' \Omega \epsilon X$$

subject to $\quad X'E = \mu \qquad\qquad\qquad$ (II)

$$X \in C(X) \quad \text{or} \quad X \in C_{NS}(X).$$

If we let $\sigma^2(\mu)$ be the minimum objective function value of (II) for a given mean return μ, then the efficient frontier containing admissible portfolios for all risk-averse investors is some subset of this minimum variance boundary. Although, as we show presently, $\sigma^2(\mu)$ is strictly convex with a unique minimum, the efficient frontier is not $\sigma^2(\mu)$ in the region $\mu \geqslant \mu^{**}$ (the mean of the minimum $\sigma^2(\mu)$ portfolio) as it is under the mean-variance selection rule. Rather, as seen directly from theorem 1, it is the subset of $\sigma^2(\mu)$ in the region $\mu \geqslant \mu^*$ (the mean of the minimum $S^2(\mu)$ portfolio). From (5) it is clear that μ^* is the value of μ which solves $\min_\mu \{\sigma^2(\mu)/\mu^2\}$.

The solution to optimization problem (II) is facilitated by the following result:

Theorem 2. $\quad \epsilon' \Omega \epsilon$ is a positive definite matrix.

Proof. See Ohlson and Ziemba [20].

Theorem 2 implies that in (II), a convex quadratic function is being minimized over a convex set. Thus, if the feasible set of portfolios is $C_{NS}(X)$, (II) is a quadratic programming problem that is identical to the optimization problem solved to obtain the traditional mean-minimum variance efficient frontier (see, for example, Bawa [3]). Thus, one would use the same mathematical programming algorithms to obtain the mean-logarithmic variance efficient frontier as are used to obtain the traditional mean-variance frontier. Since (II) is in the form of a convex quadratic function subject to linear constraints, one could use the Markowitz critical-line algorithm, Markowitz [15], or the Markowitz-Sharpe critical-line algorithm, Sharpe [25], to obtain the mean-variance efficient portion of $\sigma^2(\mu)$, i.e., $\sigma^2(\mu)$ for $\mu \geqslant \mu^{**}$.

In either case, it is a simple matter to compute the point which minimizes $\sigma^2(\mu)/\mu^2$. The mean-logarithmic variance efficient frontier is then completely determined.

It should be noted that except for the subtle difference that the mean-logarithmic variance efficient frontier is for $\mu \geqslant \mu^*$ rather than $\mu \geqslant \mu^{**}$, the traditional mean-variance analysis still holds. It should also be noted that the use of the afore-mentioned algorithm generates the entire set of admissible portfolios. The optimal portfolio choice for a specific utility function can the be obtained from among the admissible portfolios. In the case of certain classes of utility functions, e.g., iso-elastic utility function, the optimal portfolio choice can alternatively be obtained directly by using the Frank–Wolfe algorithm. (See Ohlson and Ziemba [20] for details and referneces to Frank–Wolfe algorithm.)

If the feasible set of portfolios is $C(X)$, then (II) is the minimization of a convex quadratic function subject to two linear equality constraints. It can be rewritten, using Lagrange multipliers, as

$$\min_{X} \{1/2\, X'\epsilon'\Omega\epsilon X + \lambda_1(\mu - X'E) + \lambda_2(1 - X'I)\} \tag{II$'$}$$

where λ_1, λ_2 are the Lagrange multipliers and $\mathbf{1}$ is a $1 \times n$ vector of ones. The first order conditions are,

$$X'\epsilon'\Omega\epsilon - \lambda_1 E' - \lambda_2 I = 0, \tag{6}$$

$$\mu - X'E = 0, \tag{7}$$

$$1 - X'I = 0. \tag{8}$$

Since, by Theorem 2, $\epsilon'\Omega\epsilon$ is positive definite, the second order conditions for a minimum are satisfied and the optimal portfolio $X^*(\mu)$ for each value of μ, $-\infty \leqslant \mu \leqslant \infty$, is given by the unique solution to (6)–(8). We note that since (II$'$) is except for notational differences, identical to the problem considered in Merton [17], the solution to (6)–(8), following the method detailed in [17], is given by the following: [9,10]

$$X^*(\mu)' = \frac{(B\mu - A)I'\Omega^{-1}\epsilon^{-1} + (C - A\mu)I'\epsilon^{-1}\Omega^{-1}\epsilon^{-1}}{D}. \tag{9}$$

---

[9] These constants are defined so as to agree, as closely as possible, with Merton's notation. As is the case in Merton's derivation, since Ω is symmetric and positive definite, Ω^{-1} is symmetric and positive definite. Thus, B and C are positive since they are quadratic forms of Ω^{-1}.

[10] As Merton shows $D > 0$ follows from the fact that Ω^{-1} is positive definite. Also, in the solution to (II$'$), $\lambda_1 = (B\mu - A)/D$ and $\lambda_2 = (C - A\mu)/D$.

where

$$A \equiv 1'\epsilon^{-1}\Omega^{-1}1 = 1'\Omega^{-1}\epsilon^{-1}1,$$

$$B \equiv 1'\epsilon^{-1}\Omega^{-1}\epsilon^{-1}1,$$

and

$$C \equiv 1'\Omega^{-1}1.$$

Using (5), the minimum variance $\sigma^2(\mu) \equiv X^*(\mu)'\epsilon'\Omega\epsilon X^*(\mu)$ can be easily shown to be

$$\sigma^2(\mu) = (B\mu^2 - 2A\mu + C)/D. \tag{10}$$

Since B and D are positive, $\sigma^2(\mu)$ is strictly convex with a unique minimum at $\mu_{\sigma^2_{\min}} = A/B$, with $\sigma^2_{\min} = 1/B$. To find the point of minimum logarithmic variance we solve

$$\min_{\mu}\left\{(e^{S^2(\mu)} - 1) = \sigma^2(\mu)/\mu^2 = \frac{B - 2A\mu^{-1} + C\mu^{-2}}{D}\right\}. \tag{III}$$

Examining the first and second derivatives of (III) we note that it has a critical point at

$$\mu_{S^2_{\min}} = C/A,$$

with

$$\sigma^2_{S^2_{\min}} = C/A^2, \qquad S^2_{\min} = \ln\left(1 + \frac{1}{C}\right),$$

and that this critical point is a minimum. A further examination of the objective function reveals that this point is indeed the solution to (III). [11]
   Thus, we have derived the mean-logarithmic variance efficient frontier in mean-variance space as

$$\sigma^2(\mu) = (B\mu^2 - 2A\mu + C)/D, \qquad \mu \geq C/A.$$

Alternatively, we may express the minimum variance boundary in the more familiar

---

[11] One must examine the objective function at the points $\mu = -\infty, 0$ and ∞. At $-\infty$ and $+\infty$ $\sigma^2(\mu)/\mu^2$ goes to B/D. But $B/D > 1/C$, i.e., $BC > D$, since B, C and D are positive and $BC = D - A^2 > D$ (unless all $E_i = 0$). Finally, as μ goes to 0, $\sigma^2(\mu)/\mu^2$ goes to ∞ since $C > 0$.

form of μ as a function of σ^2, i.e.,

$$\mu = \frac{A}{B} \pm \sqrt{\frac{D}{B}\left(\sigma^2 - \frac{1}{B}\right)},$$

(11)

and the efficient frontier containing all admissible portfolios for risk-averse investors as

$$\mu = \frac{A}{B} + \sqrt{\frac{D}{B}\left(\sigma^2 - \frac{1}{B}\right)}, \qquad \sigma^2 \geqslant C/A^2$$

$$= \frac{A}{B} + \sqrt{\frac{D}{B}(\sigma^2 - \sigma_{\min}^2)}, \qquad \sigma^2 \geqslant C/A^2$$

(12)

From (11) it is clear that we may draw the minimum variance boundary as the right-hand branch of a hyperbola in mean-standard deviation space. In figure 1 we represent the efficient frontier (12) as the solid portion of the minimum variance boundary.

Finally, if we define

$$\omega = e^{S^2} - 1,$$

then using (1), we may translate (11) and (12) into mean-logarithmic variance space as

$$\mu = 1 \Big/ \left(\frac{A}{C} \pm \sqrt{\frac{D}{C}\left(\omega - \frac{1}{C}\right)}\right),$$

(13)

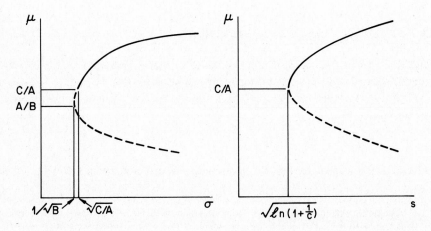

Fig. 1.

and

$$\mu = 1 \Big/ \left(\frac{A}{C} - \sqrt{\frac{D}{C}\Big(\omega - \frac{1}{C}\Big)} \right)$$

$$= \mu_{S^2_{\min}} \Big/ \left(1 - \mu_{S^2_{\min}} \sqrt{\frac{D}{C}(\omega - \omega_{S^2_{\min}})} \right) \tag{14}$$

respectively. In μ/S space, equation (13) takes the form of a hyperbola, the right-hand branch of which is also shown in figure 1. The efficient frontier (14) is again the solid portion of the curve. Thus we see from figure 1 that at least for the case when the set of feasible portfolios is $C(X)$, the mean-logarithmic variance efficient frontier is precisely the traditional mean-variance efficient frontier less those portfolios which have standard deviations $\sigma < \sqrt{C/A}$. It is interesting to note that the minimum variance portfolio is not mean–logarithmic variance efficient. In fact, it is not even on the mean-logarithmic variance boundary. Thus, in a lognormal securities market, no risk-averse individual would ever buy the minimum variance portfolio.

We note that the inclusion of a riskless asset with certain one-period return R_F does not change the determination of optimal portfolio choice in any significant manner. [12] For the case where $C_{NS}(X)$ is the feasible set of portfolios, the changes are identical to the change in the construction of the mean-minimum variance boundary as outlined in Bawa [3]. For the case where $C(X)$ is the feasible set of portfolios, inclusion of a riskless asset changes the efficient frontier identically as obtained by Merton [17] for the mean-variance case. We do not repeat these analyses here, but in the next section, explicitly include the riskless asset in the development of the market equilibrium relationships.

3. Equilibrium in a lognormal securities market

From (9) it is clear that for any portfolio on the minimum variance boundary, the allocation of wealth among the n risky assets may be written as a linear function of the mean μ on that portfolio, i.e.,

$$X' = \mu G + H \tag{15}$$

---

[12] We are aware that a linear combination of a riskless asset with a risky asset with lognormal returns is a displaced lognormal distribution, (i.e., portfolio returns are defined on some range (θ, ∞) instead of $(0, \infty)$ and that except for this displacement, the distribution is lognormal. However, in keeping with our basic assumption, we assume (viewing riskless asset as a degenerate lognormal distribution) that portfolios that include riskless asset have lognormal distribution.

where for notational convenience X denotes $X^*(\mu)$,

$$G = (BI'\Omega^{-1}\epsilon^{-1} - AI'\epsilon^{-1}\Omega^{-1}\epsilon^{-1})/D,$$

$$H = (CI'\epsilon^{-1}\Omega^{-1}\epsilon^{-1} - AI'\Omega^{-1}\epsilon^{-1})/D.$$

Since $X'1 = 1$, this implies that $G'1 = 0$ and $H'1 = 1$. As Merton [17] shows, (15) implies that any portfolio on the minimum variance boundary may be expressed as a linear combination of two linearly independent minimum variance portfolios. We refer to these two portfolios as M and Z. Since the mean-logarithmic variance efficient frontier is a subset of the minimum variance boundary, all risk-averse individuals will be indifferent between portfolios composed of the original n securities and combinations of the two portfolios or "mutual funds" M and Z. Thus, the separation or mutual fund property still holds in a lognormal market when all securities are risky. [13]

If, in addition to the n risky securities, there exists a riskless asset with certain return R_F, then we prove that the more traditional separation property still holds in a lognormal security market. Under this form of separation, individuals are indifferent between portfolios of the original $n + 1$ securities (n risky and 1 riskless) and combinations of two mutual funds, one of which contains only risky assets and the other composed only of the riskless asset. To see this, consider a portfolio P which is a linear combination of the riskless asset and some risky fund M. The return on this portfolio R_P may be written as

$$R_P = \alpha R_M + (1 - \alpha)R_F,$$

where α is some constant. The expected value of R_P is

$$\mu_P = \alpha\mu_M + (1 - \alpha)R_F, \tag{16}$$

and the standard deviation is

$$\sigma_P = \alpha\sigma_M. \tag{17}$$

Solving (17) for α and plugging into (16) gives the well-known relationship

$$\mu_P = R_F + \lambda_M\sigma_P \tag{18}$$

---

[13] Typically, fund M is chosen to be an efficient portfolio and is referred to as the "market portfolio". Given M, portfolio Z is chosen as the unique portfolio which is both on the minimum variance boundary and uncorrelated with M. Portfolio Z is called the "zero beta portfolio." This type of separation was first introduced by Black [4]. Thus, the results of Black carry over to the lognormal securities market case.

where

$$\lambda_M = (\mu_M - R_F)/\sigma_M.$$

Since portfolio returns are lognormally distributed, (18) is translated into μ/S space as

$$\mu_P = R_F/[1 - \lambda_M(e^{S_P^2} - 1)^{1/2}]. \tag{19}$$

(19) defines the relationship between the mean and logarithmic variance of any portfolio that is a linear combination of the risk-free asset and some risky fund M. Thus, in order to establish the separation property, we must show that for some risky fund, (19) is in fact the efficient portfolio frontier. Since (19) describes a parabola in μ/S space and since the efficient frontier of only risky securities (14) is concave in μ/S space, it is clear from Figure 2 that the optimal choice of M is defined by the point of tangency between (19) and (14). For this fund, M^* (often referred to as the "market portfolio" or "the market"), (19) is clearly the efficient portfolio frontier and thus the separation property holds in a lognormal market with the inclusion of a riskless asset.

One additional point worth mentioning is the fact that since, from (19), $d\mu_P/d\lambda_M > 0$, M^* must be the point which maximizes λ_M. From Figure 2, it is clear that the portfolio which maximizes λ_M is defined by the point of tangency, in μ/σ space, between the efficient frontier composed of only risky securities and the line described by (18). Thus, for M^*, (18) describes the efficient portfolio frontier in μ/σ space.

The results shown above are summarized by the following:

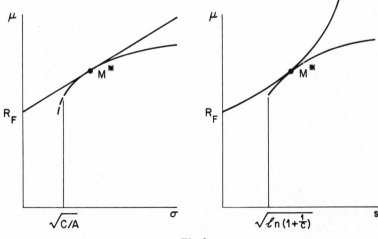

Fig. 2

Theorem 3.   The optimal portfolio choice for all risk-averse investors in a log-normal securities market admits separation between two portfolios ("mutual funds") of assets. If the riskless asset exists, the riskless asset and the "market" portfolio of risky assets are the two mutual funds. Otherwise, two portfolios on the mean-minimum logarithmic variance boundary serve as the two mutual funds.

Having established theorem 3, it is now a simple matter to derive the asset valuation model in a lognormal market under conditions of market equilibrium. In equilibrium, if investors have homogeneous expectations and risk-free borrowing and lending is permitted without limit at the riskless rate, then the prices of all securities will adjust so that their expected returns, in relationship to their riskiness, place them on the efficient frontier. Since as seen from Figure 2, the analysis is still done in the mean-variance framework, the analytic cum graphical technique of Sharpe [24] or equivalently the analytic method of Merton [17] still holds and one obtains directly the following security market line:

$$E_j = R_F + \beta_j(E_M - R_F) \tag{20}$$

where we recall that $E_j = E(R_j)$, $E_M = E(R_M)$ and define $\sigma_{jM} = \mathrm{cov}(R_j, R_M)$ and $\beta_j = \sigma_{jM}/\sigma_M^2$. Thus, it would appear that the equilibrium results in the mean-variance framework still holds. However, it should be noted that in the case of lognormal distributions, σ_{jM} and σ_M^2 and hence β_j are parameters that are not independent of the means E_j and E_M. Indeed, from (5), it follows that

$$\sigma_M^2 \equiv \mathrm{var}(R_M) = E_M^2(e^{S_M^2} - 1) \tag{21}$$

and it can be shown easily that

$$\sigma_{jM} \equiv \mathrm{cov}(R_j, R_m) = E_j E_M(e^{S_{jM}} - 1). \tag{22}$$

Thus, substituting (21), (22) in (20) yields

$$E_j = R_F + (E_M - R_F)\frac{E_j E_m(e^{S_{jM}} - 1)}{E_M^2(e^{S_M^2} - 1)}. \tag{23}$$

In the traditional model β_j represents the systematic or undiversifiable risk of security j. However, in a lognormal securities market, writing the valuation model in this form ignores the fact that E_j is a component of σ_{jM} and thus appears on the right-hand side of (20). β_j, as defined in (20), is thus not the correct measure of systematic risk since it includes the return measure as well. This directly leads to a new Capital Asset Pricing Model summarized by the following:

Theorem 4.   Under the standard assumptions employed in the analysis of capital market equilibrium, including homogeneous expectations and risk-averse investors, market equilibrium prices in a lognormal securities market satisfy the following relationship:

$$\frac{E_j - R_F}{E_j} = \frac{E_M - R_F}{E_M} \beta'_j ,$$
(24)

where

$$\beta'_j = (e^{S_{jM}} - 1)/(e^{S^2_M} - 1).$$
(25)

Thus, the difference between the new equilibrium model and the traditional Capital Asset Pricing Model, evident from a comparison of (20) and (24), is that in the new valuation model, the expected excess return on a security, expressed now as a fraction of its own expected return, is linearly related to its risk measure β'_j. Also, in the lognormal securities market, empirical validation of the new testable hypothesis is different from that under the normality assumption and is discussed in the next section.

4. Towards empirical verification of the valuation model

The difference between (20) and (24) is perhaps the single most important difference between the results in a normal and lognormal securities market. This difference has important implications for a large body of empirical work done to verify the traditional capital asset pricing model and to estimate the systematic risk of individual securities. If the underlying distribution of security returns is in fact more closely lognormal than normal, then the structural difference between (20) and (24) might explain the poor results of the numerous empirical tests of the traditional model (Lintner [12], Douglas [8], Miller and Scholes [18]).

Typical attempts to verify (20) begin with a time series index model of security returns. The returns on an individual security over time, R_{jt}, are assumed to be indexed on the returns, R_{Mt}, of some proxy for the market portfolio. The most commonly used index model is the Sharpe single index model, Sharpe [25],

$$R_{jt} = \alpha_j + \beta_j R_{Mt} + \epsilon_{jt},$$
(26)

where the ϵ_{jt} terms are the normally distributed disturbances associated with the jth security. The disturbance for any security is assumed to have zero mean, finite variance and zero covariance with the market return. If we make the necessary stationarity assumptions, the ordinary least squares regression estimate of β_j in (26) is   an   estimate   of   the   traditional   systematic   risk   coefficient σ_{jM}/σ^2_M.

These estimates, $\hat{\beta}_j$, $j = 1, 2, ..., n$, are then used in the cross sectional regression

$$\bar{R}_j = \gamma_0 + \gamma_1 \hat{\beta}_j + v_j,$$

where $\bar{R}_j$ is the average return on security j over some time period and v_j is a random disturbance term. The validity of the traditional model is then judged by comparing the ordinary least squares estimates of γ_0 and γ_1 with R_F and $\bar{R}_M - R_F$ respectively, for the relevant time period. R_F is typically taken to be the return on a government obligation and $\bar{R}_M$ is the average return on the market index.

As mentioned before, the result of these regressions have been quite disappointing. In particular, Miller and Scholes [18] found the estimate of γ_0 to be significantly larger than R_F and the estimate of γ_1 to be significantly smaller than $\bar{R}_M - R_F$. Among a number of feasible explanations of these results, Miller and Scholes suggest a possible nonlinearity in the risk return relationship. In addition, they suggest a significant source of the difficulty could be a skewness in the returns distribution.

In light of these facts, it behooves us to develop an econometric procedure for testing the validity of the alternative valuation model described in (24). Barring a complete estimation of the logarithmic variance-covariance matrix, the first step is to suggest an appropriate index model. The natural analog of the Sharpe single index model, under the lognormality assumption, would be the power model

$$R_{jt} = \alpha_j'' R_{Mt}^{\beta_j''} \epsilon_{jt}'', \tag{27}$$

where the ϵ_{jt}'' terms are assumed to be lognormally distributed disturbances with unit means and finite variance. In practice, one would run a time series regression on the logarithmic transformation of this model,

$$\ln R_{jt} = \ln \alpha_j'' + \beta_j'' \ln R_{Mt} + \ln \epsilon_{jt}''. \tag{28}$$

The ordinary least squares estimate of β_j'' is an estimate of S_{jM}/S_M^2. Thus, if we define $\hat{\beta}_j''$ as the estimate of β_j'', then we may in turn define

$$\hat{\beta}_j' = (e^{\hat{\beta}_j'' S_M^2} - 1)/(e^{S_M^2} - 1)$$

as an estimate of β_j' as described in (24). The final step in the procedure would be to run a cross-sectional regression on the model

$$(\bar{R}_j - R_F)/\bar{R}_j = \gamma_0' + \gamma_1' \hat{\beta}_j' + v_j',$$

where v_j' is the disturbance term, and to compare the estimates of γ_0' and γ_1' with zero and $(\bar{R}_M - R_F)/\bar{R}_M$, respectively.

Jensen [11] provides a detailed discussion of alternative empirical tests employed to validate the CAPM in the mean-variance framework. We note that except for the appropriate changes resulting from using (27) instead of (26), the procedures outlined in [11] still hold.

5. Concluding remarks

In the foregoing analysis, we have presented a viable alternative to the classic mean-variance approach to portfolio selection and capital market equilibrium analysis. This alternative is in the form of an equally simple portfolio selection rule derived from an equally robust theoretical basis. Although equally robust, this new theory is derived from assumptions which are more consistent with institutional realities and empirical evidence. The same econometric methods used to test the traditional theory may be used to test this alternative hypothesis and the same computational procedures that have been used to implement the mean-variance portfolio selection rule may be used to implement the mean-logarithmic variance selection rule. These facts seem to suggest a clear dominance of the lognormal assumption and that its use in portfolio theory and market equilibrium analysis and thus, in turn, in modern finance theory, is preferred over the classic mean-variance approach.

References

[1] K.J. Arrow, Theory of risk aversion, Essays in the Theory of Risk Bearing, Chapter 3 (Markham, Chicago 1971).
[2] V.S. Bawa, Optimal rules for ordering uncertain prospects, Journal of Financial Economics, Vol. 2 (1975).
[3] V.S. Bawa, Admissible portfolios for all individuals, Journal of Finance, Vol. 31 (1976).
[4] F. Black, Capital Market Equilibrium with Restricted Borrowing, Journal of Business, Vol. 45 (1972).
[5] R.C. Blattberg and N.J. Gonedes, A comparison of stable-paretian and student distributions as statistical models for stock prices, Journal of Business, Vol. 47 (1974).
[6] P.H. Cootner, The Random Character of Stock Market Prices (MIT Press, Cambridge, Massachusetts, 1974).
[7] A.S. Dexter, J.N.N. Yu and W.T. Ziemba, Portfolio selection in a lognormal market when the investor has a power utility function: computational results, Proceedings of the International Conference on Stochastic Programming, M.A.N. Dempster, Editor (Academic Press, forthcoming).
[8] G.W. Douglas, Risk in the equity markets: an empirical appraisal of market efficiency (University Microfilms, Inc., Ann Arbor, Michigan 1968).
[9] E.J. Elton and M.J. Gruber, Portfolio theory when investment relatives are lognormally distributed, Journal of Finance, Vol. 29 (1974).
[10] J.R. Hicks, Liquidity, Economic Journal, Vol. 72 (1962).
[11] M.C. Jensen, Capital markets: theory and evidence, The Bell Journal of Economics and Management Science, Vol. 3 (1972).

[12] J. Lintner, Security Prices, Risk and Maximal Gain from Diversification, Journal of Finance, Vol. 30 (1965).

[13] J. Lintner, Equilibrium in a random walk and lognormal securities market, Harvard Institute of Economic Research, Discussion Paper No. 235 (Harvard University, Cambridge, Massachusetts, 1972).

[14] H. Markowitz, Portfolio selection, Journal of Finance, Vol. 7 (1952).

[15] H. Markowitz, Portfolio Selection: Efficient Diversification of Investment (Wiley, New York, 1970).

[16] R.C. Merton, Optimum consumption and portfolio rules in a continuous-time model, Journal of Economic Theory, Vol. 2 (1971).

[17] R.C. Merton, An analytic derivation of the efficient portfolio frontier, Journal of Financial and Quantitative Analysis, Vol. 7 (1972).

[18] M.H. Miller and M. Scholes, Rates of return in relation to risk: a re-examination of some recent findings, in Studies in the Theory of Capital Markets, M.C. Jensen, ed., (New York, 1972).

[19] J. Mossin, Equilibrium in a Capital Market, Econometrica, Vol. 34 (1966).

[20] J.A. Ohlson and W.T. Ziemba, Portfolio selection in a lognormal market when the investor has a power utility function, Journal of Financial and Quantitative Analysis, Vol. 11 (1976).

[21] B. Rosenberg, The behavior of random variables with non-stationary variance and the distribution of security prices, unpublished paper, University of California, Berkeley (1973).

[22] S.A. Ross, Portfolio and capital market theory with arbitrary preferences and distributions − the general validity of the mean-variance approach in large markets, Working Paper No. 12-72, Wharton School of Finance, University of Pennsylvania (1972).

[23] P.A. Samuelson, The fundamental approximation theorem of portfolio analysis in terms of means, variances and higher moments, Review of Economic Studies, Vol. 37 (1970).

[24] W.F. Sharpe, Capital asset prices: a theory of market equilibrium under conditions of risk, Journal of Finance, Vol. 29 (1964).

[25] W.F. Sharpe, Portfolio Theory and Capital Markets (McGraw-Hill, New York, 1970).

[26] J. Tobin, Liquidity preference as behavior towards risk, Review of Economic Studies, Vol. 25 (1958).

[27] J. Von Neumann and O. Morgenstern, Theory of Games and Economic Behavior (Wiley, New York, 1967).

TIMS Studies in the Management Sciences 11 (1979) 63–71

DOES DIVERSIFICATION ALWAYS PAY?

Haim LEVY *

Jerusalem School of Business Administration
Hebrew University, Israel

In a recent article, Fisher and Lorie provided us with valuable data on investment profitability in common stocks for the period 1926–1965. The most interesting data, in my view, refer to the frequency distribution of returns for portfolios of different sizes. [1] The purpose of this paper is to apply some investment criteria in order to examine empirically to what extent diversification of investment is worthy.

Theoretically, Samuelson [19] has proven that if all available distributions are identical and independent then every risk averter would diversify his investment, and the optimal investment proportions are given by $P_i = 1/n$ ($i = 1, 2, ..., n$) where P_i is the proportion invested in security i and n is the number of available securities. When Samuelson drops the assumption of independence and replaces it by the assumption of "symmetric joint distribution" (see Samuelson [19, p. 3]), he still arrives at the conclusion that "diversification pays", i.e., every risk averter will diversify his investment in all the securities available in the market.

In a more recent paper [20] Samuelson shows that under a given condition, the mean-variance rule is useful and yields very good approximation. He obtains the results without assuming normality of the distributions or a quadratic utility function.

Hadar and Russell [5] show that if investors are risk averters, and the two securities under consideration have identical means, then a diversified portfolio dominates the specialized portfolios. Obviously, the above theoretical results depend on some assumptions with regard to the distribution of the rates of return.

The practical validity of the assumptions of Samuelson and Hadar and Russell is not clear. For example, in order to prove that diversification pays, they assume that all securities are characterized by the same mean, an assumption which does not have strong empirical support. However, the above theoretical results give us some

---

[1] See Fisher and Lorie [2, table 5]. This table presents the deciles and the 5th and 95th percentiles of the final wealth on investments with the horizons of 1, 5, 10, and 20 years. The mean, the variance, the maximum and the minimum of each distribution are also given. For each of the above investment horizons, two sampling techniques were applied. The meaning and the implications of these techniques are discussed below.

indications of the merits of diversification and empirical results can shed more light on this issue.

On the empirical side, few papers deal with the merit of diversification. Evans and Archer [1] analyze the relationship between the portfolio variance (risk) and the number of stocks in the portfolio. They come to the conclusion that an increase of the portfolio's size beyond 10 securities is unjustified since the impact of the marginal security in the portfolio on its variance is negligible. However, Evans and Archer analyze only the impact of a change in the portfolio's size on its variance, while it is clear that in general in order to determine if diversification pays, one has to examine the detailed distribution of returns.

Recently Levy and Markowitz [13] have shown that the mean-variance rule provides an excellent approximation to the maximum of expected utility for an important group of utility functions. The excellent approximation is achieved when the rates of return of mutual funds have been examined and even for rates of return of random portfolios of stocks, as long as the sample includes at least five different securities.

In this paper we test empirically if diversification pays. As a by-product, we shall examine to what extent our results are approximated by those obtained by the mean-variance criterion. Doing so, we have to bear in mind that the empirical test gives us only a rough indication and the results are limited to the particular available data. We do not claim that the empirical results are generalizations of the theory but rather a verification for it.

Most of the empirical results reported in this paper support the theoretical finding that diversification pays, especially when the portfolio is diversified between industries rather than randomly. However, beyond certain size the benefit from an increase in the number of securities included in the portfolio is very small.

1. The methodology

As mentioned above, the main drawback of most empirical works which examine the merit of diversification is that they are limited to the analysis of the reduction in the portfolio variance, stemming from an increase in the number of securities included in the portfolio. However, it is well known that, unless one is ready to assume normal distribution of return, the whole detailed distribution should be examined rather than only the variance. In the empirical work reported in this paper we shall use the following two decision rules which are, by now, well known in the economic literature as second degree stochastic dominance (SSD):

Rule I. Let F and G be the cumulative distributions of two prospects, then under conditions of risk aversion, a necessary and sufficient condition for prospect G to be dominated by prospect F (or FDG) is that $\int_{-\infty}^{x} [G(t) - F(t)] \mathrm{d}t \geqslant 0$ for every x, and that $G \neq F$ for some x_0. Thus, if rule I holds we say that F dominates G by the SSD criterion. For formal proof of this rule, see Hadar and Russel [4], Hanoch and Levy [7], and Fishburn [3].

Rule II. Let F, G be two cumulative distributions with mean values μ_1, μ_2 respectively, for which the following relations hold:

(i) for some $x_0 < \infty$ $F \leqslant G$ for all $x < x_0$ and $F < G$ for some $x_1 < x_0$;

(ii) $F \geqslant G$ for all $x > x_0$;

. Then, FDG for all concave utility functions (i.e., FDG by the SSD rule) if and only if $\mu_1 \geqslant \mu_2$. For formal proof see Hanoch and Levy [7, p. 341].

Obviously, rule II is a special case of rule I and is applicable whenever there is only one intersection between the two cumulative distributions F and G. If the above conditions hold, by rule II $\mu_1 \geqslant \mu_2$ implies FDG. If these conditions are not satisfied, we have to turn to rule I and conduct the cumbersome computations of the areas under the two distributions. In some cases of multi-intersections, some work can be saved by using the fact that a necessary condition for dominance of F over G is that $\mu_1 \geqslant \mu_2$. (See [7, p. 340].)

Efficiency procedure

A checking rule for dominance will be:

(a) See if rule 2 is applicable. If yes, $\mu_1 \geqslant \mu_2 \rightarrow$ FDG.

(b) If rule 2 is not applicable, compare μ_1 with μ_2 and $\min_F X$ with $\min_G X$, where $\min_F X$ and $\min_G X$ are the lowest observations under distribution F and G, respectively. In case that $\mu_1 > \mu_2$ and $\min_F X < \min_G X$, we cannot determine dominance, i.e., F$\not D$G and G$\not D$F. The fact that $\mu_1 > \mu_2$ rules out the possibility GDF (by the necessary condition) and $\min_F X < \min_G X$ rules out the possibility FDG (by rule 1). [2]

(c) If neither a nor b is applicable, compute the area under the distributions and use rule I to determine which one (or both) will be included in the efficient set. Unfortunately, in many of the comparisons reported below we had to perform this computation.

Before we apply decision rule I (or II) to empirical data one remark is called for. This decision rule assumes that F and G represent the population cumulative distributions, i.e., that no sampling errors are involved. In most empirical work in the area of portfolio selection it is implicitly assumed that the ex-post empirical distributions serve as the population distributions. The necessity to assume such an assumption stem, from the difficulty involved in testing the significance of the portfolio efficient set. This is true even in the mean-variance framework, a fortiori in the stochastic dominance framework. Employing stochastic dominance rules one assumes nothing about the distributions of rates of return. Recently [18] a nonparametric statistical test has been developed for the null hypothesis which asserts that $F = G$ where the alternative hypothesis is either $F < G$ or $F > G$. Unfortunately, this test is not applicable for testing the significance of the SSD rule, since

---

[2] Since for the value $x_0 = \min_G X$ we get $\int_{-\infty}^{x_0} [G(t) - F(t)]\, dt < 0$, and hence F does not dominate G by the SSD.

in this case F may dominate G in spite of the fact that $F < G$ in some part of the range.

Johnson and Burgess [8] examine the statistical accuracy of the mean-variance rule as well as the SSD rule. They assume that the distributions under comparisons are normal with given means and standard deviations. Performing a series of Monte Carlo experiments they investigate the impact of changes in the number of observations in the sample on the possible statistical errors. They show that in general the larger the number of observations in the sample the better is the performance of these decision rules and that the SSD rule and the mean-variance rule perform almost the same. However, the research on the statistical accuracy of stochastic dominance rules is still underdeveloped, and according to my knowledge very little on this topic has been done. This is true, in particular when one does not assume normal distributions.

Though the empirical research represented below is not precise, since we are dealing with samples rather than populations, we believe that the sampling errors are not significant, because we use very large samples which are provided by Fisher and Lorie [2]. The sample size varies but the smallest one includes approximately 32,000 portfolios.

In their table 5, Fisher and Lorie give the cumulative distributions of return for portfolios of different sizes. All the portfolios were taken from the same period 1926–65 but they differ in their investment horizon. Let us start with the one-year investment. In this case, Fisher and Lorie assume that the investor draws at random one year out of the forty years studied (1926–1965), and also chooses at random portfolios which contain the following alternative sizes: 1, 2, 8, 16, 32 or 128 stocks. Hence, we have six distributions which differ only with respect to the number of stocks included in the portfolio. By comparing these distributions, one can find if "diversification actually pays." Let us denote by F_i the cumulative distribution functions of return from a portfolio which contains i securities. Hence, if F_{128} dominates F_{32}, we will have shown that every risk averter would prefer a random portfolio with 128 securities rather than a portfolio with only 32 securities. More specifically, if $F_{128}DF_{32}$, $F_{32}DF_{16}$, $F_{16}DF_8$, F_8DF_2 and F_2DF_1, we can conclude, on empirical grounds that in the above cases diversification always pays.

In order to use rule I, we must have the detailed distributions $F_i(x)$ and $G_i(x)$ for every x. Unfortunately, Fisher and Lorie supply us only with partial information: eleven specific points on the cumulative distributions. Therefore, some approximations are called for. We assume that between two successive percentiles: x_i, x_{i+1}, the random return from the portfolios is distributed uniformly. This enables us to assume linearity of the cumulative distributions between any two successive percentiles calculated by Lorie and Fisher. However, in many cases we would determine dominance precisely even without full information (see the above suggested procedure).

2. The empirical results

Using the data of Fisher and Lorie for the one-year investment case, we obtain the following results:

$$F_2DF_1, \ F_8DF_2, \ F_{16}DF_8, \ F_{32}DF_{16}, \ F_{128}DF_{32}$$

That is to say, for one-year horizon, diversification always pays and the larger the number of securities in the portfolio, the better off will be the investor. In other words, if the past distributions represent well the future distributions, then every risk-averter who wishes to invest for one year should diversify his investment. [3]

Fisher and Lorie provide us also with the cumulative distributions for periods longer than one year, more specifically: five-year, ten-year and twenty-year investment horizons. Comparison of these distributions, together with the one-year results, is summarized below:

One-year horizon	Five-year horizon	Ten-year horizon	Twenty-year horizon
F_2DF_1	F_2DF_1	F_2DF_1	F_2DF_1
F_8DF_2	F_8DF_2	$F_8\not{D}F_2, F_2\not{D}F_8$	F_8DF_2
$F_{16}DF_8$	$F_{16}DF_8$	$F_{16}DF_8$	$F_{16}\not{D}F_8, F_8\not{D}F_{16}$
$F_{32}DF_{16}$	$F_{32}\not{D}F_{16}, F_{16}\not{D}F_{32}$	$F_{16}\not{D}F_2, F_2\not{D}F_{16}$	$F_{32}\not{D}F_8, F_8\not{D}F_{32}$
$F_{128}DF_{32}$	$F_{128}DF_{16}$	$F_{32}\not{D}F_2, F_2\not{D}F_{32}$	$F_{32}\not{D}F_{16}, F_{16}\not{D}F_{32}$
	$F_{128}DF_{32}$	$F_{32}\not{D}F_{16}, F_{16}\not{D}F_{32}$	$F_{128}DF_{32}$
		$F_{128}\not{D}F_2, F_2\not{D}F_{128}$	$F_{128}\not{D}F_8, F_8\not{D}F_{128}$
		$F_{128}\not{D}F_{16}, F_{16}\not{D}F_{128}$	$F_{128}\not{D}F_{16}, F_{16}\not{D}F_{128}$
		$F_{128}\not{D}F_{32}, F_{32}\not{D}F_{128}$	

As we have previously seen, for investors who commit their investment for one year, the efficient set includes only the portfolio F_{128}. For investors characterized by five-year investment horizon, the results are almost unchanged. We cannot determine dominance only with respect to F_{16} and F_{32}. That is to say, if we limit the investors to portfolios which contain no more than 32 stocks, it is not obvious that all of them would choose F_{32} since for some concave utility functions F_{16} is better than F_{32}. On the other hand, if there is no constraint on the portfolio size, the investor will choose neither F_{16} nor F_{32} because F_{128} dominates both. Hence, like the one-year result, for the five-year horizon, the efficient set includes only one portfolio: F_{128}.

The results for periods longer than five years are not crystal clear. For the ten-year case, we still get that portfolio with two securities is better than one which is not diversified at all (F_2DF_1). But no other portfolio which dominates F_2 can be found, and therefore the efficient set includes this portfolio. Making the other

---

[3] Obviously we ignore transaction cost, etc.

relevant comparisons, we find that the efficient set includes: $F_2, F_{16}, F_{32}, F_{128}$. Similarly, for the twenty-year horizon, it is always worthwhile to diversify in at least eight securities, but diversification beyond this size may not pay.

The above data reveal that to some extent diversification pays. Independent of the investment horizon, it is always better to invest in two-securities portfolios rather than concentrating on one security, but, in general, the longer the investment horizon the more difficult it is to determine dominance. This result might stem from the fact that a portfolio of, say, eight securities for twenty years is diversified not only between eight stocks but also diversified over time; i.e., the hypothesis is that diversification over time reduces the importance of the diversification between securities.

However, if the returns are indeed independent over time, this hypothesis has no theoretical support. It has been shown elsewhere [10] that under the assumption of independence over-time, if F_1 dominates G_1 and F_2 dominates G_2, then $F^{(2)}$ dominates $G^{(2)}$, where F_1 and G_1 are the cumulative distributions of the first period (e.g. first year), F_2 and G_2 are the cumulative distributions of the second period, and $F^{(2)}$ and $G^{(2)}$ are the two-period cumulative distributions. Applying this theoretical finding we would expect, in general, to find that diversification over time does not reduce the portfolio risk, since, if say, F_{32} dominates F_{16} for a one-year period, F_{32} must also dominate F_{16} for the two-year horizon. [4] Obviously, if returns are not independent over time, the above theoretical argument does not hold and diversification over time may count for the empirical findings.

It is interesting to note that in all four horizons the efficient sets which have been constructed for all risk averters (i.e., we assume concave utility function) are identical with the efficient set constructed under the well-known mean-variance rule. This implies that in the above cases the simple mean-variance criterion yields a good approximation. However in some cases, as will be shown below, the mean-variance rule yields unsatisfactory results.

3. Diversification by industry groups

Fisher and Lorie used two methods of random sampling. The first method (denoted by S) is a simple random sampling without replacement. By the second method (denoted by R), Fisher and Lorie ensure that portfolios are well diversified between industry groups. All the stocks on the New York Stock Exchange were assigned to 34 industry groups, from which only one stock can be included in each portfolio. Does it pay to diversify between industries? Portfolios which are diversified between industries (method R), are carried out by Fisher and Lorie only

---

[4] The assumed investment horizon plays a very important role in measuring the portfolio risk, and the portfolio performance. For more details see Levhari and Levy [9] and Levy [10], [12].

for the sizes of 8, 16 and 32 securities. Hence, we are limited to the comparison of portfolios of these sizes. The comparisons which are relevant in answering this question are given below:

One-year horizon	Five-year horizon	Ten-year horizon	Twenty-year horizon
$F_8(R)DF_8(S)$	$F_8(R)DF_8(S)$	$F_8(R)DF_8(S)$	$F_8(R)\not{D}F_8(S)$
$F_{16}(R)DF_{16}(S)$	$F_{16}(R)DF_{16}(S)$	$F_{16}(R)DF_{16}(S)$	$F_8(S)\not{D}F_8(R)$
$F_{32}(R)DF_{32}(S)$	$F_{32}(R)\not{D}F_{32}(S)$	$F_{32}(R)\not{D}F_{32}(S)$	$F_{16}(R)DF_{16}(S)$
	$F_{32}(S)\not{D}F_{32}(R)$	$F_{32}(S)\not{D}F_{32}(R)$	$F_{32}(R)\not{D}F_{32}(S)$
			$F_{32}(S)\not{D}F_{32}(R)$

Here $F_i(R)$ and $F_i(S)$ denote the portfolio distribution with i securities with sampling methods R and S, respectively. It is interesting to mention that in none of the periods the relation $F_i(S)DF_i(R)$ occurs, which means that the portfolio which is diversified between industries is always included in the efficient set. On the other hand, in many cases we have $F_i(R)DF_i(S)$ and hence diversification between industries pays in most cases. Once again, we can see from the above data that diversification between industries is particularly important for relatively short-period horizons.

Finally, let us compare the above results with those obtained by the mean-variance rule.

	Portfolio size	Dominance by the risk aversion criterion [a]	Dominance by the mean-variance rule [a]
One-year horizon	8	RDS	RDS
	16	RDS	RDS
	32	RDS	RDS
Five-year horizon	8	RDS	$R\not{D}S$ $S\not{D}R$
	16	RDS	$R\not{D}S$ $S\not{D}R$
	32	$R\not{D}S$ $S\not{D}R$	$R\not{D}S$ $S\not{D}R$
Ten-year horizon	8	RDS	$R\not{D}S$ $S\not{D}R$
	16	RDS	$R\not{D}S$ $S\not{D}R$
	32	$R\not{D}S$ $S\not{D}R$	$R\not{D}S$ $S\not{D}R$
Twenty-year horizon	8	$R\not{D}S$ $S\not{D}R$	RDS
	16	RDS	RDS
	32	$R\not{D}S$ $S\not{D}R$	SDR

[a] R – portfolio diversified by industry groups.
 S – portfolio diversified randomly.

Bearing in mind that the risk aversion criterion (SSD) is an optimal criterion for every risk averter (i.e., for every concave utility function), the above table shows that in some cases the results obtained by the mean-variance rule are not satisfactory. With the exception of the one-year horizon case, the approximation of the mean-variance rule is not too impressive. Moreover, in the twenty-year horizon case, we get SDR according to the mean variance rule, while it is clear from the risk aversion criterion that we are not able to determine dominance in this case (i.e., RDS and SDR). The identity of the result of SSD and the M-V rule for the one-year horizon support the hypothesis that annual rates of return distribute approximately normally. For the annual data the risk-aversion decision rule and the mean variance rule coincide. However, for longer horizons, the distributions are not normal, hence the discrepancy in our results. [5]

In the one-year horizon, diversification by industry groups (method R) proved to be better than the random diversification (method S). However, going into longer investment horizons, we can see that in many cases one cannot determine dominance, which means that it is not certain that all risk averters would prefer to diversify their portfolio by industry groups.

4. Concluding remarks

It has been proven theoretically that under several strong assumptions every risk averter will diversify his investment. Since most of the assumptions needed in the theoretical argument are questionable, we empirically test in this paper whether diversification pays. The empirical test does not intend to replace the theoretical argument but to complement it. Moreover, the results are limited to the analyzed data, i.e., the New York Stock Exchange, and any generalization to other markets or other types of investments is dangerous. Moreover, it is assumed that the ex-post data are the true distributions of the portfolios under consideration. Though we deal with huge sample sizes, some statistical errors are still possible.

The empirical results show that diversification almost always pays, but the larger the investment horizon the smaller is the merit of the diversification. By the same token, portfolios which are diversified by industry groups tend to be better than portfoilios which are diversified randomly. These conclusions have been derived under the assumption that investors are risk averters; no other assumptions have been employed with regard to the investors' preferences or the distribution of the portfolio's rate of return. Nevertheless, as far as the size of the portfolio is concerned, the mean-variance rule leads to the same results of those obtained by the risk-aversion criterion. In analyzing the advantages of diversification between industry groups, the mean-variance rule yields unsatisfactory approximations for long investment horizons, and in many cases we obtain results which are inconsistent with the results of the risk-aversion criterion, which is the optimal rule for

---

[5] Note that if one assumes that investors revise their portfolios instantaneously, then the distribution for every finite horizon are log normal (see Merton [17]). In this case the mean-coefficient of variation is the optimal decision rule for risk averters (see Levy [11]).

all risk averters. For short investment horizons (one year) the mean-variance and the risk-aversion rule provide identical (empirical) ranking.

In short, if one assumes that most investors in the stock market invest for one year or less, we conclude that diversification always pays, diversification between industries is preferable to a random diversification, and finally that the mean-variance and stochastic dominance criteria yield identical ranking of portfolios.

References

[1] J.L. Evans and S.H. Archer, Diversification and the reduction of dispersion: an empirical analysis, Journal of Finance 23 (1968).

[2] L. Fisher and H.L. Lorie, Some studies of variability of returns on investments in common stocks, Journal of Business 43 (1970).

[3] P.C. Fishburn, Decision and Value Theory (Wiley, 1964).

[4] J. Hadar and W.R. Russell, Rules of ordering uncertain prospects, American Economic Review 59 (1969).

[5] J. Hadar and W.R. Russell, Stochastic dominance and diversification, Journal of Economic Theory 3 (1971).

[6] J. Hadar and W.R. Russell, Diversification of interdependent prospects, Journal of Economic Theory 7 (1974).

[7] G. Hanoch and H. Levy, The efficiency analysis of choices involving risk, Review of Economic Studies 66 (1969).

[8] K.H. Johnson and R.C. Burgess, The effects of sample size on the accuracy of EV and SSD efficiency criteria, Journal of Financial and Quantitative Analysis 10 (1975).

[9] D. Levhari and H. Levy, The capital asset pricing model and the investment horizon, Reviews of Economics and Statistics (February 1977).

[10] H. Levy, Efficiency criteria and efficient portfolio: the multi-period case, American Economic Review 63 (1973).

[11] H. Levy, Stochastic dominance among log-normal prospect, International Economic Review 14 (1973).

[12] H. Levy, Portfolio performance and the investment horizon, Management Science 36 (1972).

[13] H. Levy and H. Markowitz, Mean-variance approximations to expected utility, American Economic Review, forthcoming.

[14] H. Levy and M. Sarnat, Investment and Portfolio Analysis (Wiley, 1972).

[15] H. Markowitz, Portfolio selection, Journal of Finance 7 (1952).

[16] H. Markowitz, Portfolio selection: efficient diversification of investment (Wiley, 1959).

[17] R.C. Merton, An intertemporal capital asset pricing model, Econometrica 41 (1973).

[18] A. Raviv, Problems in nonparametric statistics: comparison of two distributions without assumption of independence, unpublished Ph.D. dissertation, Hebrew University (1976).

[19] P.A. Samuelson, General proof that diversification pays, Journal of Financial and Quantitative Analysis 2 (1967).

[20] P.A. Samuelson, The fundamental approximation theorem of portfolio analysis in terms of means, variances and higher moments, Review of Economic Studies 37 (1970).

TIMS Studies in the Management Sciences 11 (1979) 73–77
©North-Holland Publishing Company

MEASURING RISK AND EXPECTATION BIAS IN WELL DIVERSIFIED PORTFOLIOS *

George M. FRANKFURTER
Syracuse University

and

Herbert E. PHILLIPS
Temple University

1. Introduction

It has been shown [4] that, in models which follow the Markowitz tradition [7], the mere existence of random error in estimation is sufficient to introduce selection bias in applications. This source of bias was recognized by Black, Jensen and Scholes [1, p. 85], though in a different context, and was observed in some empirical work by Blume [2, pp. 7–8]. Blume's empirical design, unfortunately, was neither rich nor flexible enough to provide any insight regarding the magnitude, consistency, or importance of selection bias. In the present work, the authors re-examine the impact and implications of selection bias in the context of portfolio selection. By resort to Monte Carlo methods, a much richer framework for analysis is provided. The purely theoretical [4] and the purely empirical [1],[2] results previously reported are verified and expanded in this paper.

2. Portfolio selection models: a Monte Carlo experiment

According to the market model formulation,

$$r_{it} = \alpha_i + \beta_i r_{mt} + \epsilon_{it}, \qquad t = 1, 2, ..., T, \tag{1}$$

where:
r_{it} = the rate of return in period t on security i;
r_{mt} = the rate of return in period t on a market portfolio;
α_i = the rate of return on security i when $r_{mt} = 0$;

* Appreciation is expressed to Mrs. Joanne Hill, a Ph.D. candidate at Syracuse University, for valuable assistance.

β_i = the slope of a line showing the extent to which the rate of return on security i is affected by r_{mt};

ϵ_{it} = a random deviate, with zero mean and variance $Q_i = \text{var}(\epsilon_i)$.

The rate of return on a portfolio of risky assets can be viewed as the result of

1. a series of investments in n basic securities,

and

2. an investment in the market portfolio.

An analytic process is one which begins with data collection, and culminates when a decision is made. The object in this Monte Carlo model is to replicate the analytic process for selecting portfolios which are efficient according to the mean-variance criteria [7]. The market model framework of (1) is used [8].   In order to replicate the estimation functions for the parameters α_i, β_i, and Q_i, which are employed in applications, we exploit the fact that (1) describes a regression structure. Regression estimators have well-known and tractable distributions [6, pp. 16–21]:

$$\tilde{\beta}_i \sim N\{\beta_i, \text{var}(\tilde{\beta}_i)\}, \tag{2}$$

$$\tilde{Q}_i \sim (Q_i/T)\chi^2_{T-2}, \tag{3}$$

$$\tilde{\alpha}_i = E(\tilde{r}_{it}) - \tilde{\beta}E(\tilde{r}_{mt}), \qquad t = 1, 2, ..., T, \tag{4}$$

where T = length of sample history, and the tilde distinguishes an estimator from a parameter. The expectation $E(\tilde{r}_{mt})$ and variance $\text{var}(\tilde{r}_{mt})$ are treated as constants in the Monte Carlo approach, but the expectation

$$E(\tilde{r}_{it}) \sim N(\mu_i, \sigma_i/\sqrt{T}) \tag{5}$$

is a normal deviate. It follows from (4), and is otherwise well known [6, p. 21], that $\tilde{\alpha}$ and $\tilde{\beta}$ are jointly distributed, bivariate normal random variables. Monte Carlo methods are used to generate $\tilde{\alpha}$ and $\tilde{\beta}$ directly.

In order that the simulations be held within realistic bounds, the parameters of (2), (3) and (5) are obtained by means of standard estimation procedures applied to actual data. A total of 72 observations on monthly rate of return were obtained for each of 760 securities, starting with February 1964; these were used as parameters for the simulation model. Values for the index, r_{mt}, were obtained by calculating rate of return on the geometric mean return for the 760 stocks. In order to hold the number of simulation trials required to produce meaningful results to a manageable level, the existence of a risk-free asset is exploited. In each simulation trial, therefore, only one collection of risky assets is considered.

A simplification of the portfolio selection problem is possible if one assumes that investors can borrow or lend at the same risk-free rate [8, p. 287], r_f; then,

---

[1] We wish to emphasize to the reader that the Capital Asset Pricing Model is not invoked in this paper. No general equilibrium conditions are expressed or implied.

with just one exception, every point on the efficient frontier [7] will be dominated by at least one point which lies on the locus of a straight line tangent to that frontier that passes through the point r_f on the expectations axis. The single exception, quite obviously, is provided by the point of tangency itself. This point identifies a unique collection of risky assets which we denote, τ. [2]

Given a set of simulation parameters, 200 repetitions for joint estimation of $\tilde{\alpha}_i$, $\tilde{\beta}_i$ and $\tilde{Q}_i$ were performed for each of the 760 securities in the universe. As a check on the system, the expectations $E(\tilde{\alpha}_i)$, $E(\tilde{\beta}_i)$ and $E(\tilde{Q}_i)$ were calculated by averaging over the 200 simulated observations on each random variable. The system showed excellent convergence, and was, thus, regarded as appropriate for use in the following application.

3. Monte Carlo experiment and results

The effect of random estimation error on the statistical characteristics of portfolio mean and variance estimates is to be studied. The market model of (1) is invoked, and it is assumed that the investor can borrow or lend at the risk-free rate r_f. The risk-free rate is set, on a monthly basis, at $r_f = 0.625$ percent, which is equivalent to an annual rate of $r_f = 7.5$ percent. For each of 11 simulated sample histories, an efficient frontier is obtained, and a single point on that simulated efficient frontier is identified by finding the tangent of the line in E-V space [8] which passes through the point r_f on the expectations axis.

Various characteristics of efficient portfolios obtained in a simulated environment are described in table 1. A portfolio whose expectation and variance depend on simulation parameters is said to be in "parameter space;" a portfolio whose expectation and variance is calculated from simulated sample statistics is said to be in "sample space." The results of 11 simulation trials are shown by rows 1 through 11 of the table; these portfolios are sample space portfolios. The expectations displayed near the bottom of the table were formed by averaging over the sample results. The characteristics of the parameter space portfolios are shown in the table by the row labeled "parameter space." Any difference in the characteristics of efficient sample space portfolios (rows 1 through 11 of the table) and the parameter space portfolios is a result of random sampling error.

Referring to the table we see that for each efficient portfolio in sample space, the expected rate of return shown in parameter space is overstated, and the total risk is understated. The binomial probability of obtaining this result given unbiased estimation of the portfolio parameters would be less than 0.5^{11}, which is less than the 0.01 percent figure used as a stopping rule for the simulation trials. On average, moreover, the degree of misstatement is in excess of 100 percent for both char-

---

[2] The portfolio τ is not a market portfolio in that, in the absence of any general equilibrium assumptions, it would not be comprised of a weighted average of every stock in the universe.

Table 1

Simulation No.	No. of Securities in Portfolio	Expected Return	Risk		
			Systematic	Nonsystem	Total
1	45	4.41	1.46	1.55	3.01
2	46	3.89	1.59	1.14	2.73
3	51	4.01	1.66	1.44	3.10
4	51	3.61	1.77	1.25	3.02
5	57	3.94	2.56	1.38	3.94
6	38	4.17	1.96	1.27	3.23
7	49	3.98	2.51	1.18	3.69
8	51	3.88	1.54	1.25	2.79
9	48	3.98	1.91	1.24	3.15
10	43	3.82	2.31	1.06	3.37
11	45	4.45	2.57	1.38	3.95
Expectation	47.63	4.01	1.99	1.28	3.27
Parameter space	39	1.72	5.26	1.66	6.92

acteristics. The selection bias identified by [1] and explained by [4] is no mere mathematical curiosity, therefore; the multiple effects of this bias are very significant. Further insight is provided by the simulation.

According to often stated gospel [9], where equilibrium is assumed, all but the systematic component of risk will have been diversified away in efficient portfolios. Referring to that block of the table which is devoted to risk, we see that for a universe as large as 760 stocks efficient diversification will not, *in general,* result in the elimination of nonsystematic risk. The nonsystematic component of risk accounts for approximately 24 percent of total risk in this parameter space, and rises to nearly 40 percent, on average, in sample space. What explains this rise and what is its consequence?

From (1) we see that the constants α_i and β_i are treated as independent constants by the market model. From (4), however, it is clear that the regression estimates $\tilde{\alpha}_i$ and $\tilde{\beta}_i$ are not independent; they are jointly distributed and thus tied together by an error structure. The regression estimator $\tilde{Q}_i$, by contrast, is independently distributed. The table shows that both systematic and nonsystematic components of risk will be understated. Because of the joint relationship between $\tilde{\alpha}$ and $\tilde{\beta}$, however, and the model's thirst for high alpha and low beta, the systematic component of risk will be more seriously understated that the nonsystematic component. Faced with a higher proportion of nonsystematic risk in sample space than in parameter space, what does the portfolio selection algorithm do? It attempts to run down nonsystematic risk by bringing in more stocks. Notice that efficient portfolios are significantly larger in sample space than in parameter space. Moral: selection bias results not only in overstatement of expectation and in understatement of risk, but in superfluous diversification as well.

References

[1] F. Black, M.C. Jensen and M. Scholes, The capital asset pricing model: some empirical tests, in Studies in the Theory of Capital Markets, Michael Jensen (ed.) (Praeger, New York, 1972).

[2] Marshall E. Blume, On The assessment of risk, The Journal of Finance XXVI (March 1971) 1–10.

[3] John L. Evans and Stephen H. Archer, Diversification and the reduction of dispersion: an empirical analysis, The Journal of Finance XXIII (December 1968) 761–768.

[4] George M. Frankfurter, Herbert E. Phillips and John P. Seagle, Bias in estimating portfolio alpha and beta scores, The Review of Economics and Statistics LVI (August 1974) 412–414.

[5] George M. Frankfurter, Herbert E. Phillips and John P. Seagle, Performance of the Sharpe portfolio selection model: a comparison, Journal of Financial and Quantitative Analysis VI (June 1976) 191–204.

[6] J. Johnston, Econometric Methods (McGraw-Hill Book Company, New York, 1963).

[7] Harry M. Markowitz, Portfolio Selection (Yale University Press, New Haven, 1959).

[8] William F. Sharpe, A simplified model for portfolio analysis, Management Science 9 (January 1963) 277–293.

[9] William F. Sharpe, Capital asset prices: A theory of market equilibrium under conditions of risk, Journal of Finance XIX (September 1964) 425–442.

TIMS Studies in the Management Sciences 11 (1979) 79–98
© North-Holland Publishing Company

THE IMPACT OF INFLATION ON PORTFOLIO SELECTION *

Menachem BRENNER
and
Marshall SARNAT
Hebrew University

1. Introduction

Economic motivation is almost invariably defined in *real* terms; individuals are assumed to react solely to changes in relative prices and/or to changes in their initial real wealth, including real security and money holdings. [1] Despite this, the normative theory of portfolio selection, associated with the pioneering studies of Harry Markowitz [15,16] was set out in nominal terms. Although Markowitz was aware of the potential impact of purchasing power considerations on the decision-making process (Markowitz [16, p. 34]), the relatively low inflation rates of the 1950s combined with his understandable and justifiable desire "to keep the analysis simple," led him to the conclusion that the essential properties of securities could be analyzed in practice using a model based on nominal returns. Writing in the relatively tranquil 1960s, William Sharpe, John Lintner, Jan Mossin and Jack Treynor derived a market equilibrium model, based on the Markowitz two-parameter portfolio analysis. Once again, price level considerations were ignored; all of the models incorporate nominal interest rates and returns. [2]

The dramatic world-wide resurgence of inflationary pressures in the 1970s, which resulted in an increase in both the level and variability of inflation, has refocused attention on the long neglected issue of the impact of price changes on portfolio choice and market equilibrium. [3] This paper builds on the suggestion, originally made by Markowitz, that the degree of inflation is potentially an impor-

* The authors gratefully acknowledge the helpful comments of Dan Galai, Yoram Landskroner and Meir Schneller, and the research assistance of Ephraim Edelman.

[1] This, of course, is Don Patinkin's classic definition of the absence of money illusion.

[2] This dependence on nominal, rather than real, returns also holds for Tobin's classic analysis of Keynes' monetary theory and Black's version of the two-parameter market model. Although the Black model does not require the assumption of risk-free borrowing and lending, his analysis is set out explicitly in terms of the nominal return on risky assets.

[3] See, for example, Roll's analysis of the relationship of interest rates to commodity prices; the studies of index-linked bonds by Sarnat [23] and Fischer [9], and the papers by Sarnat [22], Fama and McBeth [7]; Levy and Sarnat [12]; Biger [2], Friend et al. [10] and Solnik [26].

tant variable to be considered in portfolio selection:

"Also of importance in many cases is the rise and fall in the costs of fulfilling the needs and obligations of the investor. To account for this the anslysis may be performed in terms of 'real returns' rather than money returns" (Markowitz [16, p. 34]).

The purpose of the present paper is to examine the impact of changing inflationary conditions on investors' portfolios, and to estimate empirically the opportunity cost, in terms of decision errors, of basing normative portfolio selection on an efficiency analysis which ignores inflation. These findings should be of interest for individual and institutional investors who base their portfolio decisions on a Markowitz-type of analysis, as well as for academic researchers who have hitherto based their research on nominal returns.

§ 2 examines the properties of empirically generated distributions of real returns on U.S. common stocks for periods of varying levels and degrees of variability of inflation. In § 3 some factors affecting the relationship between nominal and real portfolio decisions are examined.

In § 4 empirical efficiency loci are generated and the nominal and real efficient portfolios are compared. § 5 concludes the paper with a brief summary of findings and some suggestions for further research.

2. The distribution of real vs. nominal returns

As Tobin [27] has shown, a mean–variance portfolio analysis can rest upon either one of the following assumptions:
   (a) individuals have quadratic utility functions;
   (b) they have concave utility functions and the distribution of returns are Gaussian.
In the absence of money illusion, we further assume that all individuals are expected utility maximizers of real wealth.

Hence, if for the usual reasons the quadratic utility assumption is dropped, the existence of significant levels of uncertain inflation implies that the distribution of real returns should be normal if the optimality of the mean–variance selection criterion is to be assured.

Despite this, empirical tests of the shape of the distribution of returns have been limited to nominal returns. The most common assumption which has been made regarding the behavior of nominal financial asset prices is that they are distributed log-normally, [4] i.e., the logs of the price relatives have a normal distribution. [5] Prior to Mandelbrot's seminal [14] paper, most studies concluded that common stock

---

[4] This is implied by the random walk model or, in continuous time, by the geometric Brownian-motion model.

[5] Alternatively, the price relatives themselves are assumed to approximate a normal distribution. Since for values below 15 percent, returns as measured by the log of the price relative are indistinguishable from returns defined as the periodic percentage change, this distinction has no relevance for empirical studies using monthly stock returns.

returns are distributed approximately normally; however, Fama [6] reached the contrary conclusion that $\ln(P_t/P_{t-1})$ has a stable nonnormal distribution. Officer [19] and others have tested the normal vs. the nonnormal stable hypothesis without reaching definitive conclusions. The nominal returns on common stock combine some characteristics of a nonnormal generating process (fat tails) with others that approximate the normal hypothesis. [6] Although the evidence is far from conclusive, the current consensus would appear to be that the distribution of returns is approximately normal; the fat tails may have been obtained by a mixture of normals. These results have some important implications for the distribution of real returns, which, as we have already noted, has not been tested at all.

If nominal returns are normal, the real returns may or may not be normal depending on the joint returns–inflation distribution. Testing the distribution of the rate of inflation is not sufficient, especially when the distribution of nominal returns is not strictly normal. Moreover, since the purpose of the present paper is to compare the implications of a nominal vs. a real analysis, it is desirable to assess the real returns distribution directly and then compare it with its nominal counterpart. This can be accomplished by adapting the methodology developed in previous studies for distinguishing the normal from nonnormal stable distributions to the problem at hand.

The normal is just one member of the so-called class of "stable" distributions. This family of distributions has three parameters: α, δ, σ. In the case of the normal distribution, the characteristic exponent (α) has the value of two. Fama and Roll [8, p. 333] provide an estimator for α and a test of stability designed to verify the stability property and to distinguish such distributions from a "mixture" of normal distributions. [7]

Two samples were used to assess the empirical distribution: [8]
(1) a sample of 25 industries comprising 1832 companies;
(2) a random sample of 49 companies. Both samples covered the 600 months from January 1926–December 1975. The nominal monthly returns (R) and real returns (r) for this period were used in estimating the characteristic exponent (α). [9]

[6] For example, there is some evidence that sums of returns have "thinner tails," for larger sums.

[7] For a detailed account of the estimation procedure, see Fama and Roll [8]. They find that "for $0.95 \leqslant f \leqslant 0.97$ the simple interfractile estimator $\hat{\alpha}_f$ has sampling properties that are 'robust' against variation in the true value of α". It is more efficient and free of bias when N is large and $\alpha \leqslant 1.7$. For $N < 99$ and/or $\alpha > 1.7$, there is a downward bias in $\hat{\alpha}$. The estimator $\hat{\alpha}_{0.96}$ was used in this study.

[8] The composition of these samples is described in more detail in § 3 below.

[9] The nominal monthly return is defined as $R = \ln(P_t/P_{t-1})$; the inflation rate is defined as $I = \ln(\Pi_t/\Pi_{t-1})$, where Π denotes the general price level and the real monthly return is given by $R - I$.

It is interesting to note that if the log of price relatives has a stable distribution, the price relative itself cannot have a stable distribution (see Elton, Gruber and Kleindorfer [5]). We have also tested the distribution using percentage returns and, as expected with monthly data, obtained virtually identical results.

Table 1

Estimates of the characteristic exponent (α) for distribution of monthly nominal and real rates of return on common stock, January 1926–December 1975.

Statistics	Sample of individual shares		Sample of industrial branches	
	Using nominal rate (R)	Using real rate (r)	Using nominal rate (R)	Using real rate (r)
$\hat{\bar{\alpha}}$	1.55	1.56	1.53	1.55
$s(\alpha)$	0.14	0.14	0.11	0.12
$\max(\hat{\alpha})$	1.87	1.85	1.69	1.74
$\min(\hat{\alpha})$	1.21	1.22	1.26	1.25

Table 2

Testing the "stability" of the characteristic exponent of nominal and real returns for the period January 1926–December 1975. [a]

$\hat{\bar{\alpha}}$ [b]	N [c]	Samples of individual shares		Samples of industrial branches	
		Nominal	Real	Nominal	Real
$\hat{\bar{\alpha}}_2$	300	1.56 (0.17)	1.57 (0.16)	1.54 (0.14)	1.55 (0.14)
$\hat{\bar{\alpha}}_4$	150	1.54 (0.20)	1.54 (0.20)	1.50 (0.19)	1.49 (0.17)
$\hat{\bar{\alpha}}_6$	100	1.62 (0.26)	1.61 (0.25)	1.59 (0.24)	1.57 (0.22)

[a] Numbers in parentheses are standard deviations.
[b] $\hat{\bar{\alpha}}_2$, $\hat{\bar{\alpha}}_4$, $\hat{\bar{\alpha}}_6$ denote $\hat{\bar{\alpha}}$ for sums of returns over 2, 4 and 6 months, respectively.
[c] N denotes the number of observations.

Estimates of the characteristic exponent (α) using nominal and real returns for both of the sample populations are given in Table 1, which sets out the mean of the estimated exponent ($\hat{\bar{\alpha}}$), its standard deviation [$s(\hat{\alpha})$] and the maximum and minimum values of $\hat{\alpha}$. The estimated exponents ($\hat{\bar{\alpha}}$) are much smaller than the appropriate value (2) for the normal distribution, and are about the same for both samples. [10] More important for the purposes of this paper, the nominal and real distributions have characteristic exponents which can be considered identical.

The estimated $\hat{\alpha}$ using time-series data to measure the "fatness" of the tails does not necessarily imply that the underlying distribution is not normal. It is quite possible that the low values of $\hat{\alpha}$ were generated by a "mixture" of normals, and

[10] The values of $\hat{\alpha}$ are also similar to those reported by Officer [19].

Table 3
Estimates of the characteristic exponent (α) for real and nominal returns for four subperiods [a]
distinguished by intensity of inflation.

Periods	Samples of individual shares				Samples of industrial branches			
	Nominal returns		Real returns		Nominal returns		Real returns	
	$\hat{\bar{\alpha}}_1$	$\hat{\bar{\alpha}}_2$	$\hat{\bar{\alpha}}_1$	$\hat{\bar{\alpha}}_2$	$\hat{\bar{\alpha}}_1$	$\hat{\bar{\alpha}}_2$	$\hat{\bar{\alpha}}_1$	$\hat{\bar{\alpha}}_2$
1/1926–12/1940	1.44	1.52	1.44	1.51	1.43	1.53	1.45	1.54
	(0.13)	(0.17)	(0.13)	(0.17)	(0.12)	(0.20)	(0.12)	(0.18)
1/1941–12/1950	1.75	1.64	1.75	1.68	1.84	1.72	1.83	1.80
	(0.19)	(0.23)	(0.18)	(0.22)	(0.23)	(0.23)	(0.24)	(0.18)
1/1951–12/1965	1.83	1.84	1.82	1.85	1.71	1.77	1.71	1.78
	(0.19)	(0.19)	(0.19)	(0.19)	(0.14)	(0.17)	(0.16)	(0.17)
1/1966–12/1075	1.76	1.62	1.75	1.62	1.89	1.78	1.90	1.78
	(0.20)	(0.26)	(0.20)	(0.26)	(0.18)	(0.23)	(0.19)	(0.22)

[a] $\bar{\alpha}$ denotes sums of returns over two months.

this "mixture" could be different for nominal and real returns. To test whether the observed fat-tails resulted from a "mixture" of normal distributions or from non-normal stable distributions, Table 2 examines the behavior of $\hat{\bar{\alpha}}$ as the sums of observations increase. Using Fama and Roll's [8] test for stability, characteristic exponents were estimated for nonoverlapping sums of 2, 4 and 6 months. For a mixture of normal distributions, one would expect a relatively rapid convergence of the mean characteristic exponent to the value of 2 (Fama and Roll [8]). This was not the case here; after 6 months the value of $\hat{\bar{\alpha}}$ did increase, but only slightly, and this increase was the same for both nominal and real returns.

The small increase in $\hat{\bar{\alpha}}$ may be a result of using data from periods with different exponents. It has been suggested (Brenner [4]) that the underlying α has changed significantly over time. The results reported in Officer [19] and Brenner [4] indicate that the distribution of returns in the period 1926–1950 may have been significantly different from that of the following 25 years ($\hat{\bar{\alpha}} = 1.5$ in the first period and 1.8 in the second). Hence, we decided to split the overall period of study of 600 months into two periods of 300 months each. And in a further effort to identify any differences between the nominal and real distributions, each of these periods was subdivided into two additional periods in accordance with the level and variability of inflation. Altogether, we have four periods of 180, 120, 180 and 120 months, respectively. For these smaller periods, we could recalculate $\hat{\bar{\alpha}}$ for sums of two months only. [11]

[11] Since relatively long periods are required to estimate α, the breakdown is not very accurate. For example, the last 10 years (1966–1975) were considered as one period. A more refined breakdown is used in the following section.

As table 3 shows, the estimated characteristic exponent for the first 15 year period was significantly lower than in later periods. However, the results for other periods are mixed. Using the sample of shares, $\hat{\alpha}$ exceeds 1.8 in period 3; but on the basis of the industries sample this result is found in periods 2 and 4. These findings are consistent with Brenner [4] and suggest that the post World War II distributions of returns are much closer to normal than their prewar counterparts. This probably has nothing to do with inflation; the fat tails in the early period were not caused by inflation hikes. Finally, table 3 again shows that the real and nominal distributions had similar characteristic exponents in each subperiod. Thus, despite our efforts to distinguish between them, the nominal and real distributions look more or less alike. In the following sections, we shall assume that both nominal and real returns have approximately normal distributions.

3. Factors affecting nominal and real portfolio choice

The fact that the empirical distributions of nominal and real returns cannot be distinguished one from another has no necessary consequence for the multivariate distribution of nominal vs. real returns. It is still possible for portfolio choice in nominal and real return space to be significantly different.

Before going on to the relevant empirical tests of portfolio choice based on real vs. nominal returns, some insight can be gained by considering a simple hypothetical example. For convenience, let us assume that the nominal returns and the inflation rate (as previous defined) are distributed multivariate normal. The real return is given by the difference between the nominal return (R) and the inflation rate I; [12] and the parameters of the real distribution can be rewritten in terms of nominal and inflation parameters:

$$E(r) = E(R) - E(I),$$

$$\sigma^2(r) = \sigma^2(R) + \sigma^2(I) - 2\sigma(R, I),$$

$$\sigma(r_i, r_j) = \sigma(R_i, R_j) + \sigma^2(I) - \sigma(R_i, I) - \sigma(R_j, I)$$

where: the notation $\sigma^2(\cdot)$ and $\sigma(\cdot,\cdot)$ denote variances and covariances, respectively. The relationship between the nominal and real parameters depends on the relative value of the nominal parameters and the combined values of the inflation parameters, e.g., positive values of $\sigma(R_i, I)$ will reduce $\sigma^2(I)$ while negative values will increase, the spread. However, we are not concerned with these differences per se,

---

[12] Empirically there is no difference between computing the real rate as $R\text{-}I$ or deflating the nominal price relatively by the inflation index relative.

but rather with their potential effect on the composition of portfolios.

Consider the example of two risky and one risk-free asset (R_f). [13] $R_i' = r_i' = E(R_i) - R_f$.

To simplify the notation, the subscripts $(i = 1, 2)$ denote the appropriate risky asset and the term for the nominal return (R) is omitted. Thus $\sigma^2(R)$ is given by σ_1^2. Now let's derive the investment proportions of the "tangent" portfolio in nominal and real terms. Employing real returns, the proportion invested in the first risky asset (1) is given by: [14]

$$W_1' = \frac{r_i \sigma^2(r_2) - r_2' \sigma(r_1, r_2)}{r_2' [\sigma^2(r_1) - \sigma(r_1, r_2)] + r_1' [\sigma^2(r_2) - \sigma(r_1 r_2)]} \tag{1}$$

If we restate the real parameters in nominal terms, we get:

$$W_1' = \frac{r_1' [\sigma_2^2 + \sigma_I^2 - 2\sigma_{2I}] - r_2' [\sigma_{12} \sigma_I^2 - \sigma_{1I} - \sigma_{2I}]}{r_1' [\sigma_2^2 + \sigma_{1I} - \sigma_{12} - \sigma_{2I}] - r_2' [\sigma_1^2 + \sigma_{2I} - \sigma_{12} - \sigma_{11}]} . \tag{2}$$

To separate the components of the nominal rate from the real rate, we rewrite (2) as:

$$W_1' = \{r_1' \sigma_2^2 - r_2' \sigma_{12} + r_1' [\sigma_I^2 - 2\sigma_{2I}] - r_2' [\sigma_I^2 - \sigma_{1I} - \sigma_{2I}]\}$$

$$\times \{r_2' \sigma_1^2 + r_1' \sigma_2^2 - (r_1' + r_2')\sigma_{12} + r_2' [\sigma_{2I} - \sigma_{1I}] + r_1' [\sigma_{1I} - \sigma_{2I}]\}^{-1} . \tag{3}$$

Where the proportion of asset 1 using nominal rates is given in (3) by:

$$W_1 = \frac{r_2' \sigma_2^2 - r_2' \sigma_{12}}{r_2' \sigma_1' + r_1' \sigma_2^2 - (r_1' + r_2)\sigma_{12}} , \tag{4}$$

which is the same as (1) except that it is set out in nominal terms.

The difference between W_1' and W_1 will be determined by the four extra terms in (3) relative to (4). While W_1 consists solely of nominal terms, the additional four terms that make up W_1' are all inflation related. If the size of the terms if negligible relative to the nominal terms, then W_1' will be close to W_1. It is clear from (3) that no simple relation exists between W_1' and W_1. If, in general, the correlation between the rate of return on stock i and the rate of inflation, denoted by $\rho(I, I)$, is close to

---

[13] The riskless asset is not essential to the analysis and is introduced solely to reduce the efficiency frontier to one specific point. For this purpose, we can either assume the existence of a real riskless asset or that the investor, as he does for risky assets, simply subtracts the rate of inflation from the nominal riskless asset.

[14] The proportion of the risk portfolio invested in the second asset is given by $W_2' = 1 - W_1'$.

zero, the difference will be determined by $(r'_1 - r'_2)\, \sigma_1^2$. If σ_1^2 is small, the differences between the proportions will also be small.

Given the complex form of (3) and the need to incorporate numerous assets (and therefore many additional inflation-related terms) in the analysis, these generalizations are not too helpful. The problem of determining the extent of inflation's impact upon portfolio choice is not a theoretical question and, therefore, requires an empirical analysis, using actual data on nominal and real returns. [15]

Even a cursory examination of (3) suggests that the variability of the rate of inflation is an important, and perhaps the main, factor which could potentially create significant differences between real and nominal portfolio choices. To isolate this factor, the overall 600 month period (January 1926—December 1975) was divided into five subperiods, using a drastic shift in the variance of the inflation rate as our partition criterion. The five periods are classified as "high" or "low" in terms of their inflation parameters [16] (mean and standard deviation) in table 4. An F test on the difference in variances between the five consecutive variances shows that no two consecutive variances belong to the same population. [17] During the period under study, the rate of inflation reached an unprecedented level (0.75 percent per month) in the last subperiod (1973—1975); however, it is noteworthy that the variability of inflation was the highest during the period 1940—1951.

Another important factor which may affect the analysis is the relative size of the correlation between nominal rates of return and the rate of inflation. The relevant correlation coefficients, for each subperiod were estimated using data drawn from the following sample population:

(1) 25 industries whose composition and number of companies included are given in the Appendix, table A-1. Taken together, these industries included about 1800 companies.

(2) A random sample of 49 stocks out of the 127 for which data are available for the entire 600 months. This will be called "stock sample 1."

(3) A random sample of 49 stocks, selected each period from all stocks, with available data for that period. This sample will be referred to as "stock sample 2." Most tests were carried out using all three samples, but not all cases are reported here due to the similarity of the results. [18]

---

[15] A theoretical simulation could also be carried out, but we are primarily interested in the differences which arise in practice, and therefore actual data have been used in the analysis.

[16] Periods III, IV and V are consistent with many recent studies of inflation; periods I and II typically are treated as a single period.

[17] These results were confirmed using the Pitman test, which unlike the F test, does *not* require the assumption of independence (Snedecor and Cochran [25, pp. 196–198]).

[18] The number of available stocks each period was: I 295, II 724, III 729, IV 918 and V 1370. In principle, each period had a different sample, although the same share could have been chosen in more than one period.

In this context, it should be noted that the size of the two stock samples (49) has no significance beyond computational convenience.

Table 4
Period of analysis (1/1926–1975) classified by rate of inflation and its variability (in percent) [a]

Period	Mean inflation rate $\bar{I}$	Standard deviation $\hat{o}_I$	Inflation rate $\bar{I}$	Variability of inflation $\hat{o}(I)$	F_c	F_{n_1, n_2}
I 1/1926– 11/1940	−0.135 (5)	0.713 (2)	Low	High	2.07	1.32
II 12/1940– 2/1951	0.500 (2)	1.025 (1)	High	High	19.69	1.32
III 3/1951– 6/1965	0.121 (4)	0.231 (4)	Low	Low	1.64	1.34
IV 7/1965– 1/1973	0.331 (3)	0.175 (5)	High	Low	3.62	1.57
V 2/1973– 12/1975	0.750 (1)	0.333 (3)	High	Low		
Overall period Jan 1926– Dec. 1975	0.191	0.682				

[a] The numbers in parentheses rank the means and standard deviations by size. F_c is the computed value $\hat{o}_1^2/\hat{o}_2^2$ where 1 in the subscript is the period with the larger variance and 2 is the period with smaller variance. F_{n_1, n_2} is the critical value of F at the 5% level with n_1 and n_2 degrees of freedom.

The correlation between nominal return and inflation, using the industry sample, is shown in table 5. The estimated correlation coefficients $(\hat{\rho}_{i,I})$ are positive, but generally insignificant in period I; negative and generally insignificant in periods II and III; and negative, but generally significant, in periods IV and V. In the former period, 21 out of 25, and in the latter, 18 out of 25, industries have negative coefficients which are significant at the 5% level. [19] Since period V shows nontrivial correlations between inflation and nominal returns, relative to the correlation between nominal returns, [20] and a relatively high variance of inflation (σ_I^2), while period II exhibits only a high variance of inflation, the former period might be expected to show greater differences when real returns are substituted for

[19] This is consistent with the known results of a negative correlation between the market index and inflation for the period 1950–1975.
[20] The correlation among the nominal returns is on the order of 0.8 and 0.5 for industries and individual shares, respectively.

Table 5
Correlation of nominal rates of return with inflation, for major industrial branches, selected periods, 1926–1975.

Industry classification	Period				
	I 1926–1940	II 1940–1951	III 1951–1965	IV 1965–1973	V 1973–1975
1	0.09	−0.04	−0.12	−0.28 [a]	−0.27
2	0.08	−0.04	−0.10	−0.22 [a]	−0.23
3	0.03	−0.15 [a]	0.10	−0.23 [a]	−0.35 [a]
4	0.07	−0.06	−0.10	−0.23 [a]	−0.29 [a]
5	0.04	−0.02	−0.13	−0.16	−0.29 [a]
6	0.03	−0.09	−0.08	−0.25 [a]	−0.32 [a]
7	0.08	−0.05	−0.12	−0.16	−0.32 [a]
8	0.10	−0.08	−0.10	−0.28 [a]	−0.37 [a]
9	0.08	−0.09	−0.09	−0.25 [a]	−0.32 [a]
10	0.11	−0.04	−0.06	−0.16	−0.42 [a]
11	0.02	−0.07	−0.10	−0.26 [a]	−0.31 [a]
12	0.06	−0.10	−0.07	−0.21 [a]	−0.31 [a]
13	0.07	−0.08	−0.06	−0.23 [a]	−0.26
14	0.05	−0.08	−0.12	−0.27 [a]	−0.31 [a]
15	0.08	−0.07	−0.08	−0.25 [a]	−0.36 [a]
16	0.06	−0.08	−0.10	−0.32 [a]	−0.38 [a]
17	0.04	−0.11	−0.06	−0.28 [a]	−0.31 [a]
18	0.03	−0.07	−0.15 [a]	−0.38 [a]	−0.29 [a]
19	0.09	−0.12	−0.09	−0.34 [a]	−0.33 [a]
20	0.15 [a]	−0.07	−0.08	−0.21 [a]	−0.18
21	0.09	−0.12	−0.09	−0.30 [a]	−0.24
22	0.14 [a]	−0.14	−0.15 [a]	−0.32 [a]	−0.34 [a]
23	0.04	−0.10	−0.03	−0.11	−0.27
24	0.01	−0.07	−0.14 [a]	−0.26 [a]	−0.31 [a]
25	0.07	−0.09	−0.15 [a]	−0.28 [a]	−0.21

[a] Significant at 5 percent level.

nominal ones. However, this must be examined empirically because the values of $\hat{\rho}_{i,I}$ may offset one another.

A somewhat different picture emerges from table 6 which presents the correlation coefficients derived from "stock sample 2." Here again the coefficients in period I are mostly positive while in periods IV and V they are largely negative. However, in all periods, the correlations do not generally differ significantly from zero. In period V only 11 out of 49 coefficients are significant. This suggests the possibility of different results when the analysis is based on the two different types of sample populations, i.e., individual shares and industrial branches. [21]

[21] As we shall see below, this difference in the correlation between nominal returns and inflation was not sufficiently pronounced to produce significantly different results for the two samples.

Table 6
Correlation of nominal rates of return with inflation, stock sample 2, selected periods, 1926–1975.

Stock	Period				
	I	II	III	IV	V
1	0.16 [a]	−0.10	−0.06	−0.03	−0.22
2	0.05	0.01	−0.08	−0.17	−0.20
3	0.00	−0.05	0.00	0.01	−0.23
4	0.08	−0.23 [a]	0.05	−0.07	−0.03
5	−0.02	−0.07	−0.06	−0.22 [a]	−0.37 [a]
6	0.06	−0.05	−0.07	−0.08	−0.26
7	0.00	−0.07	−0.14 [a]	−0.04	0.36 [a]
8	0.08	−0.06	−0.12	−0.20 [a]	0.26
9	0.00	−0.15 [a]	0.02	−0.05	0.25
10	0.07	−0.01	−0.15 [a]	−0.15	0.22
11	−0.02	−0.08	−0.09	−0.12	−0.14
12	0.09	−0.01	−0.04	−0.07	−0.12
13	0.08	−0.07	−0.10	−0.01	−0.34 [a]
14	0.11	−0.03	−0.13 [a]	−0.12	−0.27
15	0.11	−0.08	0.04	−0.17 [a]	−0.07
16	0.10	0.02	−0.12	−0.15	−0.15
17	0.03	−0.08	−0.03	−0.05	−0.19
18	0.04	−0.07	0.12	−0.20 [a]	−0.33 [a]
10	0.08	−0.10	0.00	−0.14	−0.24
20	0.08	−0.04	0.05	0.04	−0.27
21	0.10	−0.04	−0.15 [a]	−0.11	−0.28 [a]
22	0.03	−0.04	0.03	−0.20 [a]	−0.14
23	0.04	−0.02	−0.10	−0.15	−0.15
24	0.10	−0.07	0.07	−0.24 [a]	−0.20
25	0.04	−0.08	−0.01	−0.11	−0.17
26	0.05	−0.11	−0.02	−0.17	−0.39 [a]
27	0.06	0.01	0.01	−0.16	−0.23
28	−0.05	−0.12	0.11	−0.19 [a]	−0.02
29	0.11	−0.02	−0.06	−0.24 [a]	−0.12
30	0.16 [a]	−0.07	0.09	−0.02	−0.20
31	0.07	−0.10	−0.09	0.00	−0.21
32	−0.02	−0.10	−0.10	−0.06	−0.11
33	0.03	−0.04	−0.17	−0.08	−0.05
34	0.23 [a]	0.03	−0.02	−0.18 [a]	−0.21
35	0.04	−0.04	−0.06	0.00	−0.07
36	0.13 [a]	0.06	−0.05	−0.13	−0.18
37	0.05	−0.08	−0.10	−0.22 [a]	−0.37 [a]
38	0.06	−0.02	−0.07	−0.12	−0.38 [a]
39	0.06	−0.04	−0.16 [a]	−0.04	−0.32 [a]
40	0.07	−0.05	−0.02	−0.10	−0.15
41	0.06	−0.08	0.03	−0.08	−0.19
42	0.05	−0.09	−0.0'	−0.18 [a]	−0.19
43	0.02	−0.07	0.02	−0.24 [a]	−0.20
44	0.09	0.12	−0.05	−0.20 [a]	−0.41 [a]
45	0.12	0.01	−0.02	−0.17	−0.16
46	−0.02	0.05	−0.05	−0.22 [a]	−0.19
47	−0.01	−0.15 [a]	0.00	−0.32 [a]	−0.11
48	0.04	−0.05	−0.09	−0.13	−0.25
49	0.12	−0.07	−0.08	−0.06	−0.32 [a]

[a] Significant at 5 percent level.

4. Nominal vs. real efficiency frontiers

The empirical implications of the preceding analysis are straightforward. The error engendered by the reliance upon nominal, rather than real, returns, can only be assessed by a direct empirical examination of the differences in the nominal and real efficient sets at comparable points along the efficiency locus. To this end, the parameters required to generate the nominal and real efficiency frontiers (i.e., means, variances and covariances) were calculated for all three samples in each of the five subperiods under study. These parameters were then used to estimate the mean-variance efficiency frontier in real and nominal space.

Let us initially assume that an investor chooses that portfolio of risky securities which is tangent to the market line rising from the risk-free interest rate (R_f), i.e., he makes his portfolio choice in nominal terms. Using the mean monthly rate of return on Treasury bills as a proxy for the risk-free rate, the tangent nominal portfolio, denoted as P', was selected and the investment proportions of this portfolio were used to compute the portfolio's mean and variance in *real* terms. This defines a point in the real space; the latter representing the risk-return implications, in real terms, of the nominal portfolio which was originally chosen. Clearly, this point may be relatively close or far from the *real* efficiency frontier.

The decision error (i.e., deviation from the *real* efficiency locus) can be assessed in several ways. If we draw a vertical line in the real space from the portfolio chosen by the investor, P' to the corresponding point on the real efficiency frontier, we find (assuming the two points do not coincide) a portfolio, denoted by P, with a higher rate of return for the same variance (see Figure 1). In this case, the error which results from the reliance on nominal returns can be measured by the differ-

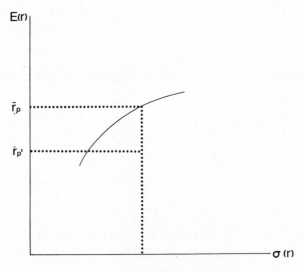

Fig. 1.

Table 7
Percentage point deviations of the mean real returns on nominal tangent portfolios from their corresponding real efficient portfolios. [a]

	Period					Total
	I	II	III	IV	V	
Industry	−0.01	−0.03	–	−0.02	–	–
sample	(13.09)	(4.92)	(2.58)	(4.90)	(7.97)	(6.64)
Stock	−0.01	−0.01	–	–	−0.02	–
sample 1	(6.07)	(4.42)	(2.91)	(4.95)	(8.17)	(5.28)
Stock	–	−0.02	−0.01	–	−0.02	
sample 2	(12.01)	(4.22)	(2.92)	(5.66)	(7.27)	
Addendum:						
Risk-free	0.11	0.04	0.19	0.41	0.56	0.19
Rate (R_f)						

[a] Figures in parentheses are portfolio standard deviations.

ence in expected returns of the two portfolios. This approach has much to recommend it. The differences in mean return have a meaningful and straightforward economic interpretation, and their significance can easily be determined using a t-test. [22]

Table 7 sets out the mean percentage point deviations of $\bar{r}_{p'}$ from $\bar{r}_p$ for the tangent portfolios of each sample in all of the time periods for which data are available. Even a cursory examination is sufficient to see that the deviations are not meaningfully different from zero. And this conclusion holds for all periods and all samples. No statistical tests are required. Even if the deviations should prove to be statistically significant, they are too small to be economically relevant as a measure of potential loss to investors. Nevertheless, it is interesting to note that the deviations, although very small, do appear consistently in periods II and V. [23]

For high levels of mean and variance (the far right-hand side of the frontier) only a few stocks (or industries) are included in the portfolios; hence, the potential

[22] Alternative tests could be designed which compare the variances for the same expected return, or the proportions of the portfolio on the frontier with those of the one actually chosen. However, these deviations are somewhat more difficult to interpret. Although a test on variances could be constructed, the properties of this test are less well known. Testing the differences in proportions is even more difficult and without additional assumptions nonparametric tests must be used.

[23] The absence of any deviation for the industry sample in period V results from the fact that the tangent nominal portfolio is a "corner" portfolio comprised of only one industry and therefore this portfolio's real counterpart is the same as the corner portfolio on the real efficiency frontier.

Table 8

Percentage point deviations of the mean real return on selected nominal portfolios from their corresponding real efficient portfolios, based on stock samples 1. [a]

Period	Portfolios							
	A_1	A_2	A_3	A_4	A_5	A_6	A_7	A_8
Total	−0.01 (4.91)							
I	−0.04 (4.83)	−0.02 (4.86)	−0.01 (5.03)	−0.02 (5.83)				
II	−0.06 (3.31)	−0.04 (3.46)	−0.02 (3.56)	−0.01 (3.79)	−0.01 (4.36)	−0.01 (5.38)		
III	−0.02 (2.31)	−0.01 (2.33)	−0.01 (2.48)					
IV	−0.06 (2.89)	−0.03 (3.24)	−0.02 (3.75)	−0.01 (4.19)	−0.01 (6.09)			
V	−0.31 (3.69)	−0.14 (3.71)	−0.11 (3.76)	−0.07 (3.91)	−0.06 (4.00)	−0.04 (5.49)	−0.02 (5.98)	−0.02 (7.42)

[a] Figures in parentheses are portfolio standard deviations.

differences are smaller than for lower mean-variance combinations. Since the risk-free rate was usually tangent to the efficiency locus at relatively high mean-variance combinations, this reduced the changes of detecting meaningful deviations. [24]

To avoid this problem and eliminate the essentially unnecessary dependence on the assumption of a risk-free interest rate, the same procedure for measuring deviations was applied to many different points along the efficiency frontier. The portfolios were chosen as follows: first, all portfolios at the (nominal) corner points were selected (on the average 20 portfolios); then other portfolios were chosen at random from the lower part of the frontier. [25] In each period about 30 portfolios were chosen from the nominal efficient set, and, as before, their real mean returns and variances were computed. These portfolios were then compared with a portfolio on the real efficiency frontier having the same real variance.

The deviations of $\bar{r}_{p'}$ from $\bar{r}_p$ for the two stock samples [26] are given in tables 8

[24] For example, the average "tangent" portfolio includes only five individual shares; the relevant figure for portfolios with lower levels of mean and variance is eleven.

[25] A corner-point is one in which an individual share is added (or dropped) from the portfolio. Low was defined as being left of the fifth corner-point (counting from the right).

[26] Results for the industry sample are not presented since they showed even fewer deviations. For example, in period III no differences between the relevant rates of return could be detected.

Table 9
Percentage point deviations of mean real returns on selected nominal portfolios from their corresponding real efficient portfolios, based on stock sample 2 in first four periods. [a]

Time period	Portfolios						
	A_1	A_2	A_3	A_4	A_5	A_6	A_7
I	−0.07	−0.02	−0.03	−0.01	−0.02	−0.02	−0.01
	(7.70)	(7.75)	(7.83)	(8.34)	(9.33)	(16.81)	(18.23)
II	−0.12	−0.06	−0.05	−0.03	−0.03	−0.02	−0.01
	(3.16)	(3.32)	(3.35)	(3.44)	(3.62)	(4.96)	(6.95)
III	−0.02	−0.01	−0.01				
	(2.60)	(2.72)	(2.85)				
IV	−0.08	−0.02	−0.03	−0.02	−0.01	−0.01	
	(2.81)	(2.83)	(2.90)	(4.89)	(5.53)	(6.20)	

[a] Figures in parentheses are portfolio standard deviations.

and 9. Only points for which the real rates of return on the equal variance portfolios differed are included in the two tables. Thus, in table 8, which is based on stock sample 1, at most, eight out of the thirty portfolios examined, displayed differences in their mean returns. (period V). Once again, with the exception of a few portfolios in period V, the deviations are too small to be economically meaningful. For example, the largest deviation in period II is 0.06 percent a month which amounts to an annual loss of 0.7 percent. This does not hold for period V. (The portfolio denoted in period V by A_1 shows a deviation of 0.31 percent per month which represents an annual loss of about 3.8 percent.) Since the deviations in period V could be meaningful to some investors a statistical test of the significance of the differences in mean returns was applied to the results in that period.

Choosing an appropriate test presented some problems. It could be argued that the real efficient frontier, as derived, accurately represents all available efficient portfolios, and therefore, if we assume normality, the appropriate confidence interval for $\bar{r}_p$ is twice the standard deviation, $s(r)$. The hypothesis tested is that the investment proportions of portfolio p' (derived from the accurate nominal frontier) are not different than the proportions of portfolio P, i.e., $\bar{r}_{p'}$ should fall within the confidence interval for $\bar{r}_p$. Using this test, it is clear that even in period V, no deviation is large enough to reject the zero difference hypothesis.

On the other hand, it could be argued that since we have derived the real frontier (and therefore P,) from a sample of real stock returns, and p' is based on a sample of nominal stock returns, deviations of $\bar{r}_{p'}$ from r_p should be tested by a statistic designed to test the difference between two correlated means. This is simply done by computing the standard deviation of the differences and computing the t-test

$$t(\bar{D}) = \frac{\bar{D}\sqrt{n}}{s/(D)}$$

where $D = r_p - r_{p'}$. Since period V is the only one with nontrivial differences, we applied the test only to that period.

Table 10 reports the results of this test (using stock sample 2) for the eight points (portfolios) which had deviations. Table 11 sets out the composition of these eight nominally derived portfolios (P') and their efficient counterparts (P).

At five of these points ($A_1 \dashv A_5$) the t-statistic indicates that $\bar{D}$ is significantly different from zero. These five points all lie in the lower mean-variance range of the efficient frontier. In other words, investors who choose very conservative portfolios may face losses on the order of two to four percent annually. (It should also be noted that the size of the deviation increases as the mean-variance level decreases.) However, the only nontrivial differences found were very close to the point of minimum variance, where very few investors presumably would choose to be.

5. Summary and conclusions

Given the level of inflation in the United States during the past 50 years, the failure to include cost-of-living considerations in portfolio analysis has done no harm. Subject to the usual caveat regarding the use of expost data for the ex ante expectations of portfolio theory, the substitution of real for nominal returns does not significantly alter investment decisions.

The two main parameters that may potentially affect portfolio decisions are the

Table 10

Test statistics for the percentage point differences between the mean of real returns for selected portfolios in period V (1973–1975), based on stock samples 2.

Test statistics	Portfolios							
	A_8	A_7	A_6	A_5	A_4	A_3	A_2	A_1
$\bar{D}$	−0.02	−0.03	−0.06	−0.11	−0.14	−0.19	−0.13	−0.36
$s(D)$	0.33	0.34	0.22	0.30	0.41	0.57	0.36	0.70
$t(\bar{D})$	−0.38	−0.43	−1.57	−2.06 [a]	−2.04 [a]	−1.96 [a]	−2.18 [a]	−2.81 [a]
max	0.83	0.70	0.29	0.55	0.92	1.40	0.72	1.29
min	−0.80	−0.73	−0.63	−0.68	−1.00	−1.23	−0.76	−1.55

[a] Significant at 5 percent level.

Table 11

Investment proportions of portfolios whose differential returns are included in Table 10.

Individual stocks	Portfolios [a]															
	A_8 P'	P	A_7 P'	P	A_6 P'	P	A_5 P'	P	A_4 P'	P	A_3 P'	P	A_2 P'	P	A_1 P'	P
2	0.16	0.17	0.14	0.15	0.06	0.06	—	—	—	—	—	—	—	—	—	—
23	0.19	0.16	0.25	0.23	0.24	0.25	0.12	0.14	0.11	0.13	0.10	0.13	0.10	0.11	0.04	0.09
32	0.65	0.67	0.56	0.60	0.26	0.28	0.11	0.13	0.09	0.12	0.08	0.11	0.08	0.10	0.02	0.08
11			0.05	0.02	0.12	0.12	0.08	0.08	0.07	0.08	0.07	0.08	0.07	0.07	0.06	0.07
22					0.15	0.13	0.39	0.36	0.41	0.37	0.43	0.39	0.43	0.40	0.44	0.43
28					0.02	0.01	0.11	0.10	0.12	0.11	0.12	0.12	0.12	0.12	0.13	0.13
33					0.15	0.15	0.06	0.09	0.04	0.08	0.02	0.06	0.01	0.06	0.00	0.02
15							0.03	0.03	0.03	0.03	0.03	0.03	0.03	0.03	0.02	0.03
36							0.10	0.07	0.13	0.08	0.14	0.09	0.14	0.11	0.09	0.14
14											0.01	0.00	0.02	0.00	0.09	0.01
3															0.02	0.00
43															0.08	0.00
47															0.01	0.00
r̄	1.48	1.50	1.41	1.44	0.90	0.96	0.13	0.24	0.05	0.19	-0.03	0.16	-0.04	0.10	-0.36	0.00
s(M)		7.44		7.18		6.07		5.22		5.19		5.15		5.13		5.07

[a] P' denotes the "nominally" chosen portfolio and P denotes its real efficient counterpart.

variance of the inflation rate and the covariance between the inflation rate and nominal returns, *relative* to the variance of the nominal returns and their covariances. However, as we have already noted in § 3, the two inflation parameters may offset each other, even if they are large, relative to the nominal ones. Of course, if they are relatively small, then one cannot expect significant differences between the real and the nominal.

To get some idea of the relative magnitudes, it is convenient to substitute the variance of the "market" portfolio and the covariances of nominal returns with the market, for the variances and covariances of the individual returns. In all periods the ratio of the variance of inflation to the variance of the return on the market was very small. (The largest value was four percent in period II.) A similar conclusion holds for the ratio of the relevant covariances: $cov(R, I)/cov(R, R_m)$. This is equiva-

Appendix Table A-1
Industry classification and number of stocks in industry groups

	Name of Industry	Two (or three) SIC Digits included	Number of companies included	
			Total	600 months sample
1	mining (except fuel)	10, 11, 12, 14	71	34
2	petroleum and gas	13	55	36
3	construction	15, 16, 17	21	16
4	food and kindred products	20	142	71
5	tobacco	21	24	8
6	textile and apparel	22, 23	95	55
7	lumber, furniture and paper	24, 25, 26	78	48
8	painting and publishing	27	42	26
9	chemicals	28	141	85
10	petroleum ref.	29	65	20
11	rubber and plastic	30	30	18
12	stone, clay and glass	32	55	44
13	primary metal	34	79	44
15	machinery except electrical	35	150	99
16	electrical machinery	36	127	77
17	motor vehicles	371	71	31
18	aircraft and parts	372	29	15
19	scientific instruments	38	65	47
20	railroad transp.	40	80	55
21	transportation (all)	41, 42, 44, 45, 46, 47	68	35
22	communication	48	25	17
23	utilities	49	149	121
24	banking and credit	60, 61	40	13
25	motion pictures	78	20	9

lent to the ratio of $\rho(R, I)\sigma_I\sigma_r$ to $\rho(R, R_m)\sigma_r\sigma_m$. Hence, even if the two correlations are of the same order of magnitude, the ratio of the covariances will still be very small.

It is the low variance of the inflation rate *relative* to the variance of the returns on common stock, which probably accounts for the close correspondence between nominal and real portfolio choices. Nevertheless, the systematic, albeit slight, differences which can be detected in the period 1973–1975 are suggestive. As additional data become available, this type of study might be extended usefully to later years. A more interesting and potentially rewarding alternative (in terms of insight gained) would be to extend the analysis to countries which have experienced significantly higher rates of inflation, such as Israel or Brazil.

References

[1] J. Aitchison and J.A. Brown, Lognormal Distribution (Cambridge University Press, Cambridge, 1957).

[2] N. Biger, The asssessment of inflation and portfolio selection, Journal of Finance (May 1975) 451–67.

[3] F. Black, Capital Market Equilibrium with Restricted Borrowing, Journal of Business (July 1972).

[4] M. Brenner, On the stability of the distribution of the market component in stock price changes, Journal of Financial and Quantitative Analysis (December 1974).

[5] E.J. Elton, M.J. Gruber and P.R. Kleindorfer, A close look at the implications of the stable Paretian hypothesis, Review of Economics and Statistics (May 1975).

[6] E.F. Fama, The behavior of stock market prices, Journal of Business (January 1965).

[7] E.F. Fama and J.D. MacBeth, Tests of the multiperiod two-parameter model, Journal of Financial Economics (May 1974).

[8] E.F. Fama and J.D. MacBeth, Tests of the multiperiod two-parameter model, Journal of American Statistical Association (June 1971).

[9] S. Fischer, The demand for index bonds, Journal of Political Economy (June 1975).

[10] I. Friend, Y. Landskroner and E. Losq, The demand for risky assets under uncertain inflation, Journal of Finances (December 1976).

[11] H. Levy and M. Sarnat, Investment and Portfolio Analysis (John Wiley and Sons, New York, 1972).

[12] H. Levy and M. Sarnat, Risk diversification and the composition of the market portfolio: an empirical investigation of the Tel-Aviv stock exchange, Bank of Israel Economic Review 42 (1975).

[13] J. Lintner, Security prices, risk, and maximal gains from diversification, Journal of Finance (December 1965).

[14] B. Mandelbrot, The variation of certain speculative prices, Journal of Business (October 1963).

[15] H.M. Markowitz, Portfolio selection, Journal of Finance (March 1952).

[16] H.M. Markowitz, Portfolio Selection (John Wiley and Sons, New York, 1959).

[17] R.C. Merton, Optimum consumption and portfolio rules in a continuous–time model, Journal of Economic Theory (December 1971).

[18] J. Mossin, Equilibrium in a capital asset market, Econometrica (October 1966).

[19] R.R. Officer, The distribution of stock returns, Journal of American Statistical Association (December 1972).

[20] D. Patinkin, Money, Interest and Prices, second edition (Harper and Row, New York, 1965).
[21] R. Roll, Interest rates on monetary assets and commodity price index changes, Journal of Finance (May 1972).
[22] M. Sarnat, Inflation and portfolio selection, Proceedings of the Conference on The Institute of Management Sciences, Tel Aviv (June 1973).
[23] M. Sarnat, Purchasing power risk, portfolio analysis and the case of index-linked bonds, Journal of Money, Credit and Banking (August 1973).
[24] W.F. Sharpe, Capital asset prices: a theory of market equilibrium under conditions of risk, Journal of Finance (September 1964).
[25] G.W. Snedecor and W.G. Cochran, Statistical Methods (The Iowa State University Press, Ames, Iowa, 1967).
[26] B. Solnik, Inflation and optimal portfolio choice, University of California, Berkeley Working Paper, Oct. 1976.
[27] J. Tobin, Liquidity preference as behavior towards risk, Review of Economic Studies (February 1958).
[28] J.L. Treynor, Toward a theory of market value of risky assets, unpublished manuscript.

TIMS Studies in the Management Sciences 11 (1979) 99–107

ON DISTRIBUTIONAL RESTRICTIONS FOR TWO FUND
SEPARATION

Robert H. LITZENBERGER *

Stanford University

and

Krishna RAMASWAMY

Bell Laboratories

The conditions under which the choice of an optimal portfolio from a set of risky assets is equivalent to choice from a given number of mutual funds have been of interest in the theory of finance. Portfolio separation, or "strong form k fund separation" obtains when, for each feasible portfolio, there exists a particular portfolio composed from k mutual funds that is at least as preferred by all risk averse investors. Separation in the "weak form" obtains when, for each risk averse investor, there exists a portfolio (possibly different across investors) drawn from k mutual funds that is at least as preferred as any other feasible portfolio. [1] From the work of Rothschild and Stiglitz [6], a given portfolio is preferred to another by all risk averse investors if and only if the return on the second can be characterized as *equal in distribution* to that of the first plus a noise term, whose expectation conditional on the first is zero. It follows that for strong form k fund separation to obtain the return on any feasible portfolio must be equal in distribution to the return on a particular portfolio drawn from these funds plus such a noise term. Requiring these funds to be made up from available assets and developing such an argument, Ross [5] shows that k fund separation obtains if and only if the return on any asset is *identically equal* to the return on a particular portfolio drawn from these mutual funds plus such a noise term. [2]

* This research was supported in part by a grant from the Dean Witter Foundation. The authors are grateful for the helpful comments of Chris Handel, Stanford University, and Stephen Ross, Yale University.

[1] See Ross [5] for a discussion of these definitions and their relation to stochastic dominance. Ross also proves the equivalence of these definitions.

This use of the term separation should be distinguished from "monetary separation," as used by Cass and Stiglitz [2]. This refers to the situation when the optimal proportions of a risk asset portfolio can be found independently from the division of investment between riskless and risky assets. Also see [2] for restrictions on individual preferences that lead to separation.

[2] The rationale for the requirement that the return on any feasible portfolio be identically equal to the return from a particular portfolio of the k funds plus noise follows from the fact that the funds are built from the assets themselves. If the returns were equal only in distribution, then any portfolio mixture between the asset and the k funds can be achieved: this must be dominated by the funds in the sense of Rothschild and Stiglitz.

This paper presents a simpler derivation of the conditions governing the return generating process that are necessary and sufficient for strong form two fund separation. The approach used here assumes that means and variances exist; it is emphasized that no further restrictions are made, either on the functional representation of the joint distribution or on asset expected returns. The analytical properties of the well-known Markowitz mean-variance efficient frontrier are exploited to show that when two fund separation obtains in market equilibrium the "zero-beta" version of the Capital Asset Pricing Model also holds. The conditions under which k fund separation leads to two fund separation are also examined.

1. Two fund separation

It is assumed that the joint probability distribution of asset rates of return is such that means and variances exist, and that the variance covariance matrix of asset returns is positive definite. From Gonzalez–Gaverra [3] and Merton [4], it is known that under unrestricted short sales, the mean-standard deviation efficient portfolio is a hyperbola. Choosing any portfolio p on this frontier (with associated return $\tilde{R}_p$), it follows from the properties of the frontier that the return on asset i, $\tilde{R}_i$, can be written

$$\tilde{R}_i = (1 - \beta_{ip})\tilde{R}_{zp} + \beta_{ip}\tilde{R}_p + \tilde{\epsilon}_{ip} \qquad \text{eq. (1)}$$

where $\tilde{R}_{zp}$ is the return on a frontier portfolio that is uncorrelated with $\tilde{R}_p$. Also from the analytics, it follows that

$$E[\tilde{\epsilon}_{ip}] = 0, \qquad \beta_{ip} = \text{cov}(\tilde{R}_i, \tilde{R}_p)/\text{var}(\tilde{R}_p). \qquad \text{eq. (2)}$$

While random variables can always be written as in (1), frontier properties are used to write (2). Other than the existence of means and variances, (1) and (2) do not depend on any specification of the multivariate distribution, nor do they depend on preferences.

It is further assumed that investor preferences are representable by von Neumann–Morgenstern utility functions defined over rates of return. Their initial wealth level is suppressed, and the utility functions redefined for different initial wealth levels. Investor utility function, $U(\cdot)$, are assumed to be weakly concave but strictly concave over some probable interval. They are not necessarily monotone. Investors with utility functions that satisfy these properties are deemed to be risk averse.

Lemma 1.   Given any two portfolios A and B, necessary conditions for portfolio A to be at least as preferred as portfolio B by all risk averse investors are

$$E[\tilde{R}_A] = E(\tilde{R}_B) \quad \text{and} \quad \text{var}(\tilde{R}_A) \leqslant \text{var}(\tilde{R}_B),$$

where: $\tilde{R}_A$ and $\tilde{R}_B$ represent the returns on portfolios A and B.

Proof. Consider the quadratic utility function

$$U(x) = x - ax^2, \qquad a > 0.$$

This is an admissible utility function, therefore $E[U(\tilde{R}_A)] \geqslant E[U(\tilde{R}_B)]$, for all risk averse utility functions implies

$$E[\tilde{R}_A] - E[\tilde{R}_B] - a(E[\tilde{R}_A]^2 - E[\tilde{R}_B]^2) - a(\text{var}(\tilde{R}_A) - \text{var}(\tilde{R}_B)) \geqslant 0.$$

This weak inequality holds for all $a > 0$ only if

$$E(\tilde{R}_A) = E(\tilde{R}_B) \quad \text{and} \quad \text{var}(\tilde{R}_A) \leqslant \text{var}(\tilde{R}_B). \qquad\qquad \text{Q.E.D.}$$

Theorem 1. When means and variances exist, strong form 2 fund separation obtains if and only if

$$E[\tilde{\epsilon}_{jp} | Q(\beta_{jp})] = 0 \qquad \text{for all assets } j \tag{3}$$

where

$$\tilde{Q}(\beta_{jp}) = \beta_{jp}\tilde{R}_p + (1 - \beta_{jp})\tilde{R}_{zp}.$$

Proof. Consider a risk averse investor (with utility function $U(\cdot)$) who invests a fraction α in asset j, and the fraction $(1 - \alpha)$ in the portfolio $\tilde{Q}(\beta_{jp})$. This last asset is constructed from two frontier portfolios and has the same mean as asset j. The problem is to

$$\max_{\alpha} EU(\alpha\tilde{R}_j + (1 - \alpha)\, \tilde{Q}(\beta_{jp})).$$

The first order condition is

$$E[U'(\alpha\tilde{R}_j + (1 - \alpha)\, \tilde{Q}(\beta_{jp}))\{\tilde{R}_j - \tilde{Q}(\beta_{jp})\}] = 0.$$

Since $U(\cdot)$ is concave (and strictly so over some interval); this condition is sufficient for a maximum, if its exists.

$\alpha = 0$ satisfies the first order condition if and only if

$$E[U'(\tilde{Q}(\beta_{jp}))\{\tilde{R}_j - \tilde{Q}(\beta_{jp})\}] = 0.$$

From (1), $\tilde{\epsilon}_{jp} = \tilde{R}_j - \tilde{Q}(\beta_{jp})$, so that $\alpha = 0$ is optimal if and only if

$$E[U'(\tilde{Q}(\beta_{jp}))\tilde{\epsilon}_{jp}] = 0. \tag{4}$$

Suppose now $E[\tilde{\epsilon}_{jp}|Q(\beta_{jp})] = 0$. Then

$$E[U'(\tilde{Q}(\beta_{jp}))\tilde{\epsilon}_{jp}] = E[U'(\tilde{Q}(\beta_{jp}))E(\tilde{\epsilon}_{jp}|Q(\beta_{jp}))] = 0$$

so that (4) is satisfied. This establishes sufficiency of (3).

Necessity is established as follows. By lemma 1, strong form separation obtains only if for every feasible asset the mean variance frontier portfolio having the same mean is at least as preferred as the asset itself. By construction this means that (4) must hold for all assets j. Suppose that (3) is violated. Then for some asset j there exists a number z such that

$$\int_{-\infty}^{z} m_j(Q)\, \mathrm{d}F(Q) = -\int_{z}^{\infty} m_j(Q)\, \mathrm{d}F(Q) \neq 0 \tag{4a}$$

where $m_j(Q) = E[\tilde{\epsilon}_{jp}|\tilde{Q})(\beta_{jp})]$ and $F(\cdot)$ is the cumulative distribution function of $Q(\beta_{jp})$. The equality in (4a) obtains because the total expectation of $\tilde{\epsilon}_{jp}$ is zero by construction. Consider a utility function that is piecewise linear:

$$U_1(R) = \begin{cases} K_1 R, & R \leqslant z, \\ K_1 Z + K_2(R - z), & R \geqslant z, \quad K_1 \geqslant K_2 \end{cases}$$

where K_1 and K_2 are real constants. Then

$$E[U_1'(\tilde{Q}(\beta_{jp}))\tilde{\epsilon}_{jp}] = K_1 \int_{-\infty}^{z} m_j(Q)\, \mathrm{d}F(Q) + K_2 \int_{z}^{\infty} m_j(Q)\, \mathrm{d}F(Q)$$

$$= (K_1 - K_2) \int_{-\infty}^{z} m_j(Q)\, \mathrm{d}F(Q) \neq 0$$

which is inconsistent with strong form separation. This proves necessity.   Q.E.D.

The theorem establishes that when means and variances exist and strong form two fund separations obtains, for every asset j the residual from a two factor model conditional on the return of the frontier portfolio with the same mean must be zero. It follows that under these circumstances, the optimal portfolios of all risk averse investors must be mean variance efficient.

Theorem 2.   When means and variances exist, weak form two fund separation is equivalent to strong form two fund separation.

Proof.   Sufficiency of strong form separation for weak form separation is straightforward. When means and variances exist the argument is even simpler and proceeds as follows: If strong form separation obtains then by lemma 1 the frontier port-folio that has the same mean as any given feasible portfolio is at least as preferred by all risk averse investors. The entire mean variance portfolio is spanned by any two portfolios on the frontier (see Merton [4], and Gonzalez–Gaverra [3]). Thus, strong form separation implies weak form portfolio separation.

To prove necessity consider the individual with the utility function defined above. If weak-form portfolio separation obtained were then the individual's optimal portfolio weights for funds, p and zp would be β_{jp} and $(1 - \beta_{jp})$ if and only if

$$E[U_1'(\tilde{Q}(\beta_{jp}))\{\tilde{R}_p - \tilde{R}_{zp}\}] = 0. \tag{4b}$$

Choose K_1 and K_2, $K_1 > K_2$ such that (4b) is satisfied. If $E[\tilde{\epsilon}_{jp} | \tilde{Q}(\beta_{jp})] \neq 0$, then the necessity proof in theorem 2 can be applied to show

$$E[U_1'(\tilde{Q}(\beta_{jp}))\tilde{\epsilon}_{jp}] \neq 0$$

which contradicts weak form separation. Hence (3) is necessary for weak form separation as well as for strong form separation. Since it has been shown that strong form separation implies weak form separation, and that weak form separation implies (3), the sufficiency of (3) for strong form separation closes this chain. Q.E.D.

Since Ross [5] does not assume that means and variances exist, his results are more general than those derived in this paper. The existence of means and variances allows us to identify the separating portfolios as mean-variance frontier portfolios. Under these circumstances the necessary and sufficient condition for two fund separa-tion is that the expectation of the residual term in a two factor model conditional on the return of the frontier portfolio having the same mean be zero. This is some-what weaker than Ross' condition which is that the expectation of the return conditional on every linear combination of the two separating funds be zero.

Capital asset pricing model

Hence when means and variances exist, and two fund separation obtains all risk averse investors will hold some linear combination of the two portfolios, $\tilde{R}_{zp}$ and $\tilde{R}_p$, which are frontier portfolios. It follows that optimal investor portfolios will be on the mean-variance frontier. For markets to clear, the market portfolio of all assets must be a convex combination of investors' portfolios. Since a convex com-bination of frontier portfolios is also a frontier portfolio, it follows that the market portfolio is on the frontier. Since $\tilde{R}_p$ was an arbitrary frontier portfolio, it can be interpreted as the market portfolio without loss of generality. Hence under (9) the first order conditions become

$$E[\tilde{R}_i] - E[\tilde{R}_{zm}] = \beta_{im}\{E[\tilde{R}_m] - E[\tilde{R}_{zm}]\},$$

where m is the market portfolio of all assets. This is the zero-beta version of the Capital Asset Pricing Model proposed by Black [1].

2. k fund separation

The conditions that are necessary and sufficient for k fund separation are from Ross [5], as follows: [3] for any asset i, the return $\tilde{R}_i$ is

$$\tilde{R}_i = \sum_{J=1}^{k} \alpha_{iJ}\tilde{R}_J + \tilde{\epsilon}_i, \qquad i = 1, 2, ..., n, \tag{6}$$

with

$$E[\tilde{\epsilon}_i | \sum_{J=1}^{k} \gamma_J \tilde{R}_J] = 0, \quad \forall\{\gamma_J\}, \forall i \tag{7}$$

where $\tilde{R}_J$, $J = 1, 2, ..., k$ represent the k mutual funds. Further, these funds are composed from the n securities with portfolio proportions $\delta_J = (\delta_{J1}, \delta_{J2}, ..., \delta_{Jn})$ such that

$$\tilde{R}_J \equiv \sum_{i=1}^{n} \delta_{Ji}\tilde{R}_i, \quad \sum_{i=1}^{n} \delta_{Ji}\tilde{\epsilon}_i = 0, \quad \forall J = 1, 2, ..., k. \tag{8}$$

The condition (7) requires that the expectation of $\tilde{\epsilon}_i$ conditional on any linear combination of the fund returns be zero. The last set requires that the funds be themselves composed from the n assets, and that these funds do not contain any $\tilde{\epsilon}$ risk. This requirement forces the $\tilde{\epsilon}$ vector to have $(n - k)$ degrees of freedom. These conditions are clearly of interest only when $n > k$.

A question of interest is the following: when means and variances exist, what further restrictions reduce k fund separation to two fund separation? To answer this, the properties of the noise term in the two cases must be examined. First note that if all risk averse investors choose from these k funds, an investor with quadratic utility will choose a mean variance efficient combination of these k funds. It follows that the entire mean–variance frontier (generated by using the n securities) must be spanned by these k funds: that is, the frontier must be identical to that generated by using the k funds as available assets. Second, note that the k funds are

---

[3] Ross [5] presents conditions (6) and (7) with $\tilde{y}, \tilde{z}', \tilde{z}^2, ..., \tilde{z}^{k-1}$ representing the k funds. Using (6) and a rank condition on the δ_J vectors in his theorem, it is easy to show that this is equivalent to writing the conditions in terms of R_J, $J = 1, 2, ..., k$. Note that (7) is required for all γ_J, whereas for our two fund representation $\gamma_J = \beta_{ip}$ is sufficient.

not unique, for portfolio combinations of a given set of k funds will yield still another set of k funds that satisfies the properties above. It is possible then to choose two of these funds that are on the mean-variance efficient frontier. From the previous section, if $\tilde{R}_p$ and $\tilde{R}_z$ are the returns from two assets on the frontier that are uncorrelated with each other,

$$\tilde{R}_i = (1 - \beta_{ip})\tilde{R}_z + \beta_{ip}\tilde{R}_p + \tilde{\epsilon}_i^*, \qquad i = 1, 2,,..., n, \qquad (9)$$

where $\beta_{ip} = \mathrm{cov}(\tilde{R}_i, \tilde{R}_p)/\mathrm{var}(\tilde{R}_p)$. The restriction

$$E[\tilde{\epsilon}_i^* | \lambda \tilde{R}_p + (1 - \lambda)\tilde{R}_z] = 0, \qquad \forall \lambda \qquad (10)$$

was shown necessary and sufficient for two fund separation. Choose the first of the k funds to be $\tilde{R}_z$, and the second to be $\tilde{R}_p$, as outlined above. The remaining funds $J = 3, 4, ..., k$ must satisfy (9)

$$\tilde{R}_J = (1 - \beta_J)\tilde{R}_z + \beta_J \tilde{R}_p + \tilde{\epsilon}_J^*, \qquad J = 3, 4, ..., k. \qquad (11)$$

This is a property of the frontier. [4] Using (11) and (6), for any asset i

$$\tilde{R}_i = [\alpha_{i1} + \sum_{J=3}^{k} \alpha_{iJ}(1 - \beta_J)]\tilde{R}_z + [\alpha_{i2} + \sum_{J=3}^{k} \alpha_{iJ}\beta_J]\tilde{R}_p + \sum_{J=3}^{k} \alpha_{iJ}\tilde{\epsilon}_J^* + \tilde{\epsilon}_i.$$
$$(12)$$

Now $\sum_{J=1}^{k}\alpha_{iJ} = 1$ and hence the sum of the first two square brackets is unity. It is then easy to show that the first is $1 - \beta_{ip}$ and the second β_{ip}; this follows from the fact that $\tilde{R}_z$ and $\tilde{R}_p$ are uncorrelated, and $\tilde{\epsilon}_J^*$ are uncorrelated with these. Comparing (9) and (12),

$$\tilde{\epsilon}_i^* = \sum_{J=3}^{k} \alpha_{iJ}\tilde{\epsilon}_J^* + \tilde{\epsilon}_i. \qquad (13)$$

The term on the left-hand side is the noise term from a two fund representation when means and variances exist. Taking $E[\cdot | \lambda\tilde{R}_p + (1 - \lambda)\tilde{R}_z]$,

$$E[\tilde{\epsilon}_i^* | \lambda\tilde{R}_p + (1 - \lambda)\tilde{R}_z] = \sum_{J=3}^{k} \alpha_{iJ} E[\tilde{\epsilon}_J^* | \lambda\tilde{R}_p + (1 - \lambda)\tilde{R}_z]$$
$$+ E[\tilde{\epsilon}_i | \lambda\tilde{R}_p + (1 - \lambda)\tilde{R}_z]. \qquad (14)$$

[4] Note that from the fact that $\tilde{R}_p$ and $\tilde{R}_z$ are on the frontier and uncorrelated,

$$\beta_J = \mathrm{cov}(\tilde{R}_J, \tilde{R}_p)/\mathrm{var}(\tilde{R}_p)$$

and $E(\tilde{\epsilon}_j^*) = 0$.

The last term on the right-hand side is zero when k fund separation obtains. Hence two fund separation obtains if for all λ

$$\sum_{J=3}^{k} \alpha_{iJ} E[\tilde{e}_j^* | \lambda \tilde{R}_p + (1 - \lambda)\tilde{R}_z] = 0. \tag{15}$$

Relation (15) is satisfied if either of the following conditions is satisfied

(i) $E[\tilde{e}_j^*] \lambda \tilde{R}_p + (1 - \lambda)\tilde{R}_z] = 0, \quad \forall \lambda, \forall J.$

This says that $\tilde{R}_J$, $J = 3, 4, ..., k$ are themselves worse, for risk averse investors than some combination of $\tilde{R}_z$ and $\tilde{R}_p$; but this is identical to the requirement for two fund separation. Note also that $\Sigma_{J=3}^{k} \alpha_{iJ} = 0$ so that

(ii) $E[\tilde{e}_j^* | \lambda \tilde{R}_p + (1 - \lambda)\tilde{R}_z] = H(\lambda \tilde{R}_p + (1 - \lambda)\tilde{R}_z)$

independently of J is also sufficient for the left-hand side of (14) to be zero.

This analysis demonstrates that if more than two funds are needed for separation when means and variances exist, then the following must hold: the conditional expectation of $\tilde{e}_j^*$, the noise term from candidate funds represented as convex combinations of two frontier funds as in (11), must be a non-null function. [5] The second condition (ii) implies still further that any nonlinear relationship between $\tilde{e}_j^*$ and $\lambda \tilde{R}_p + (1 - \lambda)\tilde{R}_z$ must not be the same for all candidate functions J. This condition says that if the additional funds provide identical risk sharing opportunities that are available from a linear combination of mean-variance efficient funds, then the latter are sufficient for separation.

3. Conclusion

When means and variances exist, two fund separation obtains if and only if in the representation of any return in a two-factor model the expectation of the residual term, conditional on the return of the mean variance frontier portfolio having the same mean, is zero. When this condition is satisfied all risk averse investors would choose mean-variance frontier portfolios and in market equilibrium the zero beta version of the capital asset pricing model obtains. When means and variances exist, for k fund separation, $k > 2$, to obtain the conditional expectation of the residual for the additional funds from a two-factor model must be a non-null function which is different across the funds.

---

[5] By a non-null function, it is meant that the function does not take zero value everywhere.

References

[1] Fischer Black, Capital market equilibrium with restricted borrowing, Journal of Business (March 1973), 444–454.

[2] David Cass and Stiglitz, J.E., The structure of investor preferences and asset returns, and separability in portfolio allocation: a contribution to the pure theory of mutual funds, Journal of Economic Theory 2 (1970), 122–160.

[3] Nestor Gonzalez–Gaverra, Inflation and capital asset market prices: theory and tests (unpublished Ph.D. Dissertation, Stanford University, 1973).

[4] Robert C. Merton, An analytical derivation of the efficient portfolio frontier, Journal of Financial and Quantitative Analysis (September 1972).

[5] Stephen A. Ross, Mutual fund separation in financial theory – the separating distributions, R.L. White Centre Working Paper 1–76, University of Pennsylvania. Forthcoming in Journal of Economic Theory.

[6] M. Rothschild and J.E. Stiglitz, Increasing risk I. A definition; II. Its economic consequences, Journal of Economic Theory 2 (1970), 225–243; 3 (1971), 66–84.

TIMS Studies in the Management Sciences 11 (1979) 109–124
© North-Holland Publishing Company

CAPITAL MARKET EQUILIBRIUM WITH PRICE AFFECTING INSTITUTIONAL INVESTORS

Eric B. LINDENBERG *

*American Telephone and Telegraph Company ***

1. Introduction

In this paper, we analyze the problem of general equilibrium in a securities market when some of the investors in that market, who are wealthy enough to make it worthwhile, take account of their effect on prices when they choose their portfolios. Sharpe [14], Lintner [7] and Mossin [10] have formulated the capital asset pricing model and have derived equilibrium prices when investors choose optimal portfolios, taking security prices as given to them. With the increasing importance of large investors, such as mutual and pension funds, the price-taking assumption becomes questionable when it is applied to all investors. [1] It is the purpose of this paper to assess the impact on the equilibrium prices of risky assets of large investors who account for price variations in selecting their optimal portfolios. In doing so, we will develop a new testable hypothesis about market equilibrium which accounts explicitly for the optimal investment behavior of large investors and can be contrasted with the traditional form of the capital asset pricing model.

Rubinstein [13] has pointed out that the relaxation of the perfectly competitive market assumption has received little attention in the literature. Only Masson [9] has sought directly to alter this assumption. In [9], individuals are taken to choose consumption levels in each of two periods, where the second period's income is a random variable. The interest rate on savings or lending depends upon the amount saved or loaned out. Masson finds that because the rate of return on nonconsumed funds is affected by the individual's decisions, the apparent level of risk aversion of the individual is altered. We will show in a later section that a similar result holds for large investors in securities markets.

* The author is indebted to V.S. Bawa for his many valuable insights and suggestions. Also, thanks are due to E.J. Elton, M.J. Gruber, J. Panzar and R.D. Willig for their comments and advice. The author, however, takes sole responsibility for any errors that may appear in this paper.
** Research for this paper was done while the author was employed by Bell Laboratories.
Recent statistics indicate that the institutional traders' volume of sales on the New York Stock Exchange has risen from 33 percent of total daily sales in 1961 to 56 percent in 1969 to 60 percent in 1971 to almost 70 percent in 1975 [12].

The analysis presented here parallels the theory of oligopoly that has been developed in the industrial organization literature (see, for example, Bertrand [1], Chamberlin [2], Cournot [3] and Edgworth [4]), in which several sellers of a product react to each other and account for their own effects on market prices when making supply decisions. Depending on each participant's assumptions about the behavior of others, a different market equilibrium will be reached. In a similar vein, the model presented here can be thought of as addressing the problem of oligopsony, in that it assumes that each of several large investors purchases a portfolio after accounting for the reactions of others as well as for his own effect on the market prices of securities. While the optimal portfolio for each particular investor depends explicitly on the assumptions that he makes about other investors' reactions to his decisions, the essence of our results is that the equilibrium relationship among securities' rates of return is invariant to the reaction assumptions made by investors.

In § 2 of this paper, we formulate the portfolio choice problem of investors, assuming that there exists a subset of investors, each of whom accounts for price variations that result from his own demands and who makes assumptions about the reactions of other investors to his own decisions. The reaction assumptions are specified by conjectural variations of demand which follow closely the concept used in the literature on oligopoly theory (see Fellner [5] for a discussion of this concept). We demonstrate that the case usually studied in the capital market literature, in which security prices are assumed to be unaffected by individual decisions, is a special case of our model and for which, in equilibrium, the traditional two factor capital asset pricing model (CAPM) results. More generally, with price affecting behavior by a subset of the investors, a three factor CAPM results in equilibrium which is invariant to the particular conjectural variations of investors, even though investors' optimal portfolios, in equilibrium, depend explictly on the conjectural variations assumed. In particular, this model provides a testable hypothesis that relates the excess expected return to the risk free interest rate, the risk of the security in relation to the market portfolio and the risk of the security in relationship to the aggregate portfolio of price affectors.

We also examine, in § 3, the equilibrium prices of risky assets within the framework of our model. We contrast these prices with those arising in the traditional perfectly competitive market. We show that the price of each risky asset can be higher or lower in the imperfect market than it would be otherwise, depending upon the relationship between the covariance of its return with the market return and its covariance with the return on the aggregate portfolio of price affecting investors.

In § 4, we illustrate the structure of the optimal portfolios of large investors by examining the problem for the case of the single price affector. We show that the large investor's optimal portfolio, in equilibrium, depends upon the level of his initial holdings of each security. Consequently, his optimal portfolio will, in general, no longer be balanced. This result contrasts with the traditional result of perfectly competitive markets in which each investor holds the same percentage of each risky asset in the market. Price taking investors, on the other hand, will hold portfolios that are balanced with respect to the market of securities excluding the portfolio of the price affector.

In § 5, we summarize our results and indicate how data on rates of return of large investors' portfolios can be used to test the model. We suggest reasons why tests of our model offer potential improvements on the results of previous tests of capital market equilibrium models.

2. Portfolio choice and capital market equilibrium with price affecting investors

In separate papers, Sharpe [14], Lintner [7], and Mossin [10] constructed a model of the structure of equilibrium prices for risky and riskless assets in a perfectly competitive market. Investors are risk averse and select optimal portfolios with respect to common estimates of expected value and variance for each asset.

The following are the standard assumptions of the basic capital asset pricing model:

(i)   All investors maximize single period expected utility and choose portfolios on the basis of mean and variance.

(ii)   Investors have homogeneous expectations of each security's probability distribution.

(iii)   All investors can borrow or lend an unlimited amount at a riskless rate of interest ρ, which they take as given. Define $r = 1 + \rho$.

(iv)   All assets are perfectly divisible and there are no transactions costs, taxes, etc.

(v)   The supplies of all assets are fixed.

(vi)   All investors choose portfolios which minimize the variance of final return for any given expected value. [2] When security returns are normal, this implies that all investors are risk averse.

(vii)   All investors assume that they can buy or sell as much of every security as they like without affecting prices. This is the standard price taking assumption.

We use the above assumptions but relax (vii) to (vii'):

(vii') Investors are of two types. Type 1 investors assume that they can buy or sell as much of every security as they like without affecting prices. Type 2 investors recognize that prices depend on their buy or sell orders and make some assumption about the reaction of other Type 2 investors to their own decisions.

Assumption (vii') reduces to (vii) if Type 2 investors believe that effect on prices of their own demands is zero.

---

[2] This assumption implies either normal distributions for security returns or quadratic utility functions for investors. Since the latter implication is severely limiting, we will use the normality assumption in this paper.

The following notation will be useful throughout the rest of this paper.

(a) There are n risky securities, issued by firms, indexed by j or $k = 1, ..., n$. Firm j has a one period return, in dollars, of X_j, $j = 1, ..., n$ which can be thought of as the liquidating value of the firm at the end of a single period. The joint probability distribution for the X_j's is normal, such that $E[X_j] = \mu_j$, $\text{var}(X_j) = \sigma_{jj} > 0$ and $\text{cov}(X_j, X_k) = \sigma_{jk}$. Furthermore, no security's return is a linear combination of the returns on any other securities; thus $[\sigma_{jk}]$ is positive definite.

(b) Let T be the set of investors in the market. Investors are indexed by $i = 1, 2, ..., m$. Let $Z_{ij} =$ the fraction of the outstanding equity of firm j chosen by investor i, for $j = 1, ..., n$. Define $Z_i \equiv (Z_{i1}, Z_{i2}, ..., Z_{in})$. Let $\bar{Z}_i \equiv (\bar{Z}_{i1}, \bar{Z}_{i2}, ..., \bar{Z}_{in})$ denote the initial holdings of investor i in each security before trading in the market. Denote the set $S \subset T$ as the set of Type 2 investors (price affectors) and $T - S \subset T$ as the set of Type 1 investors (price takers).

(c) Let $g_i =$ the total dollars invested in the riskless asset (bearing interest rate $\rho = r - 1$) by the ith investor. Let $\bar{g}_i$ denote investor i's initial position in the riskless asset.

(d) Let $s_j =$ the *total* market value of the equity of firm j. Let $d_j =$ the total market amount of debt (bearing a riskless interest rate $\rho = r - 1$) of firm j. Let $V_j = s_j + d_j =$ total value of firm j's assets.

For each investor selecting a portfolio Z_i there is a budget constraint, specified as:

$$W_i = g_i + \sum_j Z_{ij} s_j, \qquad i = 1, ..., m, \tag{2.1}$$

where $W_i \equiv \bar{g}_i + \Sigma_j \bar{Z}_{ij} s_j$. If Y_i is the final wealth of investor i after one period, then

$$Y_i = r g_i + \sum_j Z_{ij} (X_j - r d_j), \qquad i = 1, ..., m, \tag{2.2}$$

where $X_j - r d_j$ is the dollar return to equity holders after the interest and principle on debt is repaid. It follows from (2.1) and (2.2) that

$$Y_i = r W_i + \sum_j Z_{ij}(X_j - r V_j), \qquad i = 1, ..., m, \tag{2.3}$$

$$E(Y_i) = r W_i + \sum_j Z_{ij}(\mu_j - r V_j), \tag{2.4}$$

$$\text{var}(Y_i) = \sum_j \sum_k Z_{ij} Z_{ik} \sigma_{jk}. \tag{2.5}$$

Note that only the total value of each firm appears in the budget constraint. Therefore, for any given structure of debt and equity of a firm with a total value V_j, the investors' portfolio selection problem must yield the same results.

It follows from the assumption of normality that if we let $P \equiv (P_1, P_2, ..., P_m)$ denote a vector whose elements are, respectively, maximum permitted levels of variance for the portfolios of investors, each investor's problem of maximizing expected utility of final wealth reduces to

$$\max_{Z_i} rW_i + \sum_j Z_{ij}(\mu_j - rV_j) + \lambda_i(P_i - \sum_j \sum_k Z_{ij}Z_{ik}\sigma_{jk}) \tag{2.6}$$

where λ_i is the Lagrange multiplier associated with the variance constraint.

We now proceed to examine the conditions necessary for solving (2.6), recognizing that investors of the two types treat the arguments of (2.6) differently. In general, since $W_i = \bar{g}_i + \sum_k \bar{Z}_{ik}(V_k - d_k)$, and with prices dependent on some of the individual decisions, the first order conditions for (2.6) reduce to

$$\sum_k Z_{ik}\sigma_{jk} = \frac{1}{2\lambda_i}\left[\mu_j - rV_j + r\sum_k (\bar{Z}_{ik} - Z_{ik})\left(\frac{\partial V_k}{\partial Z_{ij}} + \sum_{l \neq i}\sum_{p=1}^n \frac{\partial V_k}{\partial Z_{lp}}\frac{\partial Z_{lp}}{\partial Z_{ij}}\right)\right]$$

$$j = 1, ..., n, \quad i \in S. \tag{2.7}$$

We can see that the right-hand side of (2.7) involves terms that account for:

(1) the direct effect on each price of changes in the investor i's decision variable Z_{ij},

(2) the indirect effect on prices that results from the reaction of other investors to changes in Z_{ij}.

Investors in the set $T - S$ (price-takers) assume that their own decisions do not affect market prices. Hence, both the direct effect $\partial V_k/\partial Z_{ij}$ and indirect effect $\sum_{l \neq i}\sum_{p=1}^n \partial V_k/\partial Z_{lp}\,\partial Z_{lp}/\partial Z_{ij}$ are assumed to be zero for each $i \in T - S$ and $j, k = 1, ..., n$. It follows that (2.7) reduces, in this case, to

$$\sum_k Z_{ik}\sigma_{ik} = \frac{1}{2\lambda_i}(\mu_j - rV_j), \qquad j = 1, ..., n, \tag{2.8}$$

which are precisely the conditions given by Mossin [11] for a market with all price taking investors.

On the other hand, each investor in S assumes that his direct effect is not negligible and that his indirect effect depends on the reactions of other members of S to his own decisions. As in oligopoly theory, we may define the *conjectural variation*, used by investor i in ascertaining the response of investor $l, l \neq i, l \in S$, to his own decisions, as $\partial Z_{lp}/\partial Z_{ij}, j, p = 1, ..., n$. (2.7) then fully describe the general conditions for an optimal portfolio choice by investor $i \in S$, in the sense that they account for his direct effect on prices and his indirect effect that results from his own conjectural variations.

The influence of these effects on optimal portfolio choices will, in general, depend on the level of prices that the investor sees. However, we can evaluate the equilibrium that results when investors behave according to (2.7) or (2.8), respectively. Define $R_S \equiv 1/\Sigma_{i \in S} \ 1/2\lambda_i$ and $R_{T-S} \equiv 1/\Sigma_{i \in T-S} \ 1/2\lambda_i$, which are, respectively, the harmonic mean of the mean–variance substitution rates for investors in S and $T - S$ each divided by the number of investors in that set. Since, in equilibrium, the demand for each security must equal its supply, it follows that, in equilibrium,

$$\sum_{i=1}^{m} Z_{ik} = 1, \qquad k = 1, ..., n, \tag{2.9}$$

Summing (2.7) over all $i \in S$ and (2.8) over all $i \in T - S$ and employing (2.9) yields

$$\sum_{i \in S} \frac{1}{2\lambda_i} \sum_k (\bar{Z}_{ik} - Z_{ik}) \left[\frac{\partial V_k}{\partial Z_{ij}} + \sum_{l \neq i} \sum_{p=1}^{n} \frac{\partial V_k}{\partial Z_{lp}} \frac{\partial Z_{lp}}{\partial Z_{ij}} \right]$$

$$= b_j - \frac{R_{M-S} + R_S}{R_S R_{M-S}} (\mu_j - r V_j), \qquad j = 1, ..., n, \tag{2.10}$$

where $b_j \equiv \Sigma_{k=1}^{n} \ \sigma_{jk} \equiv$ covariance of firm j's return with the total market return $\Sigma_{k=1}^{n} X_k$. Substituting (2.10) into (2.7) and then summing (2.7) over all $i \in S$ yields, after rearrangement,

$$V_j = \frac{1}{r} (\mu_j - R_{T-S}(b_j - \sum_{k=1}^{n} Z_{Sk} \sigma_{jk})), \qquad j = 1, ..., n, \tag{2.11}$$

where $Z_{Sk} = \Sigma_{i \in S} Z_{ik}$. The equilibrium, then, depends explicitly on the decisions of price affectors only through the aggregate portfolio $Z_S = (Z_{S1}, Z_{S2}, ..., Z_{Sn})$. This result holds independently of the number of price affectors or their respective conjectural variations. Individual optimal portfolios, in equilibrium, are found by differentiating (2.11) with respect to each Z_{ij} and substituting these plus the assumed conjectural variations into (2.7). Note that (2.7) depends explicitly on the initial portfolio $\bar{Z}_i = (\bar{Z}_{i1}, ..., \bar{Z}_{in})$ for each $i \epsilon S$. This contrasts with the conditions (2.8) for price takers. Consequently, since $\bar{Z}_i$ can be arbitrary, optimal portfolios for investors in S will not, in general, be balanced [3], as they are for investors in markets with all price takers (see Mossin [11]). Further discussion of this issue will be left to § 3.

The traditional valuation formula for perfect markets with all price takers falls out as a special case of (2.11) when S is empty, so that $T - S = T$. Then (2.11) reduces to

---

[3] A balanced portfolio consists of the same percentage of the outstanding shares of every firm in the market.

$$V_j = \frac{1}{r}(\mu_j - R_T b_j), \qquad j = 1, ..., n, \tag{2.12}$$

where R_T is defined similarly to R_S and R_{T-S} and is known as the market price of risk. Formula (2.12) is identical to that given in Mossin [11]. Note that in this case investors perceive prices as having zero derivatives with respect to their demand vectors.

We can compare the equilibrium values of firms in the market with price affectors to those arising in markets with price takers only. Let V_j' define the traditional, perfect market value of firm j, given by (2.12) and let V_j be the corresponding value in a market containing a subset of price affectors given by (2.11). Given the set of mean–variance substitution rates $\lambda \equiv (\lambda_1, ..., \lambda_m)$ for investors, (2.12) can be rewritten as

$$V_j' = \frac{1}{r}\left(\mu_j - \frac{R_S R_{T-S}}{R_S + R_{T-S}} b_j\right), \qquad j = 1, ..., n. \tag{2.12'}$$

Comparing V_j with V_j', we see that

$$V_j \gtrless V_j' \quad \text{as} \quad \sum_{k=1}^{n} Z_{Sk}\sigma_{jk} \gtrless \frac{R_{T-S}}{R_{T-S}+R_S} b_j, \qquad j = 1, ..., n.$$

Define $X_S \equiv \Sigma_k Z_{Sk} X_k$. Then the above condition becomes

$$V_j \gtrless V_j' \quad \text{as} \quad \sigma_{jS} \gtrless \frac{R_{T-S}}{R_{T-S}+R_S} b_j, \qquad j = 1, ..., n,$$

where $\sigma_{jS} \equiv \text{cov}(X_j, X_S)$. We have just proven the following theorem:

Theorem 1. If the covariance of a security's total return with the aggregate portfolio of the set S of investors is sufficiently large relative to its covariance with the market, then its equilibrium value will be higher in the imperfect market than in a market containing all price takers with the same mean–variance substitution rates.

In other words, when σ_{jS} is large relative to b_j, security j's return moves more closely with the return on the portfolio of investors in S than it does with the market as a whole. Such an effect is likely to occur whenever investors in S place greater weight on security j in their portfolios than does the market. Consequently, greater demand pressure is placed on security j than in the perfect market, forcing its equilibrium value upward.

We can restate the equilibrium valuation formulae in the more familiar rate of return form in order to further the comparison of our model with that arising in a perfect market. Define $r_j \equiv X_j/V_j \equiv 1 +$ rate of return on firm j's securities. Similarly, let $r_S \equiv \Sigma_k Z_{Sk} X_k / \Sigma_k Z_{Sk} V_k \equiv 1 +$ rate of return on the risky portion of the aggregate portfolio of the set S of price affectors, and define r_M similarly to r_S for the entire market portfolio. Then, for any security or efficient portfolio, (2.11) can be written as

$$E[r_j] = r + R_{T-S} V_M \operatorname{cov}(r_j, r_M) - R_{T-S} V_S \operatorname{cov}(r_j, r_S),$$

$$j = 1, ..., n, \tag{2.13}$$

where V_M and V_S are, respectively, the total value of the market and aggregate S portfolios. Since the market is efficient and each portfolio of investors in S is efficient, then the aggregate S portfolio is efficient. In equilibrium, the entire market portfolio as well as the portfolio Z_S must satisfy (2.13). Using this fact it is shown in the Appendix that (2.13) reduces to

$$E(r_j) = r + \beta_j^M \frac{[E(r_M) - r - \beta_M^S(E(r_S) - r)]}{1 - \rho_{SM}^2}$$

$$+ \beta_j^S \frac{[E(r_S) - r - \beta_S^M(E(r_M) - r)]}{1 - \rho_{SM}^2}, \qquad j = 1, ..., n, \tag{2.14}$$

where

$$
\begin{aligned}
\beta_j^M &= \operatorname{cov}(r_j, r_M)/\operatorname{var}(r_M), \\
\beta_j^S &= \operatorname{cov}(r_j, r_S)/\operatorname{var}(r_S), \\
\beta_M^S &= \operatorname{cov}(r_M, r_S)/\operatorname{var}(r_S), \\
\beta_S^M &= \operatorname{cov}(r_M, r_S)/\operatorname{var}(r_M), \\
\rho_{SM} &= \operatorname{corr}(r_S, r_M).
\end{aligned}
$$

We have thus proven the following:

Theorem 2. In a capital asset market containing both price taking investors and a group of price affectors whose portfolios are selected according to (2.7), under varying assumptions about investor interactions, the excess return for each security is linearly related to two risk measures β_j^S and β_j^M which, respectively, measure the comovement of a security's return with the return on the aggregate portfolio of price affectors and its comovement with the total market return.

The traditional capital asset pricing model stated by Sharpe [14], is a special case of (2.14) and can be derived from (2.13) by noting that if price affectors' direct and indirect effects are negligible, then conditions (2.8) apply and the portfolio Z_S will be balanced. This means that r_S and r_M are perfectly correlated. (2.13) reduces to

$$E[r_j] = r + \beta_j^M (E[r_M] - r), \qquad j = 1, ..., n, \tag{2.15}$$

which is identical to that given in Sharpe [14].

The new model (2.14) has important practical consequences. First of all, it provides a testable alternative to the traditional capital asset pricing model which has the potential for providing a better fit to the data (see Jensen [6]). Second, it suggests that biases in the slope and intercept found by regressing excess returns on securities on the "market betas" may be attributable to an omitted variable as well as to the comovement of r_S and r_M. Lastly, since $Z_i = (Z_{i1}, ..., Z_{in})$ for $i \in S$ depends explicitly on initial holdings of securities as shown by (2.7), the new model provides a theoretical reason for holding unbalanced portfolios by some investors that is based upon imperfect competition and can be tested through its effects upon market rates of return.

3. Optimal portfolio choice: the case of the single price affector

We have noted that despite the fact that the equilibrium rate of return relationship depends on price affectors' behavior only through Z_S, the individual portfolios of price affectors $Z_i = (Z_{i1}, ..., Z_{in})$ for $i \in S$ depend explicitly on the derivatives of (2.11) as well as the particular conjectural variations presumed by investors. To obtain general solutions for the optimal portfolios would be quite difficult. However, in order to gain some insight about how the optimal portfolio of a price affector may differ from that predicted by the traditional perfectly competitive market, we study the problem, in this section, for the case of the single price affector. This analysis will indicate how the price affector's unbalanced portfolio compares with a balanced portfolio of an investor with the same attitude towards risk.

In this case, the price affector, say investor 1, sees the market price of each asset as

$$V_j = \frac{1}{r}(\mu_j - R_{T-\{1\}}(b_j - \sum_k Z_{ik}\sigma_{jk})), \qquad j = 1, ..., n, \tag{3.1}$$

where $R_{T-\{1\}}$ is the harmonic mean of all the price taking investors' mean-variance substitution rates divided by $m - 1$ (or $1/\sum_{i \neq 1} 1/2\lambda_i$). Then it follows that [4]

$$\partial V_k / \partial Z_{1j} = R_{T-\{1\}}\sigma_{jk}/r, \qquad j, k = 1, ..., n. \tag{3.2}$$

---

[4] These calculations assume that $R_{T-\{1\}}$ is unaffected by small changes in Z_{1j}. Such an assumption is reasonable when the number of price affectors is large, since $R_{T-\{1\}}$ is the harmonic mean of the λ_i's $i \neq 1$, divided by $m - 1$. Therefore, while individual λ_i's may be affected by small changes in Z_{1j}, the aggregate effect on $R_{T-\{1\}}$ is likely to be small. This assumption is equivalent to investor 1 assuming that the market price of risk for the set of $m - 1$ price takers is approximately unaffected by small changes in his own portfolio. If investors have constant absolute risk aversion, this assumption is exact.

Contracting our notation a bit, for this section, let $R_1 \equiv R_{T-\{1\}}$. Then substituting (3.2) into (2.7) yields the first order conditions for investor 1:

$$\sum_k Z_{1k}\sigma_{jk} = \frac{1}{R_1 + 2\lambda_1}(\mu_j - rV_j) + \frac{R_1}{R_1 + 2\lambda_1}\sum_k Z_{1k}\sigma_{jk} \qquad j = 1, ..., n. \qquad (3.3)$$

The solution Z_{1k}^* to (3.3) is given as $Z_{1k}^* = A_{1k}^* + B_{1k}^*$, $k = 1, ..., n$, where A_{1k}^* and B_{1k}^* solve, respectively,

$$\sum_k A_{1k}^*\sigma_{jk} = \frac{R_1}{R_1 + 2\lambda_1}\sum_k \bar{Z}_{1k}\sigma_{jk},$$

$$j = 1, ..., n, \qquad\qquad\qquad\qquad\qquad\qquad\qquad\qquad (3.4)$$

and

$$\sum_k B_{1k}^*\sigma_{jk} = (\mu_j - rV_j)/(R_1 + 2\lambda_1), \qquad j = 1, ..., n, \text{ } [5] \qquad (3.5)$$

Since $[\sigma_{jk}]$ is nonsingular, (3.4) implies

$$A_{1k}^* = \frac{R_1}{R_1 + 2\lambda_1}\bar{Z}_{1k}, \qquad k = 1, ..., n.$$

To solve B_{1k}^*, we note that $B_{1k}^* = Z_k^*/(R_1 + 2\lambda_1)$ where Z_k^* solves $\Sigma_k Z_k^*\sigma_{jk} = \mu_j - rV_j$ at the equilibrium prices. This is a key step, since we already know from (2.8) that for investors $i\epsilon T - \{1\}$, $Z_{ik}^* = Z_k^*/2\lambda_i$. Therefore, in equilibrium, it must be that

$$A_{1k}^* + B_{1k}^* + \sum_{i\neq 1} Z_{ik}^* = 1, \qquad k = 1, ..., n,$$

or

$$\frac{R_1 \bar{Z}_{1k}}{R_1 + 2\lambda_1} + Z_k^*\left(\frac{1}{R_1 + 2\lambda_1} + \frac{1}{R_1}\right) = 1, \qquad k = 1, ..., n.$$

Solving for Z_k^* and substituting into the expressions for Z_{ik}^*, $i \neq 1$ and Z_{1k}^* respectively, we obtain

---

[5] We can write $Z_{1k}^* = A_{1k}^* + B_{1k}^*$ only if (3.4) and (3.5) do in fact have solutions.

$$Z_{ik}^* = \frac{1}{2\lambda_i} [R_1(2\lambda_1 + R_1(1 - \bar{Z}_{1k}))/(2R_1 + 2\lambda_1)], \quad i \in T - \{1\},$$

$$k = 1, ..., n, \tag{3.6}$$

and

$$Z_{1k}^* = R_1(1 + \bar{Z}_{1k})/(2R_1 + 2\lambda_1), \qquad k = 1, ..., n. \tag{3.7}$$

We have proven, then, the following theorem.

Theorem 3. The single price affecting investor will select an equilibrium portfolio such that his holding of each security depends linear on his initial position in that security. His optimal portfolio will be balanced only if his initial portfolio is balanced.

Equations (3.6) and (3.7) indicate that in the imperfect market with a single price affector as described in this paper, the price affector will, in general, hold an unbalanced portfolio. Furthermore, while the portfolios of price takers also appear unbalanced, it can easily be shown that their portfolios are, in fact, percentages of the market of securities remaining after the price affector chooses optimally.

Because the price affector's optimal portfolio structurally differs from that selected by price taking investors at the new equilibrium prices, it appears that his "market power" has altered the price affector's attitude towards risk. To see this, note that the portfolio $Z_1^* = (Z_{11}^*, ..., Z_{1n}^*)$ would be optimal also for a price taker if it satisfied

$$\mu_j - rV_j = 2\lambda' \sum_k Z_{1k}^* \sigma_{jk}, \qquad j = 1, ..., n, \tag{3.8}$$

where λ' is the hypothetical price taker's rate of mean-variance substitution. If we substitute the solution for Z_1^* from (3.7) into (3.8), and sum (3.8) over j, we can easily see that

$$\lambda' = (R_1(b_M - \sum_k \bar{Z}_{1k}b_k) + 2\lambda_1 b_M)/(2(b_M + \sum_k \bar{Z}_{1k}b_k)) \tag{3.9}$$

where $b_M \equiv \Sigma_k b_k$ = market variance. The natural question to ask at this point is how λ', the mean-variance substitution rate of the hypothetical price taker, compares with λ_1, the substitution rate actually displayed by the price affector. It can easily be shown that $\lambda' < \lambda_1$ whenever

$$\sum_k \bar{Z}_{1k}b_k/b_M > R_1/(R_1 + 2\lambda_1). \tag{3.10}$$

Theorem 4.   If $\Sigma_k \bar{Z}_{1k} b_k / b_M > R_1 / (R_1 + 2\lambda_1)$, the single price affecting investor will, in equilibrium, select a portfolio which is identical to that of a price taking investor in that market whose mean-variance substitution rate is lower than that exhibited by the price affector.

Theorem 4 indicates that if the covariance of the price affector's initial portfolio, as a fraction of market variance, is above a critical level, the price affector is willing to accept a lower tradeoff of mean for variance in his optimal portfolio than that portfolio would indicate for a price taker at the equilibrium prices. Intuitively, a lower acceptable tradeoff of mean for variance indicates that price affecting behavior makes the investor act less risk averse. [6]

We may ask if condition (3.10) is a reasonable one for the price affecting investor. The condition requires that the covariance of return of the price affector's initial portfolio with the market return be a sufficiently large fraction of market variance. Assuming for each security k that $b_k \geqslant 0$, condition (3.10) therefore requires that investor 1 holds a sufficiently large initial portfolio of risky securities. Price affecting behavior would seem to be more reasonable for investors whose initial resources are likely to be large. Furthermore, the critical level $R_1 / (R_1 + 2\lambda_1)$ in general will be small. To see this, note that if

$$\lambda_{\min} = \min_{l \neq 1} \lambda_l$$

then

$$R_1 = 1 / \sum_{l \neq 1} 1/2\lambda_l < 2\lambda_{\min} / (m - 1)$$

so that condition (3.10) is implied by

$$\sum_k \bar{Z}_{1k} b_k / b_M > \frac{\lambda_{\min}}{\lambda_{\min} + \lambda_1 (m - 1)}. \tag{3.11}$$

If the number of investors, m, is large, then the right-hand size of (3.11) will be quite small. It appears likely that for a price affecting investor with relatively large initial resources, condition (3.10) will be satisfied.

Because the price affector selects a portfolio as though he were price taker with a lower λ than his own, we might expect that his portfolio would contain more

---

[6] While, in general, there is not an exact correspondence between λ and risk aversion, this relationship holds precisely in the case of exponential utility functions of the form $U_i(Y_i) = -\exp(-c_i Y_i)$, for which $\lambda_i = c_i/2$.

risky assets than it would had he acted as a price taker. To verify this conjecture, we state and prove the following theorem.

Theorem 5. If the value of the single price affector's initial portfolio is sufficiently large, then his optimal portfolio will contain a greater amount of risky assets than it would if he acted as a price taker, in that market, with the same λ_I.

Proof. The price affector optimally purchases an amount

$$Z_{1k}^* = R_1(1 + \bar{Z}_{1k})/(2R_1 + 2\lambda_1), \qquad k = 1, ..., n, \tag{3.7}$$

of each risky asset. We have also shown in (3.6) that if investor i is a price taker in this market, his optimal portfolio can be written as

$$Z_{ik}^* = \frac{1}{2\lambda_i} R_1(1 - Z_{1k}^*), \qquad k = 1, ..., n, \qquad i \neq 1. \tag{3.6}'$$

Now multiply both sides of (3.7) and (3.6)$'$ by V_k, evaluated at Z_{1k}^*, and sum over k. If we assume that $\lambda_i = \lambda_1$, then

$$\sum_k Z_{1k}^* V_k > \sum_k Z_{ik}^* V_k \quad \text{as} \quad \sum_k \bar{Z}_{1k} V_k > R_1 V_M/(R_1 + 2\lambda_1)$$

where $V_M \equiv \Sigma_k\, V_k$ = total value of the market. Hence if investor 1's initial holdings of risky securities exceed $R_1/(R_1 + 2\lambda_1)$ times the total market value, investor 1's optimal portfolio will contain a greater amount of risky securities than the portfolio of a price taker in that market, with an identical mean-variance substitution rate, λ_1.

If we stipulate a stronger condition, namely that the amount of *each* risky security in investor 1's initial portfolio is sufficiently large, so that $\bar{Z}_{1k} > R_1/(R_1 + 2\lambda_1)$, then it follows immediately that for every k, $Z_{1k}^* > Z_{ik}^*$ when $\lambda_i = \lambda_1$. In general, then, if the price affector's initial holdings are sufficiently large, he is induced to hold more risky assets than would a price taker with the same λ in that market.   Q.E.D.

Intuitively, this theorem again suggests that by exercising his "market power," the price affector is induced to behave in a less risk averse manner than would be indicated by his utility function in a perfect market. This implies that when the price affector's influence is strong enough, the market valuation formulae and consequently the equilibrium rate of return relationships may be altered to reflect this change in investor behavior.

The study of the single price affector's optimal behavior in this section is suggestive of what the composition of optimal portfolios is likely to be when S contains more than one investor, namely the favoring of some securities over others in investors' optimal portfolios. Depending upon the number of price affectors and their presumed conjectural variations, the conclusions of Theorems 3 to 5 may be altered somewhat. However, our analysis indicates a structural change in the equilibrium prices which is reflected by relationship (2.14).

4. Summary and a final comment

The results of this paper incorporate into capital market theory some aspects not previously discussed in the literature, which account for the influence of large, non-price-taking investors. We have shown that by taking account of price movements that result from his transactions, a large investor may be induced to hold an optimal portfolio that is unbalanced. This result contrasts with the traditional principle of "holding the market." The consequence of this action is that securities which are weighed heavily by price affectors relative to their market weights, so that the covariance of the security's return with the return on the price affectors' portfolio is high, will have higher values than would be predicted by the traditional capital asset pricing model. We have shown that the effect of this result is to add an additional term to the traditional form of the capital asset pricing model which accounts for the risk of each security within the aggregate portfolio of price affectors. We thus provide a new testable hypothesis about capital market equilibrium which can be compared with the traditional model using the same set of market data.

While, in general, optimal portfolio selection by individual price affectors may depend on assumptions about their interactions, it is only the aggregate portfolio of these investors that affects equilibrium prices. Consequently, the testable hypothesis derived in this paper is invariant to assumptions about conjectural variations used by individual investors. Thus, suitable aggregation of rate of return data on individual price affectors' portfolios is the only additional information needed to test the equilibrium model within the same statistical framework as previous tests of the capital asset pricing model in a perfectly competitive market.

Empirical analyses of the capital asset pricing model in its traditional form have indicated that the standard model yields biased estimates of equilibrium security returns and provides an inadequate explanation of the variation of these returns. Our model offers an alternate specification of the model which has the potential for correcting some of these problems.

Appendix

We demonstrate in this Appendix that (2.14) describes the equilibrium rate of return relationship for securities. First note that since the market portfolio must satisfy (2.13), we have

$$E(r_M) = r + R_{T-S} V_M \operatorname{var}(r_M) - R_{T-S} V_S \operatorname{cov}(r_M, r_S),$$

$$j = 1, ..., n. \tag{A.1}$$

Similarly, since the aggregate S portfolio also satisfies (2.13), we have

$$E(r_S) = r + R_{M-S} V_M \operatorname{cov}(r_M, r_S) - R_{M-S} V_S \operatorname{var}(r_S). \tag{A.2}$$

If we multiply both sides of (A.1) by $\operatorname{var}(r_S)$ and both sides of (A.2) by $\operatorname{cov}(r_M, r_S)$ and subtract (A.2) from (A.1), we obtain

$$R_{T-S} V_M = \frac{\operatorname{var}(r_S)(E(r_M) - r) - \operatorname{cov}(r_M, r_S)(E(r_S) - r)}{\operatorname{var}(r_S) \operatorname{var}(r_M) - \operatorname{cov}^2(r_M, r_S)}. \tag{A.3}$$

Similarly, we obtain

$$R_S V_S = \frac{\operatorname{cov}(r_M, r_S)(E(r_M) - r) - \operatorname{var}(r_M)(E(r_S) - r)}{\operatorname{var}(r_S) \operatorname{var}(r_M) - \operatorname{cov}^2(r_M, r_S)}. \tag{A.4}$$

If we substitute (A.3) and (A.4) into (2.13), (2.14) immediately follows.

References

[1] J. Bertrand, Theorie mathématique de la richesse sociale, Journal de Savants, Paris (September, 1883).

[2] E.H. Chamberlin, The Theory of Monopolistic Competition (Harvard University Press, Cambridge, 1965).

[3] A. Cournot, Researches into the Mathematical Principles of the Theory of Wealth (Macmillan, New York, 1897).

[4] F. Edgeworth, Mathematical Psychics (Kegan-Paul, London, 1881).

[5] W. Fellner, Competition among the Few (Augustus Kelly, New York, 1965).

[6] M. Jensen, Capital markets: theory and evidence, Bell Journal of Economics and Management Science 3 (Autumn 1972).

[7] J. Lintner, The valuation of risk assets and the selection of risky investments in stock portfolios and capital budgets, Review of Economics and Statistics 47 (February 1965).

[8] J. Lintner, The market price of risk, size of market and investor's risk aversion, Review of Economics and Statistics (February 1970).

[9] R.T. Masson, The creation of risk aversion by imperfect markets, American Economic Review 71 (March 1972).

[10] J. Mossin, Equilibrium in a capital asset market, Econometrica (October 1966).

[11] J. Mossin, Theory of Financial Markets (Prentice Hall, Englewood Cliffs, New Jersey, 1973).

[12] New York Stock Exchange, Public Transaction Study (1976).
[13] M. Rubinstein, A mean–variance synthesis of corporate financial theory, Journal of Finance 28 (March 1973).
[14] W.F. Sharpe, Capital asset prices: a theory of market equilibrium under conditions of risk, Journal of Finance 19 (September 1964).

TIMS Studies in the Management Sciences 11 (1979) 125–134
©North-Holland Publishing Company

A NOTE ON THE USE OF THE CAPM FOR UTILITY RATE OF RETURN DETERMINATION

Willard T. CARLETON *

University of North Carolina, Chapel Hill

1. Introduction

One of the most profound developments in contemporary finance is the capital asset pricing model (CAPM). As with earlier theoretical advances, after some lag it has come to be employed in the arena of public utility regulation as a guide to the determination of a utility's required rate of return on equity capital. It is the thesis of this paper that because the consequences of errors in such determinations include substantial social costs, cost of capital models should be assessed as to their error generating potential. The market return generating mechanism typically employed in regulatory uses of the CAPM specifies sample statistics useful in such an assessment. Known analytical problems with the CAPM per se, coupled with sample results for ATT (the most stable utility, hence a conservative testing place), lead to the conclusion that the CAPM is of limited usability as an information framework for estimating utility costs of equity capital.

2. Rate of return regulation in practice

In the most typical scenario a period of experienced profit rates deemed excessive (by the utilities commision) or inadequate (by the company's management) leads to hearings in which an important variable to be determined is the accounting rate of return on book equity to be allowed in setting tariffs. [1] It is well known that application of allowed rate of return to either a book value or market value rate base has anomalous consequences [7]. These will not be reviewed here. What is important for this paper is the interesting investigative division of labor that arises, especially in those enlightened regulatory jurisdictions in which it is admitted that

* The author is endebted to James Jordan for computational assistance, and to a large number of colleagues in academia and in regulatory practice for ideas. The usual caveat applies.
[1] In this paper the author ignores capital structure questions and assumes the utility is all-equity financed. He also assumes that the rate base is derived from original cost rather than "fair value."

shareholder opportunity cost defines allowable rate of return. Financial economist testimony is presented in an adversarial setting, for company, commission staff and interested intervenors, as to the firm's cost of equity capital. The commissioners sit as judge and jury over the proceeding, ultimately deciding on a single number for purposes of setting customer charges. In recent years the most frequent originator of such rate hearings has been a company filing based on a plea that its cost of equity capital (among other things) has risen. That is to say, unanticipated increases in inflation rates induced therefore unanticipated rises in costs of capital.

The characteristics of this scenario to keep in mind for later discussion are:

(a) Testimony as to the value of a utility's cost of equity capital is heard by a regulatory commission in a context which is inherently, and by design, adversarial. In addition, such testimony frequently is presented by witnesses whose technical capabilities far exceed those of the commissioners.

(b) The cost of equity capital, or shareholder required rate of return, to be found is, conceptually, the single rate required expectationally by owners from the date of hearing for each period on into an indefinitely long future.

(c) Perceived changes in such capital costs have precipitated a large proportion of utility rate hearings in recent years.

(d) The cost of equity finally adopted by the commission is a point estimate, even though uncertainty always remains as to its "true" value. [2]

(e) Any errors of judgment by the commission produce immediate and permanent social costs. For example, consider a finding of cost of equity in excess of its "true" or underlying expected value. Among the consequences: (1) windfall gains to shareholders of the moment; (2) an incentive to pad the rate base through excessive investment and otherwise distort capital/labor ratios [7]); (3) charges to utility customers above the costs of producing the service; (4) output levels departing from social optima.

3. Characteristic pattern of CAPM use in utility rate cases

A quick review of the standard version of the theory is in order. To quote Black, Jensen and Scholes [2, pp. 79–80]:

> ... it is assumed that (1) all investors are single period risk-averse utility of terminal wealth maximizers and can choose among portfolios solely on the basis of mean and variance, (2) there are no taxes or transactions costs, (3) all investors have homogeneous views regarding the parameters of the joint probability distribution of all security returns, and (4) all investors can borrow and lend at a given riskless rate of interest. The main result of the model is a statement of the relation between the expected risk premiums on individual assets and their "systematic risk."

[2] The allowed rate of return is often stated as a range in commission findings. Such a procedure is motivated by a desire to minimize the frequency of future rate investigations and to give the utility an incentive for cost efficiency as well as, perhaps, an implicit admission that the original point estimate is in doubt.

Of course, none but the faithful would argue that the above is anything but a caricature of the world as it is. And it is true that individually these assumptions have been softened and a form of the theory has survived. What is important to remember is that modifications (as well as the original CAPM) serve the needs of positive — or predictive — economics.

In any event, the derived CAPM proposition is:

$$E(\tilde{R}_j) = R_F + \beta_j [E(\tilde{R}_M) - R_F] \tag{1}$$

where:

$E(\tilde{R}_j)$ = expected rate of return on financial asset j;
R_F = riskless rate of interest;
$E(\tilde{R}_M)$ = expected rate of return on a "market portfolio" consisting of an investment in every asset in proportion to its value;
β_j = $\text{cov}(\tilde{R}_j, \tilde{R}_M)/\sigma^2(R_M)$ = the "systematic" risk of the jth asset.

At this point, relation (1) is a statement about financial market equilibrium in which the expected value, variance and covariance parameters are best thought of as Bayesian estimates for single outcome experiments.

To operationalize such a model, there typically is added an assumed market return generating mechanism of the form:

$$\tilde{R}_{jt} = a_{j0} + a_{j1}\tilde{R}_{Mt} + \tilde{e}_{jt} \tag{2}$$

where:

a_{j0}, a_{j1} = constants;
$\tilde{R}_{jt}, \tilde{R}_{Mt}$ = random variables, rates of return on the jth asset and market portfolio,
 as before (the latter typically based on a broad stock market index);
$\tilde{e}_{jt}$ = disturbance term.

For purposes of regression modeling, some strong assumptions are further required, viz., $E(\tilde{e}_{jt}) = 0$, $E(\tilde{R}_{Mt}, \tilde{e}_{jt}) = 0$ and both $\tilde{e}_{jt}$ and $\tilde{R}_{Mt}$ normally and independently distributed. For present purposes, note that relation (2) is a classical statistical model.

The typical fashion in which (1) and (2) have come to be employed in cost of equity investigations involves the following steps:

(a) For arbitrarily chosen period of history and observation intervals, assemble R_{Mt} and R_{jt} series measured in first difference or log relative form.

(b) Generate $\hat{a}_{j0}$ and $\hat{a}_{j1}$ as ordinary least square estimates of a_{j0} and a_{j1}.

(c) Assuming that $\hat{a}_{j1}$ is also the best estimate of β_j, substitute into (1) along with hypothesized values (as of hearing date) of R_F and $E(\tilde{R}_M)$ to determine estimates of $E(\tilde{R}_j), E(\tilde{R}_j)$, as company j's expected cost of equity capital. The process may be simulated with alternative assumed values for R_F and $E(\tilde{R}_M)$ to derive an interval for $E(\hat{R}_j)$.

4. Known problems with this version of the CAPM and their impact in a regulatory setting

Four properties are of interest in this paper: (a) nonstationarity of parameter estimates for single securities [3]–[6],[8],[10],[12],[14]–[17]; (b) effects of alternative treatment of R_F in the estimating equation; (c) skewness of return distributions [9],[13]; (d) sensitivity of parameter estimates to measurement intervals [11].

(a) The standard resolution for parameter nonstationarity, motivated by a concern for tests of capital market efficiency and assuming the validity of the assumptions of relation (1), has been to form portfolios of individual securities clustered by $\hat{a}_{j1}$ values for purposes of final beta estimation. Unfortunately, nonstationarity of the single securities' coefficients is merely suppressed by this procedure. It necessarily remains an embarrassment for those, such as utility commissioners, who must estimate and forecast for an individual company. A further difficulty, initially noted by Roll [17], is that there is a gross inconsistency between the requirements of (1) and assumptions of (2). While CAPM theory calls for an R_F fixed over a future period of unspecified length, the reality of economic life and sampling is that R_F and $\tilde{R}_M$, even if correctly measured, are both random variables which, by long standing agreement, are correlated. This fact, and the resulting nonzero relationship of $\tilde{R}_M$ and $\tilde{e}_j$ in (2), render $\hat{a}_{j0}$ and $\hat{a}_{j1}$ asymptotically biased. A reasonable interpretation of monetary events in the last decade is that $\tilde{R}_{Ft}$ and $\tilde{R}_{Mt}$ have behaved in a nonstationary way, rendering single-factor estimates of $\hat{a}_{j0}$ and $\hat{a}_{j1}$ still less meaningful.

A final source of nonstationarity for $\tilde{R}_{jt}$, $\hat{R}_{Mt}$ and $\tilde{R}_{Ft}$ suggests that the assumption of any stationary market return generating mechanism may be unwise. There is no *economic* theory which specifies how the repricing of a financial asset in an efficient capital market over time to achieve *ex ante* equilibrium is generated by any specific random process – only that if the market is efficient the process will be random. In particular, the stronger assumptions of (2) include stationarity as an arbitrary statistical assumption. If one contemplates the economics of sequential asset pricing, it is not obvious that the resulting observations of *realized* rates of return constitute sample drawings, with random errors from a single population of possible future rates of return. The point is made most easily with bonds, but the logic also applies to equities: The price of a security at two points in time is in each instance a present value of expected cash flows discounted at a required rate of return. If the required rate of return rises between the two dates the realized rate of return will fall. The realized returns for the market and individual securities over any sequence of dates may incorporate capital market shifts in perverse fashion, e.g., abnormally high mean realized rate of return induced by sharply declining expected rate of return. It should be noted that the inverse relationship between realized and expected rates of return can afflict any empirical model, CAPM or otherwise. Brigham and Crum [4] have articulated with examples the perversity of the phenomenon in a CAPM setting.

(b) The effects of alternative specifications of (2) for regulatory purposes are, perhaps, not widely appreciated. Depending on how strongly one feels about constraining coefficient estimates in line with CAPM theory, any of the following might be appropriate regression candidates:

$$\tilde{R}_{jt} = a_{j0} + a_{j1}\tilde{R}_{Mt} + \tilde{e}_{jt}, \tag{2}$$

$$\tilde{R}_{jt} = b_{j0} + b_{j1}\tilde{R}_{Mt} + b_{j2}R_{Ft} + \tilde{u}_{jt}, \tag{3}$$

$$\tilde{R}_{jt} - R_{Ft} = c_{j1}(\tilde{R}_{Mt} - R_{Ft}) + \tilde{v}_{jt}, \tag{4}$$

where:

$\tilde{R}_{jt}$, $\tilde{R}_{Mt}$, $\tilde{R}_{Ft}$, a_{j0} and a_{j1} are as defined previously; b_{j0}, b_{j1}, b_{j2}, c_{j1} are parameters to be estimated in accordance with model specifications (3) and (4); $\tilde{e}_{jt}$, $\tilde{u}_{jt}$, $\tilde{v}_{jt}$ are disturbance terms with appropriate characteristics.

Aside from sampling error, one would hope that $\hat{a}_{j0} = \bar{R}_{Ft}(1 - \hat{c}_{j1})$, $\hat{b}_{j0} = 0$ $\hat{b}_{j2} = 1 - \hat{c}_{j1}$, and $\hat{a}_{j1} = \hat{b}_{j1} = \hat{c}_{j1}$. In most conventional uses of the CAPM as a vehicle for tests of market efficiency, choice of (2) over, say, (3) or (4) would be subordinate to structuring the "second stage," cross-sectional regression which uses the results $\hat{a}_{j1}$, $\hat{b}_{j1}$, or $\hat{c}_{j1}$. In rate-of-return studies, the choice may be critical, for at least two reasons. In the first place, estimation of (2), followed by a rate of return estimate of the form $R^*_{jt} = \hat{a}_{j1}(R^*_{Mt} - R^*_{Ft})$ is an obviously biased (though typically employed) procedure. If an $\hat{a}_{j0}$ estimate was secured, it should be used. Secondly, choice of (2), (3) or (4) will have a substantial impact on the width of confidence intervals which accompanies the resultant conditional estimated rate of return, $E(R_{jt})$. As mentioned in § 2, errors in regulatory determination of $E(R_{jt})$ can produce significant social costs.

(c) As for skewness in return distributions. Miller and Scholes [13], in an early cataloguing of difficulties with the CAPM, demonstrated that it may be the best explanation for why, in two-stage tests of the theory, mean realized rates of return were sensitive to "non-systematic risk" (i.e., residual variance) contrary to theory. Unfortunately, while their solution "works," empirically it casts considerable doubt on the validity of the underlying two-parameter theory specified in (1). In turn, from the perspective of rates of return regulation, this has to introduce, at the least, uncertainty as to the underlying value of costs of equity, when estimates are derived from two-parameter models. In this paper we will not assess the empirical adequacy of the two-parameter generating model assumption.

(d) Finally, sensitivity of parameter estimates to measurement intervals may be the most awkward problem for utility regulation, especially to the extent that it produces an intolerably wide interval of cost of equity estimates. We know already ([9], for example) that if the full CAPM — (1) and (2) — hold for one time interval, then (2) cannot hold for other intervals except under the further assumption that portfolios be continuously rebalanced. Yet, CAPM theory does not specify the length of the assumed single decision period, and (as noted) rate of return regulation presupposes a time horizon of indeterminate length.

5. Empirical significance of the CAPM problems

The catalogue of difficulties described in § IV is of course well aired in the finance literature. These are also typical of difficulties posed by any theoretical development in positive economics. Uniquely (at least to this author's knowledge), however, the empirical specification and estimation of the return generating mechanism which makes the CAPM "work" also provides sample evidence on the degree of "workability" of that theory. It is in the spirit of demonstrating this point that regression and confidence interval estimates are presented in this section.

The company chosen for this exercise is American Telephone and Telegraph Company (ATT), whose operating and financial characteristics are widely recognized to be quite stable. Thus it can be presumed that the CAPM's likely usability in rate of return determination is greater than for any other utility. Data include: monthly closing prices for ATT common stocks for the years 1967–1976 (from which, with dividends, monthly realized rates of return were calculated); monthly rates of return on Treasury bills, calculated from bills whose purchase prices and maturity dates matched ATT pricing dates as closely as possible; and monthly realized rates of return on the S&P 425 Index, as the R_M measure, again for 1967–1976. [3]

In order to determine how serious the empirical difficults are, (2), (3) and (4) were estimated for: the full ten-year period, 1967–1976; two five-year subperiods, 1967–1971 and 1972–1976; and five two-year subperiods, 1967–1968, 1969–1970, 1970–1971, 1971–1972, 1973–1974, and 1975–1976. Finally, each estimated model was used to generate a value of $E(E_{ATT})$ and associated 90 percent confidence intervals, at sample $\bar{R}_M$ and $\bar{R}_F$ and (as available) at period-ahead sample $\bar{R}_M$ and $\bar{R}_F$. Such results were then converted into annual rate of return units, both for intuitive understanding and because it is with such units that utility regulation is concerned. Table 1 contains the results. For the demonstration purposes of this paper the principal findings are:

---

[3] All of the regression results reported herein were estimated using the percentage change form of returns. Results using the log-relative form and for three-months measurement intervals were in all essential respects virtually identical.

Table 1
Regression results, equations (2), (3), (4) for ATT

Period	Equation	$\hat{a}_0, \hat{b}_0$	t	$\hat{a}_1, \hat{b}_1, \hat{c}_1$	t	$\hat{b}_2$	t	R^2	$D-W$	dof
1967–1976	2	0.0032	0.98	0.6078	8.97	—	—	0.4056	2.06	118
	3	−0.0136	−0.97	0.6307	9.00	3.689	1.23	0.4132	2.10	117
	4	—	—	0.6098	9.11	—	—	0.4110	2.07	119
1967–1971	1	−0.0034	−0.70	0.6786	6.21	—	—	0.3990	2.15	58
	3	−0.0393	−1.67	0.7212	6.47	8.2833	1.56	0.4238	2.23	57
	4	—	—	0.6677	6.17	—	—	0.3923	2.13	59
1972–1976	2	0.0093	2.22	0.5627	6.80	—	—	0.4435	2.07	58
	3	0.0108	0.63	0.5605	6.45	−0.3221	−0.09	0.4436	2.07	57
	4	—	—	0.5671	6.78	—	—	0.4381	1.97	59
1967–1968	2	−0.00411	−0.51	0.4310	2.09	—	—	0.1660	2.03	22
	3	−0.0733	−1.51	0.4092	2.03	18.2392	1.45	0.2416	2.31	21
	4	—	—	0.3718	1.93	—	—	0.1392	2.00	23
1969–1970	2	0.0049	0.64	0.8220	5.47	—	—	0.5759	2.37	22
	3	0.0335	0.46	0.8050	5.05	−5.5339	−0.39	0.5790	2.41	21
	4	—	—	0.8117	5.56	—	—	0.5737	2.34	23
1971–1972	2	−0.0013	−0.17	0.7821	3.31	—	—	0.3328	1.30	22
	3	−0.0708	−1.57	0.8432	3.63	20.5090	1.57	0.4025	1.46	21
	4	—	—	0.7568	3.47	—	—	0.3430	1.31	23
1973–1974	2	0.0109	1.23	0.5854	3.84	—	—	0.4018	2.57	22
	3	0.0761	1.25	0.5684	3.73	−11.1304	−1.08	0.4334	2.50	21
	4	—	—	0.5305	3.83	—	—	0.3389	2.53	23
1975–1976	2	0.0075	1.35	0.5480	5.18	—	—	0.5499	1.66	22
	3	0.0020	0.04	0.5443	4.84	1.3257	0.12	0.5502	1.66	21
	4	—	—	0.5919	6.10	—	—	0.6183	1.61	23

Period	Equation	$\bar{R}_M, \bar{R}_F$ (in annual units)	$E(R_{ATT}|\bar{R}_M, \bar{R}_F)$	90% Confidence Interval	Period Ahead $E(R_{ATT}|\bar{R}_M, \bar{R}_F)$	90% Confidence Interval
1967–1976	2	0.0814	0.0891	±0.0694	—	—
	3	0.0553	0.0891	±0.0652	—	—
	4		0.0712	±0.0027	—	—
1967–1971	1	0.1009	0.0255	±0.0994	0.0008	±0.0996
	3	0.0529	0.0255	±0.0981	0.0374	±0.1066
	4		0.0658	±0.0081	0.0576	±0.0008
1972–1976	2	0.0623	0.1562	±0.0872	—	—
	3	0.0576	0.1562	±0.0880	—	—
	4		0.0602	±0.0006	—	—
1967–1968	2	0.2113	0.0348	±0.1616	-0.0599	±0.1839
	3	0.0467	0.0348	±0.1560	0.2717	±0.4797
	4		0.1053	±0.0499	0.0285	±0.0307
1969–1970	2	-0.0289	0.0347	±0.1673	0.2088	±0.2009
	3	0.0640	0.0347	±0.1713	0.3579	±0.7055
	4		-0.0064	±0.0231	0.1479	±0.0308
1971–1972	2	0.1742	0.1164	±0.1571	-0.1785	±0.2387
	3	0.0409	0.1164	±0.1522	0.4892	±0.9621
	4		0.1405	±0.0465	-0.1463	±0.1188
1973–1974	2	-0.2075	-0.0037	±0.1881	0.3516	±0.2457
	3	0.0730	-0.0037	±0.1878	0.6591	±0.4873
	4		-0.0854	±0.0737	0.1975	±0.0600
1975–1976	2	0.3412	0.2841	±0.1053	—	—
	3	0.0520	0.2841	±0.1081	—	—
	4		0.1961	±0.0417	—	—

(a) Estimates of beta ($\hat{a}_1$, $\hat{b}_1$, $\hat{c}_1$) are quite insensitive to the form of the estimating equation, and the t-statistics are impressively large. This coefficient is somewhat sample-dependent, varying from around 0.4 (1967–1968) to around 0.8 (1969–1970 and 1971–1972).

(b) Intercept terms ($\hat{a}_0$, $\hat{b}_0$) and R_F coefficient ($\hat{b}_2$) are extremely sensitive to choice of sample period, even though statistically insignificantly different from zero. While some use insignificance as license to discard in developing predictive results, as noted previously such a procedure is biased on the face of the matter.

(c) Choice of estimating equation has a pronounced impact on predicted rate of return and a smaller effect on its confidence interval for ATT, when sample means of R_M and R_F are used. Quite clearly the size and nonstationarity of the intercept is the culprit. From a portfolio theory perspective one might say the beta estimates are reasonably stable, and ignore or modify the estimation procedure to avoid this embarrassment. Again, given the nature of the regulatory "experiment," it is the position of this paper that such devices are illegitimate. In general one gains efficiency by constraining the equation intercept, but at a cost that the predicted values do not pass through the sample mean of the dependent variable.

(d) Choice of next period mean values of R_M and R_F as conditioning variables leads to predicted rates of return which are extremely dependent upon model and time period, go far outside the range of values within which opposing witnesses argued at various times over the ten years (from about 8 to 15 percent), and have for the most part unusually wide confidence intervals. To the extent that the predicted mean value of R_M and R_F actually used depart even further from sample period means, of course the confidence intervals will be even wider.

6. Conclusion

Many of the empirical attributes of CAPM estimation demonstrated in this paper have been noted by finance scholars and, indeed, have led to model modifications, e.g., two-factor CAPM and Bayesian parameter estimation. In utility rate hearings in which the CAPM is introduced, however, the typical procedure is described in § II. It seems clear from the evidence, however, that when "residual risk" is employed in its traditional statistical meaning – and when all of the regression coefficients are employed in the predictive equation – the results do not appear to serve the needs of regulation very well. Since regulation is concerned with the expected rate of return (the entire equation, not just beta) and imprecision of its estimate, capital asset pricing theory does not appear to provide much comfort. The same charge may be made of other rate-of-return finding tools, it is true, but only the CAPM in its entirety provides empirical information of its intrinsic limitations for such purposes.

References

[1] W. Baumol and A. Klevorick, Input choices and the rate of return regulation: an overview of the discussion, Bell Journal of Economics and Management Science (Autumn 1970).

[2] F. Black, M. Jensen and M. Scholes, The capital asset pricing model: some empirical tests, in Studies in the Theory of Capital Markets, M. Jensen, ed. (Praeger Publishers, New York, 1972).

[3] W. Breen and E. Lerner, On the use of β in regulatory proceedings, Bell Journal of Economics and Management Science (Autumn 1972).

[4] E. Brigham and R. Crum, On the use of the CAPM in public utility rate cases, Financial Management (Summer 1977).

[5] W. Carleton, Testimony, FCC Docket No. 16070 (1972).

[6] W. Carleton, Rebuttal Testimony, FCC Docket No. 16070 (1973).

[7] W. Carleton, Rate of return, rate base and regulatory lag under conditions of changing capital costs, Land Economics (May 1974).

[8] D. Downes and T. Dyckman, Efficient market research and accounting information, Accounting Review (April 1973).

[9] M. Edesess, Reservations about the practical value of the capital asset pricing model, unpublished paper presented at meetings of the Institute for Quantitative Research in Finance, Napa, California (May 1973).

[10] R. Hagerman, Finance theory in rate hearings Financial Management (Spring 1976).

[11] N. Jacob, The measurement of systematic risk for securities and portfolios: some empirical results, Journal of Financial and Quantitative Analyais (March 1971).

[12] S. Meyers, Stationarity in the use of the market model, Accounting Review (April 1973).

[13] M. Miller and M. Scholes, Rates of return in relation to risk: a re-examination of some recent findings, in Studies in the Theory of Capital Markets, M. Jensen, ed. (Praeger Publishers, New York, 1972).

[14] S. Myers, On the use of β in regulatory proceedings: a comment, Bell Journal of Economics and Management Science (Autumn 1972).

[15] R. Pettway, On the use of β in regulatory proceedings: an empirical examination, Bell Journal of Economics (Spring 1978).

[16] R. Pettway, Structural change in risk perceptions of equity investors in the elective power industry (unpublished paper).

[17] R. Roll, Bias in fitting the Sharpe model to time series data, Journal of Financial and Quantitative Analysis (September 1969).

[18] D. West and A. Eubank, An automatic cost of capital adjustment model for regulating public utilities, Financial Management (Spring 1976).

TIMS Studies in the Management Sciences 11 (1979) 135–149
© North-Holland Publishing Company

TESTING A PORTFOLIO FOR EX ANTE MEAN/VARIANCE EFFICIENCY

Richard ROLL *

University of California, Los Angeles

1. Introduction

Among the most durable and important concepts introduced by Markowitz [9] was the mean/variance efficient set, the set of nondominated portfolios in the mean/variance space. Since 1959, a basic normative problem of investment analysis has been to ascertain whether a particular portfolio is a member of this set. For the portfolio manager and the investor, the efficient set constitutes a fundamental benchmark of investment performance: Is the selected portfolio dominated in the mean/variance space by some other portfolio?

A slightly more sophisticated version of this question should be asked: "During the sample period, was the selected portfolio *statistically significantly* dominated by some other portfolio?" There are two reasons why this version of the question is preferable. First of all, no rational investor would purposely select a portfolio that was not ex ante mean/variance efficient, based on his own ex ante subjective assessments, unless he was not an expected-return maximizer/variance of return minimizer. Secondly, because sampling variation is always present, a given portfolio does not usually turn out to be exactly in the ex post efficient set. Even if prior subjective estimates of means, variances and covariances are correct, unanticipated sampling variation can cause the selected portfolio to be dominated ex post.

The rational investor would not be troubled by such unpredictable variation, however. If his portfolio were dominated in a sample, he merely would like that fact to be attributed to chance, not ascribed to systematic errors in assessments. In addition, he would wish his selections to approach mean/variance efficiency as the time-series sample grows indefinitely large. This implies a correspondence between the parameters of the ex ante objective generating process and the subjective parameters assessed by the investor.

Such considerations are properly labeled "normative" because they are practical guides to action and they presuppose an objective function based on expected return and variance. There is also a scientific question involved with mean/variance

* The comments of Alan Kraus, James MacBeth and Stephen Ross are gratefully acknowledged.

efficiency. Building on earlier work by Sharpe [17] and Lintner [7], Black [2] showed that if all investors based choices on the mean and variance and if they shared common beliefs, the value-weighted portfolio of all assets (the market portfolio) would be ex ante mean/variance efficient. Thus, a proper test of Black's theory would ascertain whether the market portfolio is statistically significantly dominated by some other portfolio.

It has been emphasized recently (Ross [16] and Roll [13]), that the position of the market portfolio in the ex ante efficient set is mathematically equivalent to the generalized (Black) version of the "capital asset pricing model." It can be proved (and is proved in the references cited) that the following two statements are equivalent:

S1: A portfolio p is on the positively-sloped segment of the ex ante mean/variance efficient frontier (so that no other portfolio with the same expected variance of return has a higher ex ante mean return).

S2: The expected return vector of individual assets in an *exact* positive linear function of the vector of "betas" computed against the portfolio's return. In other words,

$$R = r_z\iota + (r_p - r_z)\beta \tag{1}$$

where R is the $N \times 1$ column vector of ex ante returns on the N individual assets, ι is the $N \times 1$ unit vector, β is the vector of individual (simple) regression slope coefficients computed against the portfolio p [1] (whose expected return is r_p) and r_z is the expected return on a portfolio whose return is exactly uncorrelated with portfolio p's return.

Since the market portfolio m should theoretically be ex ante efficient and satisfy S1, its measurement is seen to be the basic testing problem of the asset pricing model, which is (1). Serious consequences for the theory's testability are caused by imperfect knowledge of the market's composition (cf. Roll [13]).

On the normative level, statements S1 and S2 apply to every nondominated portfolio. If portfolio p is ex ante mean/variance efficient, then individual expected returns must be exactly linear in the vector of "betas" computed against p, and vice versa. There are, of course, an infinite number of portfolios in the efficient set and for each one, there is a unique vector of "betas" which satisfies (1) exactly.

Furthermore, statements S1 and S2 also hold for any sample of returns. If the sample covariance matrix is nonsingular, a sample efficient set can be computed. Any portfolio which is in that set can be used to calculate a vector of sample "betas" with the same data and (1) will hold *exactly* for these betas and the sample mean return vector. [2]

---

[1] I.e., for the jth element of β, $\|\beta_j\|$, we have $\beta_j = \text{cov}(r_j, r_p)/\text{var}(r_p)$.

[2] For a proof of these statements and further discussion see Roll [13, appendix].

These facts imply that either S1 or S2 can be used as the vehicle for a statistical test of the ex ante efficiency of a given portfolio p. Unfortunately, neither statement admits a straightforward econometric test. We shall see that the sample efficient set has a very complex distribution even for the most familiar return generating processes. Furthermore, for large numbers of assets, S1 is subject to computational difficulties. S2 also is a difficult testing vehicle but for a different reason. Though (1) is exactly linear ex ante for any efficient p, there is usually no a priori information about the values of r_p and r_z. Furthermore, in a finite sample it is difficult to identify those deviations from exact linearity which arise from measurement error in the individual returns (R) and in the β's and those deviations that are caused by p *not* being ex ante mean/variance efficient.

The idea that a given portfolio is the object of inquiry is formalized by the following assumption:

A particular portfolio is to be tested directly for mean/variance efficiency (a test of S1) or to be employed in calculating betas (for use in a test of S2). The investment proportions vector X_p which defines this portfolio is prespecified and held constant (i.e., "rebalanced") during the sample period.

In a more advanced discussion, we would want to do away with this assumption. Most portfolios change composition significantly over time as the relative total values of individual assets evolve. They are not continually rebalanced. Thus, we might begin with a set of investment proportions that are prespecified but allow them to change according to the observed sample returns. This would create much more difficult problems of statistical inference, insofar as ascertaining the efficiency of the resulting nonstationary portfolio; and, as we shall see, the problems are far from trivial even with a constant composition portfolio.

Given that X_p *is* fixed, we are faced with a small sample [3] problem of inference. Every efficient set is determined completely by a mean return vector and a covariance matrix [4] (either sample or population) and the product–moment sample estimates of means, variances and covariances are known to be consistent. Thus, the large sample problem is straightforward because the sample mean-variance efficient set approaches the population efficient set asymptotically. Of course, in order to make valid large (or small) sample inferences, one also must assume a stationary population. If the ex ante means, variances and covariances were changing, no test of S1 or S2 would be unambiguous unless the form of nonstationarity were known or could be estimated (as is attempted, for example, in Rosenberg and Marathe [15].

Given preselection of a portfolio and an assumption of stationarity in the population, either S1 or S2 is available for testing. Tests using S1 are outlined in the next section and tests using S2 are discussed in § 3.

---

[3] Here and throughout the paper, the sample size refers to the number of time series observations. The number of assets is assumed fixed along with X_p. Similarly, "asymptotic" refers to an indefinitely large number of *time series* observations.

[4] For a proof, see the appendix to Roll [13].

2. Directly testing a preselected portfolio for mean-variance efficiency

The most straightforward test of a preselected portfolio's efficiency employs S1. This might be termed the method of brute force. Compute the sample efficient set and infer whether the portfolio lies "insignificantly" far within. Such a procedure would be subject to the serious practical problem that the sample efficient set can only be computed with the inverse of the covariance matrix of *all* individual assets. Just computing this inverse would be a formidable task and too expensive in many applications. [5] However, if the application were for a limited number of individual assets, as would be the situation faced by many portfolio managers who make selections from an approved list of 200–300 securities, the brute force method could be recommended.

2.1. Tests based on the vector of investment proportions

Assuming that the full covariance matrix can be inverted at a feasible cost, there are several variants of tests based on the preselected investment proportions vector, X_p. Such tests should be among the most straightforward because X_p is the only *known* attribute of the portfolio. Its ex ante mean return, variance, etc., are all unknown and must be estimated from the sample. One simple example of such a test is based on a theorem of Anderson [1, p. 76]. In the present application, it can be stated as:

Let X_p denote the fixed vector of investment proportions for portfolio p. Let $\hat{X}_p$ be the vector of proportions for the sample efficient portfolio whose mean is $\hat{r}_p = X_p'\hat{R}$, [6] where $\hat{R}$ is the mean return vector for a sample of T time series ob-

---

[5] The computational problem of inversion could be alleviated by computing efficient frontiers from subsets of assets. However, the statistical significance of the preselected portfolio dominating (or not dominating) a subset's efficient frontier would be hard to determine. Binomial methods would not be available because the subsets would be correlated through correlation of the asset returns themselves.

[6] As shown in the appendix of Roll [13], the vector of investment proportions for an exactly mean/variance (ex post) efficient portfolio with return $\hat{r}_p = X_p'\hat{R}$ is given by

$$\hat{X}_p = \hat{V}^{-1}(\hat{R}:\iota)\,\hat{A}^{-1}(X_p'\hat{R}:1)'$$

where

$\hat{V}$ is the sample covariance matrix of individual assets,
$\hat{R}$ is the sample mean return vector,
X_p is the prespecified vector of investment proportions,
ι is the unit vector, and
$\hat{A}$ is the sample efficient set "information" matrix

$$\hat{A} = \begin{bmatrix} \hat{R}'\hat{V}^{-1}\hat{R} & \iota'\hat{V}^{-1}\hat{R} \\ \iota'\hat{V}^{-1}\hat{R} & \iota'\hat{V}^{-1}\iota \end{bmatrix}$$

servations. Then $y = \hat{X}_p'\hat{X}_p$ is asymptotically normal with mean $X_p'X_p$ and variance whose sample analog is $\hat{\sigma}_y^2 = X_p'\hat{X}_p\hat{X}_p'X_p/T$, where p is ex ante efficient.

For a proof, apply Anderson's theorem (which is also given in Press [12, pp. 93–94]). The result requires that $\hat{X}_p$ be asymptotically normal but this is guaranteed for any probability law whose sample mean return vector is asymptotically multivariate normal. Since returns generally display little temporal dependence, this provision would be assured for any stationary, finite-variance process. Generally, the exact sampling variance of y will be unknown but that should not matter too much in large samples.

In testing for portfolio p's efficiency, y is to be compared with its asymptotic value. A critical region is obtained in terms of

$$\sqrt{T}(\hat{X}_p'\hat{X}_p - X_p'X_p)/(X_p'\hat{X}_p\hat{X}_p'X_p)^{1/2}.$$

For large samples, this is unit normal. Notice that inversion of the full covariance matrix is required in order to compute $\hat{X}_p$. (See note 6.)

This test is not claimed to possess optimal properties relative to other tests. Indeed, the Anderson theorem can be used to construct a test based on *any* scalar function of $\hat{X}_p$. The suggestion above merely gives a "quick and dirty" statistic that leads to correct inference in large samples. Some other function of $\hat{X}_p$ may have smaller asymptotic standard error or approach the normal distribution more rapidly.

Any test that involves only the estimated proportions vector $\hat{X}_p$ should be preferred over one that involves the vector of betas or the sample means or variances. For example, the test statistic y above implicitly compares a sample quantity $\hat{X}_p'\hat{X}_p$ to a prespecified number, $X_p'X_p$. But a test involving variances would compare a sample quantity $\hat{X}_p'\hat{V}X_p$ to another sample quantity $X_p'\hat{V}X_p$ (which is the sample variance of return of the prespecified portfolio). The true variance of this portfolio is $X_p'VX_p$, but V is unknown.

The following test, again using investment proportions, would be particularly useful in the scientific question about the ex ante efficiency of the market portfolio. Every reasonable candidate for the true market portfolio has positive investments in all individual assets. [7] A sufficient condition for the existence of *some* totally positive mean/variance efficient portfolio has been obtained. [8] Unfortunately, the necessary conditions for total positivity would seem to require inversion of the full covariance matrix as well. This is actually an unsettled mathematical problem. It is possible that the necessary condition can be obtained without inver-

---

[7] This is because the true market portfolio is composed of all assets weighted in proportion to their relative market values (which are positive).

[8] See Roll and Ross [14].

sion, in which case a test might be devised from the existence or nonexistence of totally positive efficient portfolios. If it were shown that *no* totally positive portfolio is on the ex post efficient frontier, nor near enough to be adjudged insignificantly off the frontier, then the true market portfolio cannot be ex ante mean/variance efficient. This would cause rejection of the asset pricing theory along with the hypothesis that *some* totally positive portfolio was ex ante mean/variance efficient. Since the mathematical conditions are presently unknown, they would appear to constitute a promising area for further research.

2.2. Tests of S1 based on assumptions about the return generating process

A second category of "brute force" tests would require a distributional assumption about the generating process of returns. The most familiar process is Gaussian and it leads to some well-known results. Assume that the vector $\tilde{R}$ of individual returns follows a multivariate normal distribution with stationary mean vector $R = E(\tilde{R})$ and stationary covariance matrix V, and that $\tilde{R}$ is intertemporally uncorrelated. Then if $\hat{V}$ denotes the sample product moment covariance matrix from a time-series sample of T periods and N securities, $T \cdot \hat{V}$ follows an N-dimensional Wishart distribution. (See Press, [1972, p. 117].) It follows that $\hat{V}^{-1}$ follows an inverse Wishart distribution and that the sample efficient set is a complex mixture of inverse Wishart, Hotelling's T^2, and a third unnamed distribution (which is followed by the vector $\hat{V}^{-1}\hat{R}$).

The exact finite sampling properties are obviously very complex but it is possible to ascertain that the sample global minimum variance portfolio's return is upward biased. There must also be a region of the efficient frontier, adjacent to the global minimum variance position, which is biased toward high returns. [9]

It is also possible to construct probability contours around the selected portfolio's position in the mean/variance space. These could provide an *asymptotic* test of the portfolio's efficiency based on whether or not they intersect the efficient frontier.

The complexity of the efficient set's sampling distribution is remarkable, even in this case of the most familiar process, the Gaussian. The prospect for any strong small sample results thus seems rather dim and only the weak large sample results remain as the source of operational tests using the brute force approach.

3. Using the beta/return linearity relation to test for portfolio mean/variance efficiency

A portfolio's ex ante mean-variance efficiency can be tested without inversion of the full covariance matrix of individual returns by using S2, the exactly linear ex

----

[9] A proof of these statements and a more complete discussion is contained in the working version of this paper, available from the author.

ante relation (1) between individual returns and betas. The relation is easy to compute and it has been the object of attention in all published empirical work.

Unfortunately, S2 has several peculiarities that could result in ambiguous inferences. The most critical arises from the following fact: Although the ex ante relation is exactly linear when the portfolio is exactly efficient ex ante, there is no way to tell how the ex post relation might depart from linearity when the portfolio is not ex ante efficient, nor how sampling variation might appear to cause deviations from linearity even when the portfolio *is* ex ante efficient. If the portfolio is not ex ante efficient, the cross-sectional scatter of ex post returns and betas may appear to fall randomly about a line and thus deviations about the line may be ascribed to sampling variation. But such deviations would not disappear as the time series sample size grew indefinitely large. Furthermore, the deviations need not be related to any measurable quantities (such as individual asset variances or squared betas).

The slope and intercept of the return/beta line (1) are not prespecified and are not unique. If the reference portfolio, (the one used to compute the betas) is indeed ex ante mean-variance efficient, it could still lie anywhere in the efficient set. For each possible location, there would be a different value of the slope and intercept in (1). The only information provided by the fact that the reference portfolio is efficient is (a) that the sum of slope plus intercept is equal to the expected return on the same reference portfolio and (b) that the slope is positive (if the reference portfolio is on the positively-sloped segment of the efficient set).

We must, therefore, develop tests that allow for considerable ambiguity, *any* positive empirical value for the slope of (1) and any empirical value for the intercept, while providing an inference about exact ex ante linearity. This seems to be a rather unusual econometric problem.

3.1. The measurement error problem in testing linearity and the "grouping" procedure

Measurement errors are *the* problem in testing for a portfolio's efficiency via the linearity relation S2. Note that the true beta vector is defined as $\beta \equiv E(\hat{V}X_p)/\sigma_p^2$ where X_p is the $(N \times 1)$ vector of investment proportions that defines the preselected reference portfolio, $\hat{V}$ is the $(N \times N)$ sample covariance matrix of returns on individual assets, N is the total number of assets and $\sigma_p^2 = X_p' E(\hat{V})X_p$ is the true variance of the reference portfolio. If p is mean/variance efficient ex ante, then the true beta vector computed against it is an exact linear function of the true mean return vector

$$E(\hat{R}) = \gamma_0 \iota + \gamma_1 E(\hat{V}X_p) \tag{2}$$

where $\hat{R}$ is the mean sample return vector, γ_0 and γ_1 are constants (with $\gamma_1 > 0$), ι is the unit vector, and the expectation operator $E(\cdot)$ acts to denote the corresponding population parameters. If portfolio p is efficient, $\gamma_0 = E(\hat{r}_z)$ and $\gamma_1 =$

$E[(\hat{r}_p - \hat{r}_z)/\hat{\sigma}_p^2]$ where z is p's orthogonal efficient portfolio (see S2).

The operational form of (2) is

$$\hat{R} = \gamma_0 \iota + \gamma_1 (\hat{V} X_p) + \zeta \tag{3}$$

where $\zeta = \epsilon_R - \gamma_1 \epsilon_V$. $\epsilon_R = \hat{R} - E(\hat{R})$ and $\epsilon_V = \hat{V} X_p - E(\hat{V} X_p)$ are the estimation error vectors contained in R and in VX_p, respectively. Since the correct explanatory variable to have included in (3) would have been $E(\hat{V} X_p)$ and not $\hat{V} X_p$, we do indeed have an errors-in-variables problem.

The standard treatment of the errors-in-variables problem assumes that the errors, ϵ_V, in the explanatory variable are totally random. This means that ϵ_V is distributed independently of ϵ_R and that the elements of ϵ_V are independent. Unfortunately, there is ample reason to suspect that the estimation errors in $\hat{V}$ and $\hat{R}$ are cross-sectionally correlated. In fact, individual estimation errors in the mean return vector $\hat{R}$ would be mutually uncorrelated only if $E(\hat{V})$ were diagonal; that is, if the returns had no common movement. Estimation errors in the covariance matrix and thus in the vector $\hat{V} X_p$ might be related to each other and to the estimation errors in $\hat{R}$. For example, estimation errors in the sample mean return vector would be related to estimation errors in the sample covariance matrix for many underlying return generating processes. We only know that $\hat{R}$ and $\hat{V}$ would be mutually uncorrelated for some generating processes, the most familiar example being Gaussian.

Furthermore, in small samples, and again depending on the generating process, the error vector $\zeta = \epsilon_R - \gamma_1 \epsilon_V$ in (3) could be related to measurable characteristics of individual securities. For example, if returns were generated by an asymmetric process, ζ would be related to individual total sample variances. This could lead the investigator to ascribe (incorrectly) some of the cross-sectional variation in expected returns (in $E(\hat{R})$) to individual sample variances – because the cross-sectional variation in sample mean returns, (in $\hat{R}$), would indeed be related to ζ. An excellent analysis of this possibility is provided by Miller and Scholes [10].

But perhaps the most serious testing difficulty arises when portfolio p is actually not ex ante efficient. In this case, the true ex ante relation is given by

$$E(\hat{R}) = \gamma_0 \iota + \gamma_1 E(\hat{V} X_p) + \alpha \tag{4}$$

where α is a nonconstant vector of ex ante deviations from linearity. Thus, in the observable form (3), the "error" vector is

$$\zeta = \epsilon_R - \gamma_1 \epsilon_V + \alpha. \tag{5}$$

If the generating process is stationary, the actual error vectors ϵ_R and ϵ_V will approach vectors of zeros as the number of time series observations grows large. The vector α, to the contrary, will remain unchanged. Significant scatter will remain about the mean return/beta line no matter how many time series observations are collected.

The difficulties thus introduced are well illustrated in the "grouping" procedure, which was originated in this application by Blume [4]. [10] Black, Jensen, and Scholes [3], Fama and MacBeth [6], and Blume and Friend [5] all used the same technique. The basic idea is to use sample returns and sample betas of portfolios rather than of individual securities with the objective of eliminating ϵ_R and ϵ_V, or at least rendering them trivially small. Without loss of generality, suppose that the N equations for individual assets in (3) are arranged in ascending order by VX. [11] Then the first N/k equations are averaged to obtain portfolio 1, the second N/k for portfolio 2, and so on to obtain k portfolios in all. Denote the $k \times 1$ vectors of the averaged means by $\bar{R}$ and the $k \times N$ averaged covariance matrix by $\bar{V}$. Then,

$$\bar{R} = \gamma_0 \iota + \gamma_1 \bar{V} X_p + \bar{\zeta} \tag{6}$$

where $\bar{\zeta} = \bar{\epsilon}_R - \gamma_1 \bar{\epsilon}_V + \bar{\alpha}$ is the $(k \times 1)$ vector of residuals.

Now if (3) is the true state of nature and the selected portfolio p is actually ex ante efficient, all elements of α and of $\bar{\alpha}$ are zero. The only remaining components of $\bar{\zeta}$ are the average measurement errors $\bar{\epsilon}_R$ and $\bar{\epsilon}_V$ and these should be very small if N/k is large. (Note, however, that the elements of $\bar{\zeta}$ generally still will be correlated.) But if p is not ex ante efficient, what will be the magnitude of $\bar{\alpha}$? Unless VX_p and α happen to be related, $\bar{\alpha}$ will approach a vector of constants as N/k becomes large. Since the entire vector $\bar{\zeta}$ of cross-sectional disturbances will approach a constant vector, (6) will appear to be *exactly* linear in $\bar{R}$ and $\bar{V}X_p$ even when the true individual α's are nonzero. The portfolio grouping procedure not only tends to remove sampling error (in ϵ_R and ϵ_V) but it also tends to remove α, the only measure of portfolio p's inefficiency.

Clearly, the grouping procedure is biased toward supporting the hypothesis that the selected portfolio is ex ante mean-variance efficient. This is true even if VX_p and α are somehow related. Since we know nothing about this relation a priori, we must acknowledge the presence of bias if we admit any probability of less than a perfect correlation between VX_p and α.

The preceding argument does not imply that an individual asset procedure is better than a portfolio grouping procedure for *all* possible alternative hypotheses to exact ex ante linearity. It would be just as easy to find an alternative for which the portfolio procedure gives a more powerful test. It is true, however, that the grouping procedure suppresses information in the data that may be relevant at the same time that it purges irrelevant random variation.

---

[10] This is a standard technique for the "errors-in-variables" problem and can be found in any econometrics text.

[11] In the citations above, VX_p was estimated for one subperiod, ranked; and then re-estimated for a later and nonoverlapping subperiod. This reduced bias in the low-ranking and high-ranking estimates $\hat{V}$ but it has no relevance for the discussion here.

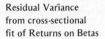

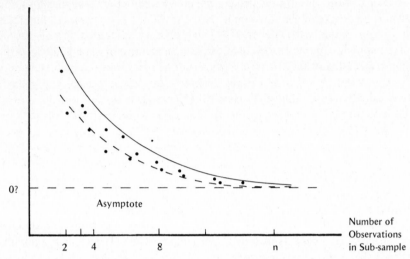

Fig. 1. Testing the linearity relation by using the cross-sectional residual variance. The esti-mated asymptote should be zero if the reference portfolio is ex ante mean/variance efficient.

3.2. Another method of testing for ex ante linearity between returns and betas

The linearity relation suggests another direct method of testing the reference portfolio's mean-variance efficiency. To my knowledge, it has not been reported in print or even calculated.

Examining the properties of (3) when the reference portfolio is truly ex ante efficient, we observe that as the time series sample size increases, the linearity between ex post mean return and beta should approach exactness. This implies that the residual variance from a cross-section regression fit of (3) should approach zero as the number of time series observations grows. [12] Unlike the standard errors-in-variables problem which does not benefit from the same two-dimensional characteristic, time series and cross-section, the linearity relation's errors can be made arbitrarily small by increasing the time series dimension.

This suggests the following procedure: *stage* 1, starting with a total sample of T time series observations, estimate the *individual* security mean returns and betas from the first two time series observations and run the cross-sectional regression (3) using individual securities. Then, repeat the same operation but with three time series observations, the third through the fifth; then with observations 6 through 9,

---

[12] Of course, the generating process is assumed to be stationary.

and so on. For each nonoverlapping time series subsample, an estimate of cross-section error variance would be obtained corresponding to a different time series sample size. The *second stage* would envisage fitting the estimates of error variance to a nonlinear function of the subsample size. See Figure 1. The number of time series observations in the last subsample, denoted "n" in Figure 1, would be equal to the largest integer less than $(\sqrt{9 + 8T} - 1)/2$ where T is the total number of time series observations.

If the estimated asymptote, drawn as a dotted horizontal line, were located at a level significantly different from zero, then the hypothesis that ex ante return and beta are exactly linearly related would be rejected.

There are several things objectionable about this procedure. First of all, it would be a heavy user of data. To obtain just 30 nonoverlapping cross-sectional regressions and thus 30 residual variances, a total of 464 simultaneous time series observations would be needed. This problem might be alleviated by using overlapping time series observations but then the residual variances would not be independently distributed (presuming that they *would* be independent for nonoverlapping observations). Secondly, the best procedure to use in the second stage (depicted by Figure 1) is not obvious. We do not have an errors-in-variables problem at this stage because the number of observations in each time series subsample is fixed. However, there is bound to be heteroscedasticity since the residual variance is a less reliable estimator the smaller the number of observations. To make things worse, the residual variance will be a biased downward estimate of the true disturbance variance in (3) because (3) itself contains an error-ridden explanatory variable. [13]

Fortunately, this bias will probably not be important. Although the residual variance scatter will appear to fall about the dashed curve of Figure 1 and the true error variance will follow the solid curve; and even though the slopes of these two curves will be different at any given point, their asymptotes will be equal. The bias will diminish with an increasing number of time-series observations, because the error vector ζ will approach the zero vector if the reference portfolio is ex ante efficient. The nonlinear fit should give an unambiguous test.

Notice that this procedure has avoided most of the econometric problems associated with (3)'s mis-specification. Although the true disturbances of (3) are cross-sectionally correlated and are also correlated with the explanatory variable, $\hat{V}X$, the suggested procedure provides an unambiguous test because it does not rely on estimates of the coefficients, γ_0 and γ_1. Instead, it relies upon S2's fundamental prediction — exact linearity — by measuring the rate of approach to this prediction as the time series sample size increases.

---

[13] The bias is easy to show: Since $\hat{R} = \gamma_0 \iota + \gamma_1(\hat{V}X) + \zeta$ is the true model and $\hat{R} = \hat{\gamma}_0 \iota + \gamma_1(\hat{V}X) + u$ is the fitted model, where u is the cross-sectional *residual* vector, we have the cross-sectional variances $\text{var}(\zeta) = \text{var}(u) + (\hat{\gamma}_1 - \gamma_1)^2 \, \text{var}(\hat{V}X) + 2(\hat{\gamma}_1 - \gamma_1) \, \text{cov}(u, \, \hat{V}X)$. The covariance is zero by the construction of least squares. Hence $\text{var}(u) < \text{var}(\zeta)$ because $\hat{\gamma}_1 \neq \gamma_1$ due to attenuation bias.

There are many ways the procedure might be improved; for example, by using a method better than ordinary least squares in the first stage cross-sectional regressions. If we assume that the returns are intertemporally uncorrelated (roughly speaking, the assumption of competitive markets), each subsample could be split into two parts in some random way; for example by taking every other observation, and *two* independent estimates of the vector VX_p, say $\hat{V}_1 X_p$ and $\hat{V}_2 X_p$, could be computed. Sample vector $\hat{V}_1 X_p$ could then be used as the instrument for $\hat{V}_2 X_p$ in order to reduce the errors-in-variables problem.

The data requirements would be only slightly more severe than when the first stage was accomplished with ordinary least squares. Time series observations 1 and 2 would have to provide the instruments for the first subsample (which would use observations 3 and 4). From that point on, each subsample could use results from the preceding subsample as instruments. Stage two would be unchanged.

3.3. The MacBeth method

MacBeth's [8] method for testing a portfolio's ex ante efficiency uses the time series sampling distribution of the vector ζ in (3). This method probably has many desirable characteristics in terms of statistical power but it too has some major disadvantages. These can be understood with only a small amount of additional notation.

Suppose the preselected portfolio p is ex ante efficient and thus (2) is true. Further, assume that estimates of $\hat{V}$ and of $\hat{\sigma}_p^2$ have been obtained from a sample exterior to the observations currently in use. Then a given time series observation on (2) can be denoted

$$R_t = \gamma_{0t} \iota + \gamma_{1t} \hat{V} X_p + \zeta_t \tag{7}$$

where the t subscripts indicate a particular time series observation of the vector of returns, R_t, the vector of disturbances ζ_t and the intercept $\gamma_{0t} \equiv r_{zt}$ and slope $\gamma_{1t} \equiv (r_{pt} - r_{zt})/\hat{\sigma}_p^2$. Thus the disturbance vector in (7) is $\zeta_t = \epsilon_{Rt} - \gamma_{1t} \epsilon_V$ and it is composed of an error vector $\gamma_{1t} \epsilon_V$ which arises partly from the estimation of $\hat{V}$ and of the usual error ϵ_{Rt}.

MacBeth's approach applies Hotelling T^2 test (cf. Morrison [11] to the random vector ζ_t with the nyll hypothesis $E(\zeta_t) = 0$. Clearly, if there are no estimation errors in $\hat{V}$, $(\epsilon_V \equiv 0)$, and no biases in the estimates of r_{zt} and $\hat{\sigma}^2$, then the expected value of ζ_t will be zero if and only if p is an ex ante efficient portfolio. Using individual security data, we immediately observe that the MacBeth test is apt to reject p's efficiency incorrectly, because ϵ_V is highly unlikely to be identically zero in every element. (There would be N elements of ϵ_V, one for each individual security.) To insure that ϵ_V is very close to zero, the investigator could do all estimations with portfolios rather than individual assets (a procedure followed by MacBeth in his original paper), but this would bring the same problem discussed earlier with the grouping procedure. Namely, if p is actually *not* ex ante efficient, the individual disturbance vector is

$$\zeta_t = \epsilon_{Rt} - \gamma_{1t}\epsilon_V + \alpha$$

and averaging ζ_t cross-sectionally could very well eliminate the nonconstant vector α. The *portfolio* disturbance vector would then be

$$\zeta_t = \epsilon_{Rt}.$$

and p's efficiency would be incorrectly supported.

Since the MacBeth test using individual security data is biased toward rejecting p's efficiency while the test using large portfolios is biased toward accepting efficiency, something might be gained by repeating the test for many different sizes of portfolios. With luck, the test would accept (or reject) for all sizes and this would be a reliable result. However, if the test rejects for small portfolios and accepts for large portfolios, no unambiguous conclusion could be drawn.

To be complete, I should mention two other problems with this test. First, there is a serious computational problem in the individual asset application (which would also be present for small portfolios). The Hotelling T^2 requires inversion of the sample covariance matrix of ζ_t. This matrix can be of an order as large as the number of individual assets, so the computational problems of the brute force method (see § 2) would also be present here. Second, there is a problem in estimating r_{zt} which may reduce the test's power. z is the portfolio which is orthogonal to p and its investment proportions actually depend on the values of $E(\hat{V})$ and $E(\hat{R})$. Thus, if ϵ_V is nonzero, or if the estimate of $E(\hat{R})$ used to construct the investment proportions for z contain errors, r_z will be biased. Whether this will offset any errors in ζ_t or aggravate them is not obvious and needs further investigation. Because of this problem, it may be better to estimate $\hat{\gamma}_0$ and $\hat{\gamma}_1$ independently, as well as $\hat{V}$, and then to apply Hotelling's T^2 directly to the random vector of returns, R_t, with the null hypothesis of p's efficiency implying $E(R_t) = \hat{\gamma}_0\iota + \hat{\gamma}_1\hat{V}X_p$.

4. Conclusions about testing for a portfolio's mean-variance efficiency

Given a willingness to preselect a vector of investment proportions that define a portfolio, there are a number of possible methods of testing its ex ante mean-variance efficiency. However, they are all subject to econometric difficulties. A "brute-force" testing method, wherein the sample efficient set is computed, is subject to two major problems. Computationally, the method is not very practical since a matrix of an order equal to the number of all assets in existence must be inverted. Furthermore, the sampling properties of the efficient set would not usually be known. Even if a simplifying assumption is made about the generating process, such as multivariate Gaussian, the statistical problems are nontrivial.

A second approach exploits the fact that "betas" computed against an efficient reference portfolio will be exactly linear (ex ante) in the mean returns (see S2). This approach is less subject to computational difficulties but it is highly subject to a different problem: the hypothesis of ex ante efficiency makes no prediction about the relation's parameters but only about its asymptotic form – exactly linear. Most standard econometric procedures are not very useful for solving this problem because they have been designed for accurate parameter estimation. The portfolio grouping procedure employed in many of the well-known empirical papers on asset returns is a case in point. Econometricians designed the grouping procedure to obtain accurate parameter estimates in an errors-in-variables context. We have seen, however, that the procedure is likely to hide important information about the *form* of the linearity relation and it may very well support the hypothesized ex ante mean/variance efficiency of the reference portfolio even when the portfolio is not efficient.

A different test procedure exploits asymptotic exact linearity. It would provide an unambiguous test of the reference portfolio's mean/variance efficiency. Much work remains to refine the test, however, and there may be many other procedures which would be better. One candidate is a test due to MacBeth, and its advantages and disadvantages are discussed.

References

[1] T. Anderson, An Introduction to Multivariate Statistical Analysis (Wiley, New York, 1958).
[2] F. Black, Capital market equilibrium with restricted borrowing, Journal of Business 45 (1972).
[3] F. Black, M.C. Jensen and M. Scholes, The capital asset pricing model: some empirical tests, in Studies in the Theory of Capital Markets, M.C. Jensen, ed. (Praeger, New York, 1972).
[4] M.E. Blume, Portfolio theory: a step toward its practical application, Journal of Business 43 (1970).
[5] M.E. Blume and I. Friend, A new look at the capital asset pricing model, Journal of Finance 28 (1973).
[6] E.F. Fama and J.D. MacBeth, Risk, return and equilibrium: empirical tests, Journal of Political Economy 81 (1973).
[7] J. Lintner, The valuation of risk assets and the selection of risky investments in stock portfolios and capital budgets, Review of Economics and Statistics 47 (1965).
[8] J.D. MacBeth, Tests of the Two-Parameter Model of Capital Market Equilibrium, unpublished dissertation, University of Chicago (1975).
[9] H.M. Markowitz, Portfolio Selection: Efficient Diversification of Investments (Wiley, New York, 1959).
[10] M.H. Miller and M. Scholes, Rates of return in relation to risk: a re-examination of some recent findings, in Studies in the Theory of Capital Markets, M.C. Jensen, ed. (Praeger, New York, 1972).

[11] D.F. Morrison, Multivariate Statistical Methods (McGraw–Hill, New York, 1967).

[12] S.J. Press, Applied Multivariate Analysis (Holt, Rinehart, and Winston, Inc., New York, 1972).

[13] R. Roll, A critique of the asset pricing theory: part I, Journal of Financial Economics 4 (1977).

[14] R. Roll and S.A. Ross, Comments on qualitative results for investment proportions, Journal of Financial Economics 5 (1977).

[15] B. Rosenberg and V. Marathe, Tests of Capital Asset Pricing Hypotheses, working Paper No. 32, Institute of Business and Economic Research, University of California, Berkeley (1975).

[16] S. Ross, A note on the capital asset pricing model, short-selling restrictions and related issues, Journal of Finance 32 (1977).

[17] W.F. Sharpe, Capital asset prices: a theory of market equilibrium under conditions of risk, Journal of Finance 19 (1964).

TIMS Studies in the Management Sciences 11 (1979) 151–168
© North-Holland Publishing Company

ON THE EXISTENCE OF SERIAL CORRELATION IN AN EFFICIENT SECURITIES MARKET

Kalman J. COHEN and Steven F. MAIER
Duke University
Robert A. SCHWARTZ
New York University
David K. WHITCOMB
Rutgers University

This paper offers a simple, efficient markets explanation of a number of diverse empirical findings involving serial correlation in common stock returns. (1) Despite the fact that there is no consistent evidence of serial correlation patterns in individual securities for differencing intervals longer than one day (see Fama [13] for a thorough survey of the extensive literature on this subject), market index returns exhibit substantial positive serial correlation. Lawrence Fisher [16] documented this observation, showed that it implies that the prices of different securities do not all adjust simultaneously to common information, and the observation of index autocorrelation without individual issue autocorrelation has come to be called the Fisher effect. [1] (2) Dimson [11] and Scholes and Williams [26] reported that autocorrelation is greater in the more broadly based indexes that give greater weight to thinner (lower value of shares outstanding) securities. (3) Fama, Fisher, Jensen, and Roll [14] and Schwartz and Whitcomb [28] reported negative autocorrelation of market model residuals, and the latter show that Fisher's price adjustment delay mechanism explains this effect as well. (4) Altman, Jacquillat, and Levasseur [1], Pogue and Solnick [24], and Schwartz and Whitcomb [27] reported that , when the differencing interval is shortened, market model R^2 diminishes substantially; the latter showed that index autocorrelation provides an explanation. (5) Altman, Jacquillat, and Levasseur [1] and Pogue and Solnick [24] reported for European data, and Scholes and Williams [26] for U.S. data, that the market model beta parameter also diminishes when the differencing interval is shortened. [2] Work

---

[1] Holbrook Working [31] had previously shown that a time series of cross-sectional averages will tend to be positively autocorrelated if the cross-sectional observations contained in each average are temporally ordered.

[2] Smith [30] and Levhari and Levy [21] report a different result for U.S. data with returns calculated in arithmetic (rather than logarithmic) terms: betas above and below one move toward one as the differencing interval is shortened. Levhari and Levy offer a theoretical explanation; Hawawini [20] shows that the apparently different results stem from the use of arithmetic returns.

by Hawawini [20] and by the present authors [4] demonstrates that these results may be due to serial cross-correlation which the model in the present paper shows will be evident in thin markets.

There is an emerging renewal of theoretical interest in dependency patterns. Recent papers by Copeland [8], Garman [18], and Scholes and Williams [26] have shown that price changes can be correlated even though the underlying processes which generate them occur randomly. None of these recent papers, however, is developed from an underlying microeconomic model based on investor demand functions to hold securities.

Our model of serial correlation builds upon a formulation of the returns generation process and an analysis of the effect of thinness on variance that we have developed elsewhere [Cohen, Maier, Schwartz, and Whitcomb [6] – henceforth referred to as CMSW]. Common to both papers is the assumption that aggregate demand shifts and idiosyncratic tenders are generated by mutually independent Poisson processes. This formulation is used in § 1, where we show that returns based on *quotation* prices have zero individual stock or index autocorrelation or serial cross-correlation. § 2 models returns based on *transaction* prices. Existence of a bid-ask spread is shown to introduce (slight) negative autocorrelation but no serial cross-correlation into transaction returns. The most important conceptual step in the analysis is also developed here: the returns generation model is altered to account for the existence of nontransaction-triggering aggregate demand shifts between the last recorded transaction and the end of a discrete measurement period. § 3 models the serial cross-correlation that results when a common informational shift is associated with a transaction in one measurement period for stock i and in the next for stock j. The magnitude of serial cross-correlation is shown to be related to the rate of idiosyncratic tender arrivals, the securities' market model betas, and to differencing interval length. § 4 then explores serial correlation in equal weighted and value weighted market indexes constructed from transaction returns. Our conclusions are presented in § 5.

1. A model of the quotation returns process

This paper assumes that, due to costs of acquiring information and of placing and executing orders, securities markets are imperfect, but satisfy the semi-strong form of the efficient markets hypothesis (see Fama [13]). Transaction costs result in incomplete transmittal of demand propensities to the market at any point in time. Thus, the aggregate limit order function for a security (which would be the order taker's "book" on a central market) is discontinuous, in contrast to the continuous latent demand to hold curve implicit in perfect markets theory. [3]

[3] Mossin [23] asserts a negatively sloping demand curve to hold securities. Cramer [9], Royama and Hamada [25], Bierwag and Grove [2], S. Fisher [17], and Epps [12] derive

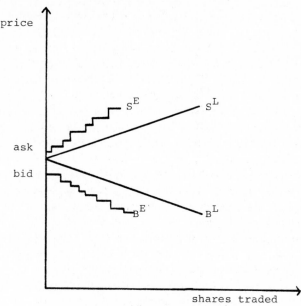

Figure 1. Market demand and supply curves.

Figure 1 depicts a limit order function in the form of *effective* buy and sell curves, drawn with the underlying *latent* buy and sell curves. The horizontal axis measures cumulative offers to alter holdings. These curves are equivalent to the trade demand and supply curves of CMSW [6], except that here we do not make the simplifying assumption of continuity. The gap between effective buy and sell curves at the vertical axis represents a bid-ask spread. [4]

The curves in Figure 1 represent (momentary) equilibrium. Trades occur when the arrival of new orders causes the effective curves to shift such that they intersect (i.e., some buy prices equal or exceed some sell prices). Following a transaction, the buy and sell curves shift left by the amount of the trade and a new momentary

Slutsky equations for assets and investigate the conditions for negatively inclined asset demand curves. Demsetz' [10] model of the determination of the bid-ask spread is the best-known example of the alternative flow formulation of a security demand curve.

[4] The existence of a spread in efficient markets is demonstrated rigorously by CMSW [5]. Demsetz [10] asserts the spread to be a price for immediacy set by marketmaker(s), but we feel the spread is more intimately related to search and transaction costs, and would exist (and would indeed be higher) even if there were no market makers or spread arbitrageurs who stand ready to offer immediacy to those who place market orders.

equilibrium results. [5] Clearly, shifts will not result in transactions unless they cause the effective buy and sell curves to intersect. [6,7]

As in CMSW [6], we distinguish two categories of demand shifts: aggregate demand shifts and idiosyncratic tenders. An aggregate demand shift is a general revision of limit orders due to e.g., GNP or interest rate announcements or specific company "news." We take an idiosyncratic tender to be a market order to buy or sell resulting from a single individual's need for or use for funds, [8] re-evaluation of a security's value, or change in risk-return preferences. [9] We do not model those idiosyncratic revisions of the limit order function which are of insufficient magnitude to result in a transaction.

Clearly some aggregate demand shifts will not result in transactions. [10] This is true in part because common information may result in similar direction and magnitude of limit order revision across individuals, causing both effective buy and effective sell curves to shift without intersecting. More realistically, the presence of the bid-ask spread means that supply can shift by more than demand (or vice versa) without an intersection necessarily resulting. For simplicity, we shall assume that *no* aggregate demand shift triggers a transaction. Under this assumption, a new transaction price is recorded following an aggregate demand shift only when a

---

[5] For a more complete description of the transaction process, see CMSW [6].

[6] For example suppose the initial quotes are 35 bid and 36 ask, and let the ask rise by 1/4 and the bid by 1. There would be no transaction. If a person who had previously offered 34 to buy then raised his price by 2 1/8, there would still be no transaction, although his offer would now be the best bid and the spread would have narrowed to 1/8.

[7] Note that with the effective demand and supply curves presented as step functions, it is clear that transactions need not necessarily change the market quotes or generate nonzero returns.

[8] In a world of zero transaction costs and fully diversified portfolios, the proportion of each stock to be liquidated to raise funds would be equal to its value weight in the investor's portfolio. However, with transaction costs and economies of scale in transaction, an individual holding a portfolio of moderate value would concentrate his sales in one or a few stocks, with the choice among stocks essentially random.

[9] Whether an individual transacts via limit order or market order depends on his assessment of the tradeoff of risks involved. A sell limit order, for instance, may be entered at any price. When the order reaches the head of the queue at that price, it will be executed if a buy order exists or comes in at that price. There is a risk that no buy order may come in, and the shares will be unsold. A sell market order is executed at the best available bid. The associated risk is that of selling at a price lower than could have been obtained with a limit order. A market order is analytically equivalent to a limit order that shifts the effective buy or sell function such that it intersects the sell or buy function.

[10] For evidence that demand shifts without transactions do occur, consider the case of the "phantom options." (See *The New York Times*, April 2, 1976, p. 39, column 4 for a most lucid explanation.) In this case AMEX specialists recorded fictitious transactions so as to bring recorded closing option prices in line with bid and ask prices and prevent a flood of orders at prices where no transaction could be struck. Such subterfuge would not have been necessary were security demand shifts always accompanied by transactions.

subsequent idiosyncratic tender is received. This feature will be exploited in the latter part of § 2 and thereafter.

In this model of the transaction process, we treat both aggregate demand shifts and idiosyncratic tenders as being generated by mutually independent compound Poisson processes. If we assume that there are $n_A(t)$ aggregate demand shifts and $n_I(t)$ idiosyncratic tenders in the tth time interval, then we could compute the return to the investor, r_t^Q, in the tth time interval as

$$r_t^Q = \log\left[\frac{P_1}{P_0} \cdot \frac{P_2}{P_1} \cdot \ldots \cdot \frac{P_{n(t)}}{P_{n(t)-1}}\right] \tag{1}$$

where $n(t) = n_A(t) + n_I(t)$. We use the superscript Q to denote that this is the return the investor would realize if he could buy the security at the price P_0 at the beginning of the time period and sell the security at the price $P_{n(t)}$ at the end of the interval. Initially, we take the bid-ask spread to be zero, a treatment which we later relax, and hence the price, which we call the quoted price, may be viewed as either the bid or ask.

We also assume that there is some correlation between the returns the investor can obtain in different securities. In order to model this interdependence of security returns, we introduce a single index market model of the returns process

$$r_{i,t}^Q = \alpha_i + \beta_i r_{M,t}^Q + \epsilon_{i,t} \tag{2}$$

where α_i is a constant whose value is dependent only on the length of the time interval over which returns are measured and the particular security i; β_i is a constant whose size is proportional to the systematic risk in security i; $r_{M,t}^Q$ is a random variable that measures the return on an underlying market portfolio M during the time interval t; and $\epsilon_{i,t}$ is a random variable that corresponds to the non-systematic return for security i that is observed in the time interval t.

The models of the return generation process given by (1) and (2) are consistent. If one associates the aggregate demand shifts of (1) with the market index $R_{M,t}^Q$ of (2) and the effect of idiosyncratic tenders on $r_{i,t}^Q$ with the nonsystematic return term $\epsilon_{i,t}$, then the two models can be viewed as alternative realizations of the same fundamental returns generation process. In the analysis that follows, we will find it convenient to make the following assumptions about the returns generation process.

(i) Idiosyncratic tenders for security i arrive at a rate of λ_i per day, where the arrival process is Poisson.

(ii) The nonsystematic return possesses the following properties:

(a) $E(\epsilon_{i,t}) = 0$ for all i and t,

(b) $\epsilon_{i,t}$ and $\epsilon_{j,\tau}$ are independent for all securities i and j and all time intervals t and τ,

(c) $\epsilon_{i,t}$ and $r_{M,\tau}^Q$ are independent for all securities i and all time periods t and τ.

(iii) $\text{cov}(r_{M,t}^Q, r_{M,\tau}^Q) = 0$ for all time intervals t and τ, as long as they do not overlap.

(iv) $E(r^Q_{M,t}) = E(r^Q_{M,\tau})$ and $\mathrm{var}(r^Q_{M,t}) = \mathrm{var}(r^Q_{M,\tau})$ for all t and τ of equal length.

In an appendix available upon request from the authors we show that assumptions (ii) and (iii) are sufficient conditions for:

$$\mathrm{cov}(r^Q_{i,t}, r^Q_{i,\tau}) = 0 \quad \text{for all securities } i \text{ and all time intervals } t \text{ and } \tau \text{ that do not overlap,}$$

and

$$\mathrm{cov}(r^Q_{i,t}, r^Q_{j,\tau}) = 0 \quad \text{for all securities } i \text{ and } j \text{ and time intervals } t \text{ and } \tau \text{ that do not overlap.}$$

The former of these assertions implies that individual securities show no serial correlation and the latter implies that the set of securities shows no serial cross-correlation. Both of these assertions are consistent with the martingale or sub-martingale form of the efficient markets hypothesis.

If we now define a market index m constructed from a sample of N quotation returns [11] as

$$r^Q_{m,t} = \sum_{i=1}^{N} w_i r^Q_{i,t}$$

where w_i are the weights each security has in the index, then

$$\mathrm{cov}(r^Q_{m,t}, r^Q_{m,\tau}) = \sum_{i=1}^{N} w_i^2 \, \mathrm{cov}(r^Q_{i,t}, r^Q_{i,\tau}) + \sum_{i=1}^{N}\sum_{\substack{j=1 \\ j\neq i}}^{N} w_i w_j \, \mathrm{cov}(r^Q_{i,t}, r^Q_{j,\tau}),$$

which from our previous assertions yields

$$\mathrm{cov}(r^Q_{m,t}, r^Q_{m,\tau}) = 0 \quad \text{for all } t \text{ and } \tau \text{ that do not overlap.}$$

It is interesting to note that this result holds for all possible weighting schemes of the securities. Therefore, if we could construct a market index from quotation

---

[11] In order for the constructed market index m (based on a sample of N securities) to be an unbiased estimator of the underlying market portfolio M, the sample must be selected and the weights chosen so that $\Sigma^N_{i=1} w_i \alpha_i = 0$ and $\Sigma^N_{i=1} w_i \beta_i = 1$. Our definition of the market index used in (2) is necessary for mathematical tractability in the current analysis; it, of course, is not identical to the log return of the aggregate market value of all securities (see, e.g., Merton [22]). The autocorrelation properties of this particular market index are not necessarily the same as the autocorrelation properties of a variety of other indexes, e.g., the S&P 500, the Fisher Index, the Value Line Index (which is essentially the antilog of the index we use), etc.; nonetheless, our theorems 3 and 4 below provide a plausible rationale for the extensive autocorrelation patterns observed by researchers in a variety of differently constructed market indexes.

returns, either value weighted or equally weighted, the index should not exhibit serial correlation.

Because the results derived in this section conflict with a number of empirical findings, it might be tempting to conclude that the assumption of efficient capital markets is fallacious. In the next section, we offer an alternative explanation. We shall show that when transaction prices are used to compute returns, the discontinuous nature of the arrival of idiosyncratic tenders in the market can cause autocorrelation and serial cross-correlation in a manner consistent with both empirical findings and the hypothesis of efficient capital markets.

2. A model of the transaction returns process

In this section, we model the generation of transaction returns in two steps. First, we incorporate the pure effect of a bid-ask spread on transaction returns and their autocorrelation and serial cross-correlation, implicitly assuming that a transaction always occurs at the end of each returns measurement period (e.g., a day, week, etc.). Then we incorporate the effect of the last transaction occurring before the end of a measurement period, which is implied by the Poisson arrival of idiosyncratic tenders.

With a nonzero bid-ask spread, transactions take place at either the bid or the ask. As a result, transaction prices show considerable variation as market orders randomly strike the bid and ask prices. For simplicity, let us assume that the prices used to determine the quotation return in (1) are the bid prices.

Then (1) can be modified to account for transaction prices as follows:

$$r_t^T = \log\left[\frac{P_0}{P_0 + G_{t-1}} \cdot \frac{P_1}{P_0} \cdot \frac{P_2}{P_1} \cdot \ldots \cdot \frac{P_{n(t)}}{P_{n(t)-1}} \cdot \frac{P_{n(t)} + G_t}{P_{n(t)}}\right]$$

where G_{t-1} and G_t are nonnegative random variables which adjust the bid prices at the end of each time interval t for the actual transaction prices. Rewriting, this expression becomes

$$r_t^T = r_t^Q + \log\left(1 + \frac{G_t}{P_{n(t)}}\right) - \log\left(1 + \frac{G_{t-1}}{P_0}\right).$$

Since the random variables G_{t-1} and G_t are small relative to P_0 and $P_{n(t)}$, we can rewrite this last expression using the approximation $\log(1 + x) \cong x$ as

$$r_t^T = r_t^Q + \frac{G_t}{P_{n(t)}} - \frac{G_{t-1}}{P_0}.$$

It is convenient to make the notational substitution

$$H_t \equiv \frac{G_t}{P_{n(t)}}$$

where $P_{n(t)}$ is the quotation price at the end of time interval t and $P_0 = P_{n(t-1)}$, so that we obtain

$$r_t^T = r_t^Q + H_t - H_{t-1}. \tag{3}$$

The form of this equation suggests that the correct form for (2), when one is measuring transaction returns, is

$$r_{i,t}^T = \alpha_i + \beta_i r_{M,t}^Q + \epsilon_{i,t} + H_{i,t} - H_{i,t-1}, \tag{4}$$

where we now make the following additional assumptions:

(v) $E(H_{i,t}) = E(H_{i,\tau})$ for all t and τ,

(vi) $H_{i,t}$ and $r_{M,\tau}^Q$ are independent for all securities i and all time periods t and τ,

(vii) $H_{i,t}$ and $\epsilon_{j,\tau}$ are independent for all securities i and j and all time periods t and τ, [12]

(viii) $H_{i,t}$ and $H_{j,\tau}$ are independent for all securities i and j and all time periods t and τ.

As a result of these assumptions, we show in the appendix that (4) leads to:

$$\text{cov}(r_{i,t}^T, r_{i,t+1}^T) = -\text{var}(H_{i,t})$$

and

$$\text{cov}(r_{i,t}^T, r_{j,\tau}^T) = 0 \quad \text{for all securities } i \text{ and } j \text{ and time intervals } t \text{ and } \tau \text{ that} \\ \text{do not overlap.}$$

Thus noting that the sign of covariance equals the sign of correlation, we have:

Theorem 1.   When a security's quotation returns are serially uncorrelated, the existence of a bid-ask spread will, ceteris paribus, introduce negative serial correlation into that security's transaction returns. The spread will not, per se, cause serial cross-correlation in transaction returns.

The returns generation model developed above is based on the assumption that we can in fact observe a transaction at the end of each measurement period. While this may be approximately correct for actively traded securities, it will not be so for infrequently traded (thin) securities. We have assumed earlier that aggregate demand shifts do not themselves result in transactions; an idiosyncratic tender is required. Thus, any aggregate demand shifts which occur between the time of the last transaction and the end of the measurement period are not reflected in the

---

[12] This assumption may not be strictly realistic if both the bid-ask spread and residual returns variance are systematically related to thinness.

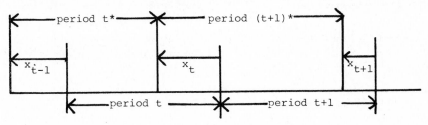

Figure 2. The relationship between time periods t and $t + 1$ in which transaction returns are nominally measured and periods t^* and $(t + 1)^*$ in which the corresponding demand shifts actually take place.

transaction returns computed for that period. Rather they are included in the next period's transaction return.

To see this more clearly, consider Figure 2. The variable x_t represents the interval between the last transaction and the end of measurement period t, and $x_t \neq x_{t-1}$ implies a difference between the lengths of the nominal transaction period, t, and the actual period over which aggregate demand shifts occur, t^*. Using this result, we can now further modify (4) to obtain

$$r^T_{i,t*} = k_{t*} \cdot \alpha_i + \beta_i \cdot r^Q_{M,t*} + \epsilon_{i,t} + \delta_{t*} \cdot (H_{i,t} - H_{i,t-1}) \qquad (5)$$

where k_{t*} = the length of the time interval t^* divided by the length of the measurement interval t, and

$$\delta_{t*} = \begin{cases} 0 & \text{if the length of } t^* \text{ is zero,} \\ 1 & \text{otherwise.} \end{cases}$$

In (5), the first and second terms of the market model are now expressed in terms of t^*, since these parameters are related to aggregate demand shifts that are measured over the time interval t^*. On the other hand, $\epsilon_{i,t}$ is related to the arrival of idiosyncratic tenders; therefore, since the interval over which we have measured idiosyncratic tenders (all of which result in transactions) is t, $\epsilon_{i,t}$ is unaffected. The dependence of $H_{i,t}$ on the variable x_t is more subtle. The key is that if no transaction occurs during a time interval t, then $H_{i,t} = H_{i,t-1}$, since then the last transaction is the last transaction during the previous time interval.

(5) permits us to analyze the serial dependence of security returns. In the next section, we use this equation to compute the serial covariance of a single security as well as the cross serial covariance between securities. These two results are then combined to obtain the serial covariance of a market index computed as a weighted sum of individual security returns.

3. Serial and cross serial covariance of transaction returns

Our objective is to obtain an expression for the serial covariance of security returns based on last transaction prices. Using an easily derived statistical identity (see the appendix), we have

$$\text{cov}(r_{i,t}^T, r_{i,t+1}^T) \equiv E[\text{cov}(r_{i,t}^T, r_{i,t+1}^T | x_{t-1}, x_t, x_{t+1})]$$

$$+ \text{cov}[E(r_{i,t}^T | x_{t-1}, x_t), E(r_{i,t+1}^T | x_t, x_{t+1})] \tag{6}$$

where x_{t-1}, x_t, and x_{t+1} are the time delay random variables between the last transaction and the end of the measurement interval. (Note that in (6) and the rest of this paper, we are omitting the * following the time period symbol for transaction returns for notational simplicity. However, the reader should be aware that for all transaction returns, the relevant interval is always t^* rather than t, as depicted in Figure 2.) Since we assume that transactions are generated by Poisson distributed idiosyncratic tenders with arrival rate λ_i, the distribution of x_t is negative exponential (see Feller [15, p. 39]) with probability density function $\lambda_i e^{-\lambda_i y}$.
The first term in (6) can be rewritten as

$$E[\text{cov}(r_{i,t}^T, r_{i,t+1}^T | x_{t-1}, x_t, x_{t+1})] = E\{E[(r_{i,t}^T - E(r_{i,t}^T | x_{t-1}, x_t))$$

$$\times (r_{i,t+1}^T - E(r_{i,t}^T | x_t, x_{t+1})) | x_{t-1}, x_t, x_{t+1}]\}. \tag{7}$$

We can now substitute for $r_{i,t}^T$ from (5) and as shown in the appendix

$$E(r_{i,t}^T | x_{t-1}, x_t) = (\alpha_i + \beta_i E[r_{M,t}^Q]) \left[\frac{l + x_{t-1} - x_t}{l} \right] \tag{8}$$

and

$$E(r_{i,t+1}^T | x_t, x_{t+1}) = (\alpha_i + \beta_i E[r_{M,t+1}^Q]) \left[\frac{l + x_t - x_{t+1}}{l} \right] \tag{9}$$

where l is the length of the measurement interval for periods t and $t + 1$. As shown in the appendix, these expressions imply

$$\text{cov}(r_{i,t}^T, r_{i,t+1}^T | x_{t-1}, x_t, x_{t+1}) = \begin{cases} -\text{var}(H_{i,t}) & \text{for} \quad x_t < l, x_{t+1} < l, \\ 0 & \text{otherwise} \end{cases}$$

from which we obtain

$$E[\text{cov}(r_{i,t}^T, r_{i,t+1}^T | x_{t-1}, x_t, x_{t+1})] = -[1 - e^{-\lambda_i l}]^2 \cdot \text{var}(H_{i,t}). \tag{10}$$

The second term in (6) can be found by substituting (8) and (9) to obtain:

$$\mathrm{cov}[E(r_{i,t}^T|x_{t-1}, x_t), E(r_{i,t+1}^T|x_t, x_{t+1})] = [\alpha_i + \beta_i E(r_{M,t}^Q)]^2$$

$$\times \frac{E[(x_{t-1} - x_t)(x_t - x_{t+1})]}{l^2} \ .$$

Using the fact that x_t has a negative exponential distribution, the final expectation is evaluated in the appendix as

$$F(\lambda_i, l) \equiv \frac{[e^{-2\lambda_i l}(4l^2\lambda_i^2 - 1) + 2\,e^{-\lambda_i l}(1 - l^2\lambda_i^2) - 1]}{l^2\lambda_i^2} \ .$$

Combining the above expression with (10), we obtain

$$\mathrm{cov}(r_{i,t}^T, r_{i,t+1}^T) = -(1 - e^{-\lambda_i l})^2 \cdot \mathrm{var}(H_{i,t})$$

$$+ [\alpha_i + \beta_i E(r_{M,t}^Q)]^2 \cdot F(\lambda_i, l). \tag{11}$$

(11) is our final form for the serial covariance. It is interesting to observe that the first term will always be negative and is positively related to the size and variability of the bid-ask spread. To show this, let the random variable $Y_{i,t}$ be the size of the bid-ask spread in return space, that is

$$Y_{i,t} = \frac{\text{Ask Price for Security } i - \text{Bid Price for Security } i}{\text{Bid Price for Security } i} \ .$$

If we assume that the arrival of an idiosyncratic tender will cause a transaction to occcur at exactly the bid or ask price, depending on the type of tender, and that each of these events is equally likely, we obtain (as shown in the appendix)

$$\mathrm{var}(H_{i,t}) = \frac{3\,\mathrm{var}(Y_{i,t}) + E^2(Y_{i,t})}{8} \ . \tag{12}$$

This last expression shows how both the size, $E(Y_{i,t})$, and the variability, $\mathrm{var}(Y_{i,t})$ of the bid-ask spread affect the serial covariance.

The second term in (11) will also be negative [13] for $\lambda_i l > 0.286$. For values of $\lambda_i l$ less than this, the second term may be slightly positive. This is a very unlikely event, since even when we are dealing with daily returns ($l = 1$ day) we would have

---

[13] This term must be zero if there is no "drift" in security i's quotation price, since by (2), $E(r_{i,t}^Q) = \alpha_i + \beta_i E(r_{M,t}^Q)$.

to have a transaction rate of less than one order every three days. [14]

It is important to realize that the first term in (11) will be substantially greater than the second term. Moreover, as $\lambda_i l$ becomes large, we obtain as expected

$$\text{cov}(r_{i,t}^T, r_{i,t+1}^T) \cong -\text{var}(H_{i,t}).$$

Consider next the cross serial covariance between security returns. An identity similar to (6) can then be written as (see the appendix)

$$\text{cov}(r_{i,t}^T, r_{j,t+1}^T) = E[\text{cov}(r_{i,t}^T, r_{j,t+1}^T | x_{t-1}, x_t, y_t, y_{t+1})]$$

$$+ \text{cov}[E(r_{i,t}^T | x_{t-1}, x_t), E(r_{j,t+1}^T | y_t, y_{t+1})] \tag{13}$$

where x_{t-1} and x_t are the random variables that describe the difference between the last transaction and the end of the measurement period for security i, while y_t and y_{t+1} are similarly defined for security j. Our analysis is simplified by the observation that since x_t is independent of y_τ for all t and τ, the second term in (13) must be zero.

In order to analyze the first term in (13), it is helpful to consider Figure 3. Notice that although there is no overlap in the periods t and $t + 1$ during which security transactions are measured, it is possible for there to be an overlap in the periods t^* for security i and $(t + 1)^*$ for security j in which aggregate demand shifts occur. In Figure 3, the length of the overlap is $y_t - x_t$. More generally, we can show that the length of the overlap will equal

$$\min[l + x_{t-1} - x_t, \max(0, y_t - x_t)]$$

if $x_t < l$ and $y_{t+1} < l$; otherwise it will be zero. In the appendix, we show that the overlap will cause cross serial covariance to be observed. This phenomenon is due to

---

[14] The negative serial correlation modeled by the first term in (11) would arise as a result of market orders striking the bid-ask quotes. For example, if we see a large positive return in period t, then the chances are that the final transaction was caused by a market order striking an ask price. Assuming the bid-ask prices remain unchanged, if the final transaction in the subsequent period is caused by a market order striking a bid price, we would observe a negative return. Therefore, if closing transaction prices are generated by market orders striking alternately bid and then ask prices, we should observe negative serial correlation. The negative serial correlation modeled by the second term in (11) would arise as a result of the upward drift in security returns and the fact that the time intervals t^* over which informational changes are measured are not necessarily of equal length. Therefore, if we observe a large positive return, it is likely that t^* is greater than usual in length, and thus the preceding and following periods $(t - 1)^*$ and $(t + 1)^*$ will be shorter than average. A shorter than average period would give rise to a less than average drift, and therefore, a smaller than average return. The possibility of positive serial correlation for small values of $\lambda_i l$ in (11), would be traceable to the occurrence of two or more consecutive days in which no transactions take place.

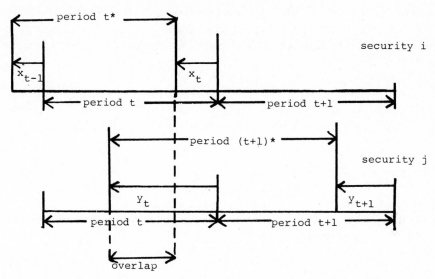

Figure 3. Example of an overlap period during which a common informational shift may affect $r^T_{i,t}$ and $r^T_{j,t+1}$.

the dependence of security returns on the market index $r^Q_{M,t}$. In particular, we can show that

$$\text{cov}(r^T_{i,t}, r^T_{j,t+1} | x_{t-1}, x_t, y_t, y_{t+1})$$

$$= \frac{\beta_i \beta_j \, \text{var}(r^Q_{M,t})}{l} \cdot \min[l + x_{t-1} - x_t, \max(0, y_t - x_t)]$$

for $x_t < l$ and $y_{t+l} < l$; otherwise the covariance is zero. Now, using the fact that $x_{t-1}, x_t, y_t, y_{t+t}$ are exponentially distributed, we show in the appendix that

$$\text{cov}(r^T_{i,t}, r^T_{j,t+1}) = \beta_i \beta_j \, \text{var}(r^Q_{M,t}) \cdot W(\lambda_i, \lambda_j, l) \tag{14}$$

where

$$W(\lambda_i, \lambda_j, l)$$

$$\equiv \frac{1}{l} \cdot \left[\frac{2(1 - e^{-\lambda_j l})(1 - e^{-\lambda_i l}) \, e^{-\lambda_j l} \cdot \lambda_j}{(\lambda_i + \lambda_j)^2} + \frac{\lambda_i (1 - e^{-\lambda_j l})^2}{\lambda_j (\lambda_i + \lambda_j)} \right] > 0.$$

Thus we have proved the following:

Theorem 2.   For the returns generation model of this paper, the first order serial cross-correlation of quotation returns between two risky securities i and j is zero, while their first order serial cross-correlation of transaction returns is nonzero and has the sign of $\beta_i\beta_j$.

In the next section, we examine the relationship between the parameters λ_i, λ_j, and l and the size of this effect, and we also show that a market index constructed from transaction returns exhibits serial covariance.

4. Serial covariance in market indices

In § 1 we showed that a market index constructed from quotation returns would exhibit no serial covariance. Now consider a market index constructed from transaction returns. Let $r_{m,t}^T$ be defined as

$$r_{m,t}^T = \sum_{i=1}^{N} w_i r_{i,t}^T$$

where w_i are again the weights each security has in the index. Then

$$\mathrm{cov}(r_{m,t}^T, r_{m,t+1}^T) = \sum_{i=1}^{N} w_i^2 \, \mathrm{cov}(r_{i,t}^T, r_{i,t+1}^T) + \sum_{i=1}^{N}\sum_{\substack{j=1\\j\neq i}}^{N} w_i w_j \, \mathrm{cov}(r_{i,t}^T, r_{i,t+1}^T)$$

which after substituting (11) and (14), becomes

$$\mathrm{cov}(r_{m,t}^T, r_{m,t+1}^T)$$

$$= \sum_{i=1}^{N} w_i^2 [(\alpha_i + \beta_i E(r_{M,t}^Q))^2 \cdot F(\lambda_i, l) - (1 - e^{-\lambda_i l})^2 \cdot \mathrm{var}(H_{i,t})]$$

$$+ \sum_{i=1}^{N}\sum_{\substack{j=1\\j\neq i}}^{N} w_i w_j [\beta_i \beta_j \, \mathrm{var}(r_{M,t}^Q) \cdot W(\lambda_i, \lambda_j, l)]. \tag{15}$$

The terms involving w_i^2 will always be *negative* for $\lambda_i l > 0.286$ and the terms involving $w_i w_j$ will be *positive* for $\beta_i, \beta_j > 0$. It may appear difficult, therefore, to determine an unambiguous sign for the covariance of a market index based on transaction returns. However, as the number of securities N in the index increases, then the terms involving w_i^2 approach zero, leaving only the positive serial covariance terms. [15] This result appears reasonable if we notice that this first term represents effects that are unique to individual securities, and therefore can be reduced by constructing the index from a large number of securities. On the other hand, the second term is more appropriately viewed as systematic, since it arises from interaction between securities, and therefore cannot be reduced by including more securities in the index. We have thus established:

Theorem 3. For the returns generation model developed in this paper, a market index constructed from quotation returns will exhibit no serial correlation, while a market index constructed from transaction returns for a large number of securities will show positive serial correlation.

Consider now the difference between a value weighted market index and an equal weighted market index. The value of $W(\lambda_i, \lambda_j, l)$ can be approximated by

$$\frac{\lambda_i}{\lambda_j \cdot (\lambda_i + \lambda_j) \cdot l}.$$

For example, if $l = 1$ day, $\lambda_i = \lambda_j = 10$ transactions per day, then $W(\lambda_i, \lambda_j, l) = 0.049998$, while the approximation $= 0.05$. Using the approximation, we find that $W(\lambda_i, \lambda_j, l)$ goes to zero as λ_i and λ_j increase. However, there is a direct relationship between the number of orders that arrive in a transaction period and the market value of the security. In particular,

$$\partial w_i / \partial \lambda_i > 0$$

for a value weighted index. Combining these two results, we find that for a value weighted index, the terms that have high values of $W(\lambda_i, \lambda_j, l)$ will have correspondingly low weights in the index. On the other hand, an equal weighted index will show much higher serial correlation, since the terms that have high W values do not have lower weights. Thus we have proved:

Theorem 4. For the returns generation model of this paper, a value weighted market index constructed from transaction returns will show lower serial correlation than a similarly constructed equal weighted market index.

---

[15] To see the effect on (15) of large N, let $w_i = 1/N$. Then the first term in (15) is proportional to $1/N$, while the second term is not proportional to N. Therefore, as N increases, the first term goes to zero, while the second term does not.

5. Conclusion

We have demonstrated that, even if capital markets are efficient and generate quotation returns that have zero autocorrelation and serial cross-correlation, then due to the existence of bid-ask spreads and because transactions do not occur simultaneously with all demand shifts, transaction returns for:

1. individual securities are negatively serially correlated;
2. securities i and j are serially cross-correlated with sign $\beta_i\beta_j$;
3. a market index based on transaction prices will be positively serially correlated;
4. a value weighted market index will show smaller serial correlation than an equally weighted market index.

The validity of the model is suggested by the empirical findings on transaction returns data cited in the introduction. We find it interesting that Hagerman and Richmond [19] found no evidence of meaningful dependence patterns in closing bid prices for a majority of stocks in their OTC sample. Our model would suggest that index returns computed from this data would show less serial correlation than similarly computed indexes using transaction prices. The quality of market model estimates for short differencing intervals may be improved substantially if quotation data are substituted for transaction data.

We do not intend to suggest that our model explains all reported phenomena relating to autocorrelation and serial cross-correlation in transaction returns data. For example, the reported predominance of positive serial correlation in individual NYSE stocks for one day differencing intervals (Fama [13]) may be due to specialist intervention (see Schwartz and Whitcomb [29]). Further, we may expect some serial correlation to arise even in quotation returns for a variety of reasons: (a) the sequential receipt of information by traders (see Copeland [8]); (b) the impact of random limit orders on an existing order book (see Garman [18] and Cohen, Maier, Schwartz and Whitcomb [7]). Finally, the persistence of index autocorrelation and serial cross-correlation for lengthy differencing intervals and value weighted indexes (see Fisher [16], Cheng and Deets [3], and Schwartz and Whitcomb [28]) suggests that some additional factors may cause price adjustment delays in stocks too "thick" to be significantly affected by the Poisson arrival of idiosyncratic tenders alone.

References

[1] E.I. Altman, B. Jacquillat and M. Levasseur, Comparative market model analysis: France and the United States, Journal of Finance 29 (December 1974).

[2] G.O. Bierwag and M.A. Grove, Slutsky Equations for Assets, Journal of Political Economy 76 (January–February 1968).

[3] P.L. Cheng and M.K. Deets, Portfolio returns and the random walk theory, Journal of Finance 26 (March 1971). See also Reply, Journal of Finance 28 (June 1973).

[4] K.J. Cohen, G.A. Hawawini, S.F. Maier, R.A. Schwartz and D.K. Whitcomb, Removing the intervaling effect bias in beta: theory and tests, working paper (1978).

[5] K.J. Cohen, S.F. Maier, R.A. Schwartz and D.K. Whitcomb, On the existence of bid-ask spreads in asset markets, working paper (1978).

[6] K.J. Cohen, S.F. Maier, R.A. Schwartz and D.K. Whitcomb, The returns generation process returns variance, and the effect of thinness in securities markets, Journal of Finance 33 (1978).

[7] K.J. Cohen, S.F. Maier, R.A. Schwartz and D.K. Whitcomb, Limit orders, market structure, and the return generation process, Journal of Finance 33 (June 1978).

[8] T.E. Copeland, A model of asset trading under the assumption of sequential information arrival, Journal of Finance 31 (September 1976).

[9] J.S. Cramer, A dynamic approach to the theory of demand, Review of Economic Studies 24 (February 1957).

[10] H. Demsetz, The cost of transacting, Quarterly Journal of Economics 82 (February 1968).

[11] E. Dimson, Dependencies in Stock Market Indices, paper presented at the Third Congress on Financial Theory and Decision Models, Garmisch-Partenkirchen, Germany (June 1974).

[12] T.W. Epps, Wealth effects and Slutsky equations for assets, Econometrica 43 (March 1975).

[13] E.F. Fama, Efficient Capital Markets: A Review of Theory and Empirical Work, Journal of Finance 25 (May 1970).

[14] E.F. Fama, L. Fisher, M. Jensen and R. Roll, The adjustment of stock prices to new information, International Economic Review 10 (February 1969).

[15] W. Feller, An Introduction to Probability Theory and Its Applications: Volume II, (John Wiley and Sons, Inc., New York, 1971).

[16] L. Fisher, Some new stock market indexes, Journal of Business 39 (January 1966).

[17] S. Fisher, Assets, contingent commodities, and the Slutsky equations, Econometrica 40 (March 1972).

[18] M.B. Garman, Market microstructure, Journal of Financial Economics 3 (June 1976).

[19] R.L. Hagerman and R.D. Richmond, Random walks, martingales, and the OTC, Journal of Finance 28 (September 1973).

[20] G.L. Hawawini, On the time behavior of financial parameters: an investigation of the intervaling effect, Ph.D. dissertation, New York University (1977).

[21] D. Levhari and H. Levy, The capital asset pricing model and the investment horizon, Review of Economics and Statistics 59 (February 1977).

[22] R. Merton, Optimum consumption and portfolio rules in a continuous-time model, Journal of Economic Theory 3 (December 1971).

[23] J. Mossin, Security Pricing Theory and Its Implications for Corporate Investment Decisions, (General Learning Press, Morristown, N.J., 1972).

[24] G.A. Pogue and B.H. Solnick, The market model applied to European common stocks: some empirical results, Journal of Financial and Quantitative Analysis 9 (December 1974).

[25] S. Royama and K. Hamada, Substitution and complementarity in the choice of risky assets, Risk Aversion and Portfolio Choice, edited by D. Hester and J. Tobin, Cowles Foundation Monograph 19 (John Wiley and Son, Inc., 1967).

[26] M. Scholes and J. Williams, Estimating betas from non-synchronous data, Journal of Financial Economics (Dec. 1977).

[27] R.A. Schwartz and D.K. Whitcomb, The time-variance relationship: evidence on autocorrelation in common stock returns, Journal of Finance 32 (March 1977).

[28] R.A. Schwartz and D.K. Whitcomb, Evidence on the presence and causes of serial correlation in market model residuals, Journal of Financial and Quantitative Analysis 11 (1977).

[29] R.A. Schwartz and D.K. Whitcomb, Assessing the impact of stock exchange specialists on stock volatility, Journal of Financial and Quantitative Analysis 11 (1977).
[30] K.V. Smith, The effect of intervaling on estimating parameters of the capital asset pricing model, Journal of Financial and Quantitative Analysis 13 (1978).
[31] H. Working, The investigation of economic expectations, American Economic Review 39 (May 1949).

TIMS Studies in the Management Sciences 11 (1979) 169-177
© North-Holland Publishing Company

A CHARACTERIZATION OF OPTIMAL MULTI-PERIOD PORTFOLIO POLICIES *

Nils H. HAKANSSON **

University of California, Berkeley

1. Introduction

In the single-period portfolio problem, the optimal investment policy is very sensitive to the utility function being used; the set of policies that are inadmissable or dominated across all utility functions is relatively small. The same observation holds in the multi-period case when the number of periods is not large. But as the number of periods does become large, the set of investment policies that are optimal for *current* investment tends to shrink drastically, at least in the simple reinvestment case without transaction costs. Many strikingly different investors will, in essence, invest the same way when the horizon is distant and will only begin to part company as their horizons near (Ross [14], Hakansson [6]).

It is tempting to conjecture that all long-run investment policies to which risk-averse investors with monotone increasing utility functions will flock, under a favorable return structure, insure growth of capital with a very high probability. Such a conjecture is false; many investors will, even in this case, converge on investment policies which almost surely risk ruin in the long run, in effect ignoring feasible policies which almost surely lead to capital growth. One purpose of this note is to set down, in simple terms, some of the relationships between the behavior of capital over time, the behavior of the expected utility of that same capital over time, and certain limits in the simple multi-period reinvestment model. A second purpose is to summarize the important role played by the isoelastic family of utility functions in this model, with particular attention given to the family member known variously as the "growth-optimal" policy, as the geometric mean policy, and as the maximization of expected logarithm policy. [1]

2. Preliminaries

In the interest of simplicity, and following Merton and Samuelson [12], Goldman [2] and others, I limit the discussion, in this and the next section, to two

* Aid from National Science Foundation grant SOC77-09482 is gratefully acknowledged.
** The author would like to thank Barry Goldman for helpful comments.
[1] For discussions of the geometric mean policy, see, for example, Williams [17], Kelly [8], Latané [9] and Breiman [1].

assets with stationary and (intertemporally) independent returns and to constant (proportion) policies. Let w_t denote wealth after t periods (where w_0 is initial wealth), r_1 the rate of return from the safe asset, and r_2 the rate of return from the risky asset, where

$$r_2 \geqslant -1, \quad 0 < r_1 < E[r_2] < M, \quad \text{some } M. \tag{1}$$

If v is the proportion (possibly greater than 1) of wealth w_{t-1} invested in the risky asset at the beginning of period t, we obtain

$$w_t(v; w_0) = w_0 \prod_{j=1}^{t} R_j(v) = w_0 [\exp \{ (\sum_{j=1}^{t} \ln R_j(v))/t \}]^t = w_0 (1 + g_t)^t, \tag{2}$$

where

$$R_j(v) = R(v) \equiv (r_2 - r_1)v + 1 + r_1,$$

provided

$$\Pr \{ R_j(v) \geqslant 0 \} = 1, \qquad j = 1, ..., t; \tag{3}$$

here, $R_t(v)$ is what is commonly known as the wealth relative in period t and g_t is the average compound growth rate of capital over the first t periods.

Consider the class of isoelastic utility of wealth functions

$$u(w_t) = \frac{1}{\gamma} w_t^\gamma, \qquad \gamma < 1, \tag{4}$$

where $\gamma = 0$ represents $\ln w_t$. Under our assumptions the optimal policy for each member of this class is stationary (Mossin [13]) and calls for investing proportion $v_\gamma > 0$ in the risky asset each period, where v_γ is the solution to

$$k(\gamma) \equiv \gamma \max_v E\left[\frac{1}{\gamma} R(v)^\gamma\right]; \tag{5}$$

as long as v_γ is an interior solution with respect to constraint (3), we note that v_γ is increasing in γ, that

$$\lim_{\gamma \to -\infty} v_\gamma = 0, \tag{6}$$

and that

$$k(\gamma) > 0, \quad k(0) = 1, \quad k'(\gamma) > 0 \tag{7}$$

[see Hakansson (1974)]. For any r_1 and r_2 satisfying (1), it follows from (6) and the continuity of v_γ in γ that there exists a $\hat{\gamma}$ such that

$$\Pr\{R(v_\gamma) \geqslant 1\} = 1, \qquad \gamma \leqslant \hat{\gamma}. \tag{8}$$

By the strict concavity of $E[R(v)^\gamma/\gamma]$ in v, (5), and (7) we obtain

$$k(\gamma, \bar{\gamma}) \equiv \gamma E\left[\frac{1}{\gamma} R(v_{\bar{\gamma}})^\gamma\right] > k(\gamma), \qquad \gamma < \bar{\gamma} < 0, \tag{9}$$

and (if (3) is not binding at v_0),

$$\frac{\mathrm{d}\, E[\ln R(v_\gamma)]}{\mathrm{d}\gamma} > 0, \qquad \gamma < 0. \tag{10}$$

3. A bounded utility discrimination theorem

We are now in a position to juxtapose the behavior of capital and the behavior of expected utility over time.

Choose numbers γ_2 and γ_2 such that

$$\gamma_1 < \gamma_2 \leqslant 0, \quad \gamma_2 \leqslant \hat{\gamma}, \quad k(\gamma_1, \gamma_2) < 1 \tag{11}$$

(property (7) makes this possible), and consider the utility function

$$u(w) = \frac{1}{\gamma_1} w^{\gamma_1}, \qquad w \geqslant \delta > 0. \tag{12}$$

The function (12) is clearly *bounded* both below and above and can be used to evaluate

$$E[u(w_t(v; w_0))] \quad \text{for} \quad v \leqslant v_{\hat{\gamma}}, \quad w_0 \geqslant \delta,$$

and all t in view of (2) and (8); the optimal policy v^* satisfies

$$v^* = v_{\gamma 1} < v_{\hat{\gamma}}$$

and gives

$$E\left[\frac{1}{\gamma_1} w_t(v^*; w_0)^{\gamma_1}\right] = \frac{1}{\gamma_1} w_0^{\gamma_1} k(\gamma_1)^t \to 0 \tag{13}$$

by (7) and (11). Applying policy $v_\gamma, \gamma_1 < \gamma \leqslant \gamma_2$, the utility function (12) gives, using (11),

$$E\left[\frac{1}{\gamma_1} w_t(v_\gamma; w_0)^{\gamma_1}\right] = \frac{1}{\gamma_1} w_0^{\gamma_1} k(\gamma_1, \gamma)^t \to 0. \tag{14}$$

Thus, policies v^* and v_γ, as noted by Samuelson [15] and others, cannot be distinguished by reference to expected utility in the limit. But by (7) and (9), $k(\gamma_1)/k(\gamma_1, \gamma) = \lambda_1 < 1$ so that in addition to (13) and (14) we also obtain

$$\frac{E[u(w_t(v^*; w_0))]}{E[u(w_t(v_\gamma; w_0))]} = \lambda_1^t \to 0, \tag{15}$$

or equivalently, defining the sequence $b_1, b_2, ...,$ by

$$E[u(w_t(v^*; w_0))] = E[u(w_t(v_\gamma; w_0 b_t))], \qquad t = 1, 2, ..., \tag{16}$$

we obtain the Goldman [2] observation

$$b_t = \lambda_2^t \to \infty. \tag{17}$$

Both (15) and (17) are incontrovertible testimony to the superiority of v^* over v_γ with respect to the (bounded) utility function (12). More importantly, either the behavior of the ratios (15) or the sequence of bribes given by (16) can be used to distinguish between policies whenever the limits (13) and (14) fail to do so.

Let us now characterize the long-run effects on capital resulting from policies v^* and v_γ. In view of (10), $E[\ln R(v^*)] < E[\ln R(v_\gamma)]$. Thus, by the law of large numbers, (2) gives (since $\exp\{x\}$ is monotone increasing) for some numbers a and $T(\epsilon)$

$$\Pr\{w_t(v^*; w_0) < w_0 a^t < w_t(v_\gamma; w_0)\} \geqslant 1 - \epsilon, \qquad t \geqslant T(\epsilon), \tag{18}$$

for every $\epsilon > 0$; in this case $a > 1 + r_1 > 1$ (Hakansson and Miller [7]). Thus, even though, in the long run, policy v_γ will almost surely produce a (compound) return above rate $a - 1 > 0$ and policy v^* will almost surely yield a return below it, some rational investors will prefer v^* to v_γ.

The preceding may be summarized as

The Rational Investor's Reassurance Theorem. For every $(1>) \epsilon > 0$, there exist bounded utility of wealth functions $u(w)$ (which are monotonically increasing and possess decreasing absolute risk-aversion), investment policies $z_1, ..., z_n$, and numbers $1 < a_1 < a_2 ... < a_{n-1}$ and $T(\epsilon)$ such that, for any initial wealth $w_0 \geqslant \delta > 0$ and any return distributions satisfying (1),

$$E[u(w_t(z_1))] > E[u(w_t(z_2))] > ... > E[u(w_t(z_n))], \qquad t = 1, 2, ..., $$

with the limits

$$\lim_{t \to \infty} E[u(w_t(z_i))] = \lim_{t \to \infty} E[u(w_t(z_1))], \qquad i = 2, ..., n,$$

and (if zero is used as the upper bound on $u(w)$)

$$\lim_{t \to \infty} \frac{E[u(w_t(z_i))]}{E[u(w_t(z_{i+1}))]} = 0, \qquad i = 1, ..., n - 1,$$

yet, as the same time,

$$\Pr\{w_t(z_1) < w_0 a_1^t < w_t(z_2) < w_0 a_2^t < ... <$$

$$... < w_t(z_{n-1}) < w_0 a_{n-1}^t < w_t(z_n)\} \geqslant 1 - \epsilon, \qquad t \geqslant T(\epsilon).$$

Paraphrased, the theorem says the following: there exist bounded utility of wealth functions reflecting a preference for more to less and (decreasing) risk aversion which rank wealth distribution 1 ahead of wealth distribution 2, which in turn is ranked ahead of wealth distribution 3, etc., despite the fact that wealth distribution 1 lies almost entirely to the *left* of wealth distribution 2, which in turn lies almost entirely to the *left* of distribution 3, etc. What makes the difference, even though the utility function is *bounded,* is the fact that the lower tail of distribution 1 is shorter and (imperceptibly) thinner than the (bounded) left tail of distribution 2, which in turn is shorter and (imperceptibly) thinner than the (bounded) left tail of distribution 3, etc. Very small adverse changes in the lower tail overpower the value of almost surely ending up with a higher compound return.

It should be noted that *no* reference has been made so far to the "growth—optimal" investment policy (denoted v_0 by reference to (5) since it maximizes $E[\ln R(v)]$, and hence $E[\ln(w_t)]$, in each period t). If the return structure is such that $\hat{\gamma} \geqslant 0$ in (8), then this policy may be associated with policy z_n in the theorem. We now turn to a classification scheme which summarizes the crucial role served by the isoelastic investment family and various branches thereof, including the "growth-optimal" twig, under pure reinvestment in a linear returns technology without transaction costs.

4. "Growth-optimal" versus other isoelastic versus all other investment policies: a classification

Let $u_h(w_h)$, $w_h \geqslant 0$, be the utility of terminal wealth at some horizon h, where $u_h' > 0$, $u_h'' < 0$, and let $v_n^*(w_{h-n})$ be the optimal fraction of w_{h-n} to invest in the risky asset with n periods to go. Then for the class (4)

$$v_n^*(w_{h-n}) = v_\gamma, \qquad n = 1, 2, ...,$$

where, as noted, v_γ is increasing in γ until constraint (3) is binding.

Modifying assumption (1) and expressions (2)–(3) to permit many risky assets and nonstationary returns (see, e.g., Hakansson [6, p. 203]), the select nature of the isoelastic family of investment policies in the "pure" multi-period portfolio model is evidenced by the following properties in relation to all other policies based on monotonically increasing and strictly concave (terminal) utility functions:

A1. When the feasible wealth relatives are exactly lognormal, [2] the set of optimal policies for the isoelastic family (4) spans the set of policies which are optimal for the class of *all* risk-averse investors in any given period.

A2. The preceding is also true when there is one risky asset (with arbitrary return distribution) and one riskless asset.

A3. Only the class (4) yields *myopic* optimal policies, i.e., the optimal policy for the current period is independent of the return structure *beyond* the current period $(v_n^*(w_{h-n})) = v_\gamma$, $n = 1, 2, ...,$ in the two-asset stationary returns case) (Mossin [13]).

A4. Convergence of $v_n^*(w_{h-n})$ to a "simple" policy has been demonstrated for a large class [3] of terminal utility functions $u_h(w_h)$ (Hakansson [6]; see also Leland [10] and Ross [14]). Significantly, convergence has always been to an isoelastic policy, [4] (i.e., of the form

$$v_n^*(w_{h-n}) \to v_\gamma, \tag{19}$$

in the case of two assets and stationary returns). [5]

For investors who lack explicit utility of (terminal) wealth functions and therefore use other criteria, such as the mean-variance criterion, we can state

A5. To obtain a "simple" approximation to the policies which yield mean-variance efficient portfolios with respect to average compound return over h periods, i.e., the mean and variance of

$$[\prod_{t=1}^{h} R_t(v)]^{1/h},$$

the class (4) for $\gamma \leqslant 1/h$ is sufficient (when there are only two assets, one risky and one riskless, and returns are stationary, this class yields the set of policies which is exactly efficient) (Hakansson [5]; Hakansson and Miller [7]).

The preceding reminds us that the simplicity of the class (4) (spelled out in A3)

---

[2] Warning: Exact lognormality does not obtain from a mixture of a riskless asset and a lognormally distributed risky asset, or mixtures of lognormal assets (except under continuous rebalancing under geometric Brownian motion). Thus, A1 is notable for its existence rather than for its usefulness.

[3] For an example in which convergence does not take place, see Hakansson [6, pp. 219–20].

[4] In view of (6), the riskless policy may be viewed as a member of class (4).

[5] (19) does not necessarily imply that v_γ can validly be substituted for $v_n^*(w_{h-n})$ for small n, i.e., *near* the horizon (Ross [14, p. 184], Hakansson [6, p. 202]).

does not detract from its richness (as evidenced by A1, A2, A5) and its strong influence over the (investment) behavior of many other families (A4). (Furthermore, as we have seen, members of the class can be chosen to prove the theorem in § 3).

The fundamental equality of the "growth-optimal" policy v_0 as a member of its immediate family (4) is evidenced by the following:

B1. Expression (5) yields a different optimal policy for each γ, i.e., $v_{\gamma_1} \neq v_{\gamma_2}$ for $\gamma_1 \neq \gamma_2$ whenever constraint (3) is not binding.

B2. In (19), the class of terminal utility functions whose optimal policies converge to v_γ, $\gamma = 0$, is no "larger" than the class whose policies converge to v_γ for any other γ.

The "equality" of the "growth-optimal" policy as a member of the *subset* of the isoelastic family (4) which insures "growth of capital" (in the sense that for any $\epsilon > 0$ we can find numbers $T(\epsilon)$ and $a > 1$ such that

$$\Pr\{w_t(z) \geqslant w_0 a^t\} \geqslant 1 - \epsilon, \qquad t \geqslant T(\epsilon)), \tag{20}$$

shows up in the following property.

C1. Suppose the return structure is as in (1) or its generalization and let z_γ denote the optimal policy (sequence) when $u_h(w_h) = (1/\gamma)w_h^\gamma$. Then (20) holds for all z_γ such that $\gamma \leqslant \bar{\gamma}$, where $\bar{\gamma} > 0$; in fact, we can (in the stationary case) set $a = 1 + r_1$ in (20) for all z_γ such that $\gamma \leqslant \gamma(r_1)$, where $0 < \gamma(r_1) < \bar{\gamma}$. Thus, all isoelastic terminal utility of wealth functions with nonpositive exponents, and at least some with positive exponents, have the property that they cause growth of capital at a rate which almost surely exceeds the return on the risk-free asset. On the other hand, isoelastic terminal utility of wealth functions with exponents close to 1 may, under certain return structures and in the long run, almost surely lead to ruin. [6]

The distinctive features of the "growth-optimal" policy (i.e., the policy based on $u(w) = \ln w$), by itself, are the following:

D1. Let z_0 be the "growth-optimal" policy and z be any other investment policy which does not converge to z_0. Then for any $\epsilon > 0$ there exist numbers $a_1 < a_2$ (where $a_2 > 1$ and a_1 is possibly less than 1) and $T(\epsilon)$ such that

$$\Pr\{w_t(z) < w_0 a_1^t < w_0 a_2^t < w_t(z_0)\} \geqslant 1 - \epsilon, \qquad t \geqslant T(\epsilon).$$

---

[6] Consider for a moment the utility function $u(w) = w^{1/2}$, one of the most frequently cited examples of "substantial" risk aversion since Bernoulli's time. Even this venerable function may, however, lead to (almost sure) ruin in the multi-period case: suppose, for example, that the riskfree asset yields 2 percent per period and that there is only one risky asset, which gives either a loss of 8.2 percent, with probability 0.9, or a gain of 206 percent, with probability 0.1. The optimal policy then calls for investing fraction 1.5792 in the risky asset by borrowing fraction 0.5792 of current wealth to complete the financing) in each period. But the average compound growth rate g_t in (2) will now tend to -0.00756, or $-3/4$ percent. Thus, expected utility $\to \infty$ as capital itself almost surely vanishes.

D2. Only the logarithmic investment policy remains myopic under serially dependent returns (Hakansson [4]).

Property D1 in effect says that one can virtually drive a wedge of arbitrary width between the capital distribution resulting from a geometric mean maximizing policy and the distribution produced by any other (significantly different) policy. In view of this, the appeal of the so-called "growth-optimal" investment policy to those who are somewhat unsure about their preferences is understandable: under the usual portfolio model assumptions it promises (and delivers) almost surely more wealth in the long run than (asymptotically) different policies. At the same time, the investor who *knows* his preferences, and is certain that they are not "close" to logarithmic, should have no difficulty discarding the "growth-optimal" policy as inferior for long-run investment purposes (see theorem in § 3). [7] Again, the reason is simply that in the long run "small" changes in the tails of the wealth distribution begin to overwhelm "large" changes elsewhere in the distribution when integrated with any given utility function. [8] Contemplation of the integral in question renders this fact rather apparent for unbounded utilities, much less so for bounded utility functions (but recall the theorem). The resulting nonoptimality of the "growth-optimal" investment policy for certain nonlogarithmic preferences was routinely noted in Hakansson [3, p. 69] and Samuelson [15, p. 246] and demonstrated by explicit counterexamples in Samuelson [16], Merton and Samuelson [12], and Goldman [2]. [9]

The author stresses again that the preceding properties do hold in the case of many risky assets and under "bounded" nonstationarity of returns (in the latter case the optimal policy will of course be nonstationary). However, the extent to which the conditions that give rise to property A4 must be strengthened when preferences based on consumption streams, as opposed to terminal utility of wealth in a pure reinvestment model, are introduced is as yet unclear. In any case, it is evident that the isoelastic family (4) occupies a rather special position in multi-period portfolio theory sans transaction costs.

[7] One might argue that the proof of the pudding is in the eating and that the test driving of cars has been known to change preferences. But once the ignorance has been dispelled, the point still remains.

[8] As an illustration of this point and of the theorem, suppose there are two investment opportunities, one yielding 5 percent per period, the other a 110 percent gain or a 47.5 percent loss with equal probabilities, the returns being independent from period to period. Consider the capital distributions obtained from repeated reinvestment over N periods in such a way that (i) the assets at the beginning of each period are divided equally between the two opportunities (distribution A_N), and (ii) a quarter of the assets are placed in the risky asset, the other three quarters in the riskless one at the beginning of each period (distribution B_N). Then A_N clearly has longer tails than B_N; furthermore, most of the probability mass of A_N is located "near" $w_0 1.05^N$ and most of the mass of B_N is "near" $w_0 1.11^N$ for large N, where w_0 is the initial asset level. For any N, a logarithmic investor will always prefer B_N to A_N while the converse is true, for example, for an investor whose utility may be measured by the square root of wealth.

[9] Less obvious, implicit counterexamples are provided by (for example) Mossin [13], Merton [11], and Hakansson [4].

References

[1] Leo Breiman, Investment policies for expanding business optimal in a long-run sense, Naval Research Logistics Quarterly 7 (1960).

[2] Barry Goldman, A negative report on the 'near optimality' of the max-expected log policy as applied to bounded utilities for long-lived programs, Journal of Financial Economics 1 (1974).

[3] Nils Hakansson, Optimal investment and consumption strategies for a class of utility functions. Ph.D. thesis, University of California at Los Angeles; also, Working Paper No. 101, Western Management Science Institute, University of California at Los Angeles (June 1966).

[4] Nils Hakansson, On optimal myopic portfolio policies, with and without serial correlation of yields, Journal of Business 44 (1971a).

[5] Nils Hakansson, Multiperiod mean-variance analysis: toward a general theory of portfolio choice, Journal of Finance 26 (1971b).

[6] Nils Hakansson, Convergence to isoelastic utility and policy in multiperiod portfolio choice, Journal of Financial Economics 1 (1974).

[7] Nils Hakansson and Bruce Miller, Compound-return mean-variance efficient portfolios never risk ruin, Management Science 22 (1975).

[8] J.L. Kelly, Jr, A new interpretation of information rate, Bell System Technical Journal 35 (1956).

[9] Henry Latane, Criteria for choice among risky ventures, Journal of Political Economy 67 (1959).

[10] Hayne Leland, On turnpike portfolios, in Mathematical Methods in Investment and Finance, G.P. Szegö and Karl Shell, eds. (North-Holland, Amsterdam, 1972).

[11] Robert Merton, Lifetime portfolio selection under uncertainty: the continuous-time case, Review of Economics and Statistical LI (1969).

[12] Robert Merton and Paul Samuelson, Fallacy of the log-normal approxiation to optimal portfolio decision-making over many periods, Journal of Financial Economics 1 (1974).

[13] Jan Mossin, Optimal multiperiod portfolio policies, Journal of Business, 41 (1968).

[14] Stephen Ross, Portfolio turnpike theorems for constant policies, Journal of Financial Economics 1, (1974).

[15] Paul Samuelson, Lifetime portfolio selection by dynamic stochastic programming, Review of Economics and Statistics LI (1969).

[16] Paul Samuelson, The 'fallacy' of maximizing the geometric mean in long sequences of investing or gambling, Proceedings of the National Academy of Sciences 68 (1971).

[17] John Williams, Speculation and the carryover, Quarterly Journal of Economics L (1936).

TIMS Studies in the Management Sciences 11 (1979) 179–196
©North-Holland Publishing Company

OPTIMAL DYNAMIC CONSUMPTION AND PORTFOLIO PLANNING IN A WELFARE STATE

S.P. SETHI and M.J. GORDON

University of Toronto

and

B. INGHAM

IBM of Canada

This paper deals with the problem of optimal multi-period consumption and investment decisions of an individual whose investment alternatives depend on his decisions in a special way. A typical example belonging to the class of problems under consideration is that of an individual living in a welfare state. This individual can count on a government income maintenance program (welfare), when his health falls below a predetermined poverty (or, subsistence) level. Obviously, the existence of such a floor level of wealth, in general, will influence the individual's decision to consume and invest. The manner in which the welfare program influences his behavior, however, depends critically on the number of periods remaining.

We assume the logarithmic utility of consumption. Furthermore, we assume that a risk-free asset and a risky asset (giving a higher return under a favorable outcome) are available alternative investments when the individual is not on welfare.

It is shown that the individual with two periods remaining consumes all his wealth when the level of his wealth is just above the welfare level. As his wealth increases, there comes a point when he switches to consuming a constant fraction which is more than half of his wealth and investing the remainder in the risky asset. This continues until a certain wealth level beyond which the individual consumes half of his wealth and invests the remainder in the risk-free asset. At this level of wealth, the individual can be considered "wealthy" since the welfare program does not distort his decisions. Note that it is possible to characterize, as intuitive, the behavior of the individual with two periods remaining.

The behavior of an individual with three periods remaining is counterintuitive. There is no systematic pattern to his investment behavior. The individual, as he becomes wealthier, can switch back and forth to risky, risk-free and intermediate-risk investments. His consumption behavior, on the other hand is quite systematic. The fraction of wealth consumed decreases as his wealth increases. The fraction changes from total consumption to one-third consumption with various intermediate stages.

Finally, we observe interesting and paradoxical behavior patterns for the individual with three periods remaining. There are levels and ranges of wealth where the individual has non-unique optimal policies. In particular cases, it is possible even to have both the extreme policies of investing entirely in the risky asset or entirely in the risk-free asset as optimal policies.

The paper contains detailed discussions of the results while relegating most of the mathematical proofs to the Appendix. It is noted that no additional patterns of behavior will arise by increasing the number of periods to more than three periods. We conclude with a plan of research for a forthcoming paper.

Dynamic models of optimal consumption and portfolio behavior over time such as Samuelson [5] and Merton [4] optimize under the assumption that the investment opportunities available to an individual are independent of his consumption and investment decisions. However, there are important classes of circumstances in which this assumption is not, in fact, true. For instance, in most modern societies, an individual can count on a government income maintenance program (welfare) when his wealth falls below a predetermined poverty level. Similarly, when the value of the income from the joint employment of a proprietor's labor and capital falls below some level, the proprietorship is liquidated and he takes a job.

In other words, an individual with a given utility function who is not on welfare or who is a proprietor need not struggle on in his existing state regardless of how low his income prospects or wealth fall in that state. Furthermore, the fact that he may go on welfare in one case or liquidate his firm in the other case may well influence his behavior short of the circumstances that force the decision.

The purpose of the present paper is to investigate this problem theoretically. Specifically, we examine how an individual allocates his wealth among consumption, a risky asset and a risk-free asset in a multiperiod world where he goes on welfare and receives a prescribed annual income when his wealth falls below that income level.

The results presented below provide theoretical support for the findings obtained from an experimental game [3] where consumption and portfolio decisions (between a risky and risk free asset) were made over time with the knowledge that a fixed periodic income would be received when wealth fell below that level. As one might intuitively expect, risk aversion fell sharply as wealth fell towards the welfare level. Recognizing that individuals in general and proprietors in particular may change their state provides an alternative and perhaps superior explanation of risk preference than previous efforts such as [2]. More important, it provides a basis for extending our knowledge of consumption and portfolio behavior.

1. The model

Let the poverty level be one, since any poverty level can be scaled to unity. We assume that the individual goes on welfare when his wealth falls below the poverty level and that consumption is equal to the income level of welfare recipients. When not on welfare the individual allocates his wealth among consumption, a risky asset and a risk-free asset. The latter provides a return of r, and the return on the risky asset is the random variable

$$Z = \begin{cases} x > 1 & \text{w.p. } p_1, \quad 0 < p_1 < 1, \\ 0 & \text{w.p. } p_2 = 1 - p_1 \end{cases} \tag{1}$$

next period for each dollar invested. For simplicity in exposition, we assume the fair game condition.

$$p_1 x = (1 + r). \text{ }^1 \tag{2}$$

The model can be generalized to the usual situation where $p_1 x > (1 + r)$. Such a generalization, however, would make the computation of the optimal policies slightly more difficult.

Let the utility of consumption c be given by

$$U(c) = \log c \quad \text{for } c \geqslant 0. \tag{3}$$

Since $\log 1 = 0$ and $\log c < 0$ for $c < 1$, we can interpret unit consumption per period as the "subsistence level." Then, the poverty level or the welfare cut-off level is set equal to the subsistence level. Finally, we set the discount rate $\rho = 0$ for simplification. The analysis can easily be extended to allow $\rho > 0$.

The problem of an individual with remaining life of T periods can be stated as follows:

$$J = \max_{\{c_t, v_t\}} E\left[\sum_{t=1}^{T} \begin{cases} 0 & \text{if } W_t < 1 \\ \log c_t & \text{if } W_t \geqslant 1 \end{cases}\right] \tag{4}$$

subject to

$$W_{t+1} = \begin{cases} 1 & \text{if } W_t < 1 \\ (W_t - c_t)[(1 + r)(1 - v_t) + v_t Z] & \text{if } W_t \geqslant 1 \end{cases},$$

$$t = 1, 2, ..., (T - 1), \tag{5}$$

with the initial condition

$$W(1) = W_1, \tag{6}$$

where

W_t = wealth in the tth period,
c_t = consumption in the tth period,
v_t = fraction invested in risky asset; $0 \leqslant v_t \leqslant 1$.

---

[1] With utility a concave function of wealth, the fair game condition (2) would make the investment problem of the individual trivial in a no-welfare state. This is not so in the welfare state.

We will solve this problem by means of stochastic dynamic programming [1]. Before doing so, we remark that the maximand in the Bellman functional equation no longer decomposes into two parts as it did in Samuelson [5] and made the portfolio decision independent of the consumption decision. The loss of decomposition renders the proposed problem quite difficult. As a result, we will solve the problem with $T = 3$, representing a 3-period problem.

2. Solution of the three period problem

The solution of our basic problem $(4, 5, 6)$ can be understood as follows. At $t = 1$, the individual knows his wealth W_1 and makes decisions c_1 and v_1. However, since Z is a random variable, these decisions must be made without knowing the exact value of the wealth W_2 in period 2. Depending upon knowledge of W_2, he will make new decisions c_2 and v_2. In period 1, however, the individual can only guess what those decisions will be. That is, period 1 decisions would depend on the probabilistic structure of decisions in future periods.

As usual in dynamic programming we state at $t = T$.

(i) $t = T$. Since we assume no bequest, the optimal decision is to consume the entire wealth. Furthermore, if $W_T < 1$, the individual goes on welfare and receives a welfare payment in the amount of $(1 - W_T)$. Thus, his one-period utility function $J_T(W)$ is given by

$$J_T(W) = \begin{cases} 0, & W < 1, \\ \log W, & W \geq 1, \end{cases} \qquad (7)$$

and is sketched in fig. 1. [2,3]

(ii) $t = T - 1$. Obviously,

$$J_{T-1}(W) = 0 \quad \text{for} \quad W < 1. \qquad (8)$$

Suppose, however, that the individual finds himself with amount of wealth $W \geq 1$ and suppose further that individual makes decisions c and v. Then his expected two-period utility would be given by

$$J_{T-1}(W; c, v) = \log c + p_1 J_T[(W - c)\{(1 + r)(1 - v) + vx\}]$$
$$+ p_2 J_T[(W - c)(1 + r)(1 - v)]. \qquad (9)$$

---

[2] Note that we have dropped the subscript on W as it is unnecessary on account of the subscript on J.

[3] It is important to remark that the analysis of this paper can be easily extended to isoelastic utility functions $U(c) = (c^\gamma - 1)/\gamma$, $\gamma < 1$. Slight modification of the usual form c^γ/γ renders $J_T(W)$ continuous.

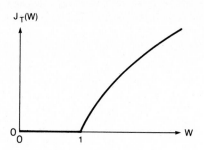

Figure 1. Sketch of $J_T(W)$.

Using Bellman's optimality principle,

$$J_{T-1}(W) = \max_{\{c,v\}} \left[J_{T-1}(W; c, v) \right]. \qquad (10)$$

Since the value of J_T in (9) depends on the argument of J_T according to (7), we denote for convenience:

$$A = (W - c)\{(1 + r)(1 - v) + vx\} \quad \text{and} \quad B = (W - c)(1 + r)(1 - v).$$

Because $A \geqslant B$ for any given policy c and v, we have only three different cases, as shown in the following table.

Table 1
Different cases for J_T

	$A < 1$	$A \geqslant 1$
$B < 1$	Case 1	Case 2
$B \geqslant 1$	–	Case 3

We shall now analyze these cases one by one.

Case 1. Since both A and B are less then one, we have

$$J^1_{T-1}(W; c, v) = \log c, \qquad (11)$$

(where the superscript refers to a case-wise analysis for case 1) and, therefore

$$c^* = W. \qquad (12)$$

Thus

$$J_{T-1}^1(W) = \log W. \tag{13}$$

Case 2. Since $A \geqslant 1$ and $B < 1$, we have

$$J_{T-1}^2(W; c, v) = \log c + p_1 \log(W - c)[(1 + r)(1 - v) + vx],$$

$$= \log c + p_1 \log(W - c) + p_1 \log[(1 + r)(1 - v) + vx]. \tag{14}$$

Obviously, J_{T-1}^2 attains its maximum with respect to v at

$$v^* = 1, \tag{15}$$

which makes

$$J_{T-1}^2(W; c, 1) = \log c + p_1 \log(W - c) + p_1 \log x. \tag{16}$$

For maximizing with respect to c, we set

$$\partial J_{T-1}^2/\partial c = 1/c - p_1/(W - c) = 0,$$

which yields

$$c^* = W/(1 + p_1). \tag{17}$$

Substituting for v^* and c^* in (14) and manipulating, we get

$$J_{T-1}^2(W) = (1 + p_1) \log \frac{W}{(1 + p_1)} + p_1 \log(1 + r). \tag{18}$$

Case 3. Since $A \geqslant 1$ and $B \geqslant 1$, we have

$$J_{T-1}(W; c, v) = \log c + p_1 \log(W - c)[(1 + r)(1 - v) + vx]$$

$$+ p_2 \log(W - c)(1 + r)(1 - v). \tag{19}$$

For maximizing J_{T-1}^3 in (19) with respect to v, we set

$$\partial J_{T-1}^3/\partial v = p_1(x - 1 - r)/[(1 + r)(1 - v) + vx]$$

$$- p_2(1 + r)/[(1 + r)(1 - v)] = 0.$$

Using (2) it is easy to see that this condition implies

$$v^* = 0, \tag{20}$$

which makes

$$J^3_{T-1}(W; c, 0) = \log c + \log (W - c) + \log(1 + r). \tag{21}$$

By the similarity of (21) with (16), we can conclude

$$c^* = W/2, \tag{22}$$

$$J^3_{T-1}(W) = 2 \log(W/2) + \log(1 + r). \tag{23}$$

In constructing $J_{T-1}(W)$, a major problem is that $J^i_{T-1}(W)$ may not be valid for the entire range $[0, \infty]$. That is, for a given W, case-wise optimal c^{*i} and v^{*i} for case i may yield A and B which fall under case $j \neq i$. Since $J_{T-1}(W)$ is the supremum of $J^i_{T-1}(W)$ restricted to their valid ranges, it may be quite complicated to obtain it. However, theorem 1 in the Appendix simplifies this task immensely by showing that the supremum taken of unrestricted $J^i_{T-1}(W)$ does not contain any invalid case-wise segment. Thus, the optimal expected two-period utility function $J_{T-1}(W)$ is given by

$$J_{T-1}(W) = \sup_{i \in \{1,2,3\}} J^i_{T-1}(W), \qquad W \geq 0. \tag{24}$$

In figure 2, we plot $J^i_{T-1}(W)$, $i = 1, 2, 3$ and take the supremum represented by the solid line. The values of intersections $\underline{W}$ and $\overline{W}$ can be easily computed as

$$\underline{W} = [1/(1 + r)] (1 + p_1)^{(1+p_1)/p_1} \tag{25}$$

and

$$\overline{W} = [1/(1 + r)] 4^{1/(1-p_1)} (1 + p_1)^{-(1+p_1)/(1-p_1)}. \tag{26}$$

Also, the intercepts or wealth levels where the various case-wise utility functions become zero can be computed as $\phi(o)$, $\phi(p_1)$, and $\phi(1)$, where

$$\phi(q) = (1 + q)/(1 + r)^{q/(1+q)}. \tag{27}$$

Furthermore, theorem 3 shows that $\underline{W} < \overline{W}$ and that $\underline{W}$ and $\overline{W}$ both increase with p_1; also by theorem 4, $\phi(q)$ increases with $q \geq 0$.

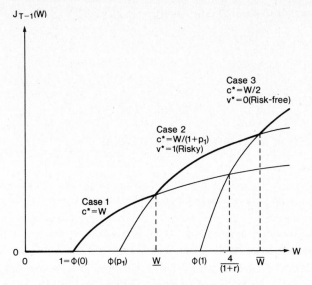

Figure 2. Sketch of $J_{T-1}(W)$.

Mathematically, we can summarize $J_{T-1}(W)$ as follows:

$$J_{T-1}(W) = \begin{cases} 0, & W \leqslant 1, \\ f(W, 0), & 1 \leqslant W \leqslant \underline{W}, \\ f(W, p_1), & \underline{W} \leqslant W \leqslant \overline{W}, \\ f(W, 1), & W \geqslant \overline{W}, \end{cases} \tag{28}$$

where the function f is defined as

$$f(W, q) = (1 + q) \log[W/(1 + q)] + q \log(1 + r). \tag{29}$$

To explain figure 2, with $1 < W < \underline{W}$, the individual consumes his entire wealth, and his utility is given by (13) which is the same as (29) with $q = 0$. He follows this policy because the amount that must be invested to avoid welfare in the next period with probability p_1 requires too great a sacrifice in current consumption.

With $\underline{W} < W < \overline{W}$ the case 2 conditions hold and optimal strategy is to consume $c^* = W/(1 + p_1)$ and put the remainder of W in the risky asset. His utility is given by (18) or (29) with $q = p_1$. Finally, for $W > \overline{W}$ case 3 holds and optimal strategy is to consume $W/2$ and put the remainder into the risk free asset. The utility in this case is given by (23) or (29) with $q = 1$.

It is interesting to note that $\underline{W}$ rises with the value of p_1. That is, the higher the probability of the favorable outcome and the smaller the amount of the payoff, the larger the range of W over which the individual consumes his entire wealth. Moreover, we have from theorem 3 that the range over which the individual consumes all his wealth tends to $[0, e/(1 + r)]$ as $p_1 \to 0$. This means that an individual with $W \leqslant e/(1 + r)$ will always consume his entire wealth regardless of the value of p_1. It also means that for any $W\epsilon(e/(1 + r), 4/(1 + r))$; there exists a $p_1\epsilon(0, 1)$ such that the individual will always gamble a part of his wealth.

We note that $\overline{W}$ also rises with p_1. This means that increasing the probability of the favorable outcome, even under the fair-game situation, attracts some wealthier individuals (who were previously not taking any risks) to the gamble. Also, we know from theorem 3 that $(\overline{W} - \underline{W})$ increases from $(4 - e)/(1 + r) \approx 1.28/(1 + r)$ at $p_1 = \delta$ to $(2e - 4)/(1 + r) \approx 1.43/(1 + r)$ at $p_1 = 1 - \delta$, where $\delta > 0$ is very small. In other words, raisng the probability of favorable outcome increases the range of W over which the individual decides to gamble. [4]

Another interesting feature of the model is the variation in consumption with W. With $\underline{W} < W < \overline{W}$ consumption is $W/(1 + p_1)$ which is a larger fraction of W than $W/2$, the optimal consumption when $W > \overline{W}$. In case 3 the individual is sufficiently rich to avoid welfare next period with certainty and chooses to avoid risk just as if he were living in a no-welfare society. In case 2, the incentive to save is reduced. The unfavorable outcome on the investment puts the individual on welfare while if the investment pays off, next period consumption will be more than the subsistence level of 1.

Finally, it should be noted that at $W = \underline{W}$ the individual is indifferent between the case 1 and case 2 strategies, and at $W = \overline{W}$ he is indifferent between the case 2 and case 3 strategies. Furthermore, at $\underline{W}$ if the individual chooses case 1, he consumes all of it and goes on welfare next period. While, if he chooses case 2, he consumes $\underline{W}/(1 + p_1) = (1 + p_1)/(1 + r)$ and invests the remaining amount to avoid welfare next period with probability p_1. Note that the consumption of the individual will never fall to a sub-subsistence level as long as $p_1 \geqslant r$. For $p_1 < r$, which makes it more of a lottery, the individual with wealth $\underline{W}$, or slight above $\underline{W}$ rather, will be tempted to consume below the subsistence level incurring a negative utility in the hope of a luxuriant consumption next period.

All these results, it must be noted, are intuitively appealing. This will not be, however, when the individual has three periods remaining. This we take up next.

(iii) $t = T - 2$. Once again,

$$J_{T-2}(W) = 0 \quad \text{for } W < 1. \tag{30}$$

Suppose, however, that the individual finds himself with $W \geqslant 1$ with three periods to go. Then his expected optimal 3-period utility would be given by

$$J_{T-2}(W) = \max_{\{c,v\}} J_{T-2}(W; c, v), \tag{31}$$

---

[4] Implicitly we have assumed that the increase in $\overline{W} - \underline{W}$ is monotonic with p_1. We have not proved the monotonicity analytically although we have verified it computationally.

where

$$J_{T-2}(W; c, v) = \log c + p_1 J_{T-1}(A) + p_2 J_{T-1}(B), \qquad (32)$$

where J_{T-1} is defined in (28) and A and B are defined after (10).

Since $J_{T-1}(W)$ for $W \geqslant 1$ has three segments, we have 10 different cases to consider:

Table 2
Feasible cases for $t = T - 2$. [5]

	$A < 1$	$1 < A < \underline{W}$	$\underline{W} < A < \overline{W}$	$A > \overline{W}$
$B < 1$	Case 1	2	3	4
$1 < B < \underline{W}$	–	5	6	7
$\underline{W} < B < \overline{W}$	–	–	8	9
$B > \overline{W}$	–	–	–	10

These cases can be analyzed in the same fashion as for $t = T - 1$. Because of this similarity, the multiplicity of cases and the length of mathematical expressions, we choose only to reproduce the results of the analysis in table 3.

To explain table 3, given the assumptions on A and B represented by each case, c^{*i} and v^{*i} represents the case-wise optimal consumption and investment policies, and $J_{T-2}^i(W)$ represent the utilities of wealth as a function of W, given these policies. The intercept column provides us with the wealth levels for which the corresponding case-wise utilities are zero. These $J_{T-2}^i(W)$ can be plotted, and by theorem 1 the supremum over them gives the optimal expected three-period utility, $J_{T-2}(W)$.

However, we do not as yet know whether all of the cases enter into the supremum or the order in which the cases that do enter. An analysis similar to that carried out for $t = T - 1$ would be quite complex and cumbersome because of the multiplicity of the cases involved. A numerical computation of the supremum for various values of r and p_1 is quite easy, and such a numerical computation has been carried out. Our immediate concern is whether the supremum can be synthesized analytically for a simple cse. This is possible with $r = 0$. Furthermore, we must emphasize that the assumption of $r = 0$, in addition to being analytically tractable, is quite adequate for the purpose of demonstrating the effect of introducing welfare on the behavior of individuals toward risk.

Analysis with r = 0

The intercepts for $r = 0$ are given by the numerators of the intercept values in table 3. [6] This enables us to analytically compare the intercepts. Indeed, by

[5] Note that in view of (28), the strict inequalities in table 2 may be changed to weak inequalities without any problem.
[6] Note that for $r = 0$, $\phi(q) = 1 + q$ from (27), i.e., the value of the intercept for $J_{T-2}^i(W)$ is simply the coefficient of log W term in its expression.

Case i	v^*_i	c^*_i	$J^i_{T-2}(W)$	Intercepts
1	—	W	$\log W$	$\phi(0) = 1$
2	1	$\dfrac{W}{1+p_1}$	$(1+p_1)\log\dfrac{W}{1+p_1} + p_1\log(1+r)$	$\phi(p_1)$
3	1	$\dfrac{W}{1+p_1+p_1^2}$	$(1+p_1+p_1^2)\log\dfrac{W}{1+p_1+p_1^2}$ $+\,p_1(1+2p_1)\log(1+r)$	$\dfrac{\phi[p_1(1+p_1)]}{(1+r)^{p_1^2/(1+p_1+p_1^2)}}$
4	1	$\dfrac{W}{1+2p_1}$	$(1+2p_1)\log\dfrac{W}{1+2p_1} + 3p_1\log(1+r)$	$\dfrac{\phi(2p_1)}{(1+r)^{p_1/(1+2p_1)}}$
5	0	$\dfrac{W}{2}$	$2\log\dfrac{W}{2} + \log(1+r)$	$\phi(1)$
6	$\dfrac{p_1^2}{1+p_1^2}$	$\dfrac{W}{2+p_1^2}$	$(2+p_1^2)\log\dfrac{W}{2+p_1^2} + (1+2p_1^2)\log(1+r)$	$\dfrac{\phi(1+p_1^2)}{(1+r)^{p_1^2/(2+p_1^2)}}$
7	$\dfrac{p_1}{1+p_1}$	$\dfrac{W}{2+p_1}$	$(2+p_1)\log\dfrac{W}{2+p_1} + (1+2p_1)\log(1+r)$	$\dfrac{\phi(1+p_1)}{(1+r)^{p_1/(2+p_1)}}$
8	0	$\dfrac{W}{2+p_1}$	$(2+p_1)\log\dfrac{W}{2+p_1} + (1+2p_1)\log(1+r)$	$\dfrac{\phi(1+p_1)}{(1+r)^{p_1/(2+p_1)}}$
9	$\dfrac{p_1p_2}{1+p_1+p_1p_2}$	$\dfrac{W}{2+p_1+p_1p_2}$	$(2+p_1+p_1p_2)\log\dfrac{W}{2+p_1+p_1p_2}$ $+\,(1+2p_1+2p_1p_2)\log(1+r)$	$\dfrac{\phi[1+p_1(1+p_2)]}{(1+r)^{p_1(1+p_2)/(2+p_1+p_1p_2)}}$
10	0	$\dfrac{W}{3}$	$3\log\dfrac{W}{3} + 3\log(1+r)$	$\dfrac{\phi(2)}{(1+r)^{1/3}}$

theorem 4,

$$p_1 < 0.5 \Rightarrow 1\text{-}2\text{-}3\text{-}4\text{-}5\text{-}6\text{-}(7,8)\text{-}9\text{-}10,$$

$$p_1 = 0.5 \Rightarrow 1\text{-}2\text{-}3\text{-}(4,5)\text{-}6\text{-}(7,8)\text{-}9\text{-}10, \tag{33}$$

$$p_1 > 0.5 \Rightarrow 1\text{-}2\text{-}3\text{-}5\text{-}4\text{-}6\text{-}(7,8)\text{-}9\text{-}10,$$

where the cases have been arranged in the order of increasing intercepts.

Furthermore, let W_{ij} denote the intersection of $J^i_{T-2}(W)$ and $J^j_{T-2}(W)$. It is easy to show that

$$W_{ij} = [(1 + q_j)^{(1+q_j)}(1 + q_i)^{(1+q_i)}]^{(q_j - q_i)}, \tag{34}$$

where q_i and q_j are the arguments of ϕ in the expression of the intercepts of case i and case j, respectively. [7] Then, by theorem 5

$$W_{ij} < W_{jk}$$

whenever i, j, and k are three consecutive cases in the same order as in (33) for the specified value of p_1. An important implication is that all cases will have their segments in the supremum.

We are now ready to sketch the case-wise utilities in figure 3 and obtain their supremum. The figure is drawn for $p_1 > 0.5$ for which the order of the intercepts is available in (33). The values of these intercepts are shown on the W-axis. Taking the adjacent cases in the ordering of the intercepts, we can compute the intersections which appear on the supremum. These are shown as W_{ij} in figure 3 and their values for $p_1 = 0.6$ are shown in parentheses. The optimal consumption and portfolios are stated for each cusp in the supremum.

Discussion of results for $t = T - 2$

In discussing the optimal policy of an individual with two periods remaining, we note that while some results are intuitive, others are not.

(i) For $W \geqslant 1$, there is a first cusp where everything is consumed. This happens until $W = W_{12}$. For $W \geqslant W_{12}$, the individual starts investing a part of his wealth while consuming the remaining part. While the fraction of the wealth consumed remains constant on a given cusp, it declines as the individual moves to higher wealth cusps. This process continues until $W = W_{9,10}$ beyond which the individual consumes one-third of his wealth irrespective of how wealthy he is.

(ii) For $W \geqslant W_{12}$, we have already mentioned that the individual starts investing part of his wealth. Initially, he goes all risky. This happens until $W = W_{35}$. Then we

[7] E.g.,

$$W_{23} = [(1 + p_1 + p_1^2)^{(1+p_1+p_1^2)}/(1 + p_1)^{(1 + p_1)}]p_1^2.$$

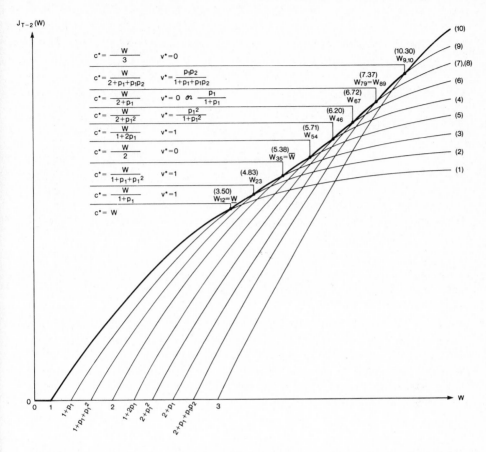

Figure 3. J_{T-2} (W) for $r = 0$ and $p_1 > 0.5$. (Numerical values in parentheses are for $p_1 = 0.6$.)

have some counterintuitive behavior when for $p_1 > 0.5$ the individual goes risk-free for wealth levels between W_{35} and W_{54} and goes all risky for wealth levels between W_{54} and W_{46}. (Note that the order of risk preference reverses for $p_1 < 0.5$ while for $p_1 = 0.5$ these two cusps coincide with both $v^* = 0$ and $v^* = 1$ being optimal.)

Between W_{46} and W_{67}, it is interesting to observe that the individual prefers an intermediate risk level by allocating between risky and risk-free investments.

In the next cusp between W_{67} and W_{79} (or, W_{89}), the optimal policy is non-unique for $0 < p_1 < 1$. The individual can go either risk-free or allocate his investment between the risk-free and the risky assets. To understand why such a result is brought about, we solve a numerical example. Let $W_{T-2} = 7$ with two periods remaining. Let $p_1 = 0.6$, and therefore $x = 1/1.6$.

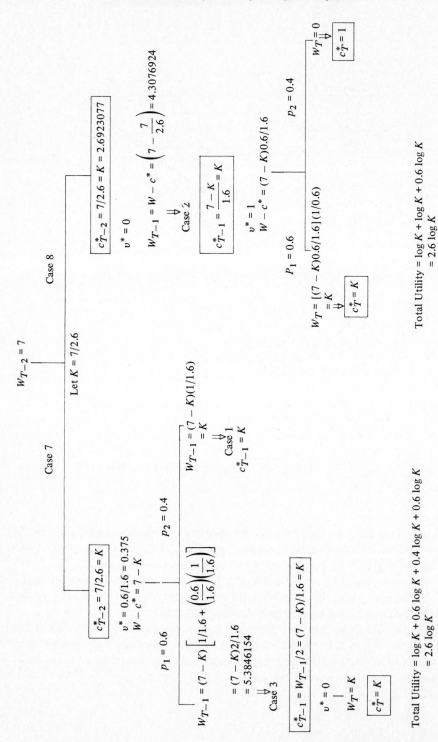

Hence, we can see that there are two different policies yielding the same total utility.

Between W_{79} and $W_{9,10}$, the individual prefers a unique intermediate risk level. For $W \geqslant W_{9,10}$, the individual is sufficiently rich and goes completely risk-free. Note that this individual behaves as if he were living in a no-welfare society.

We conclude this remark with an observation that while roughly the richer the individual, the lower his risk-preference, there are important exceptions.

(iii) At intersection wealth levels, the optimal policy is always nonunique. In particular, an individual with wealth W_{67} has three different optimal policies:

(a) $c^* = W/(2 + p_1^2)$, $v^* = p_1^2/(1 + p_1^2)$;

(b) $c^* = W/(2 + p_1)$, $v^* = 0$;

(c) $c^* = W/(2 + p_1)$, $v^* = p_1/(1 + p_1)$.

This happens only for finite number of wealth levels and therefore is fortuitous.

3. Extensions and concluding remarks

In this paper, we have analytically derived the optimal consumption and portfolio policies for a three-period problem. The results obtained in deriving these policies can be used to extend the analysis to more than three decision periods. While this can be done, it will be quite lengthy. Note that the number of possible cases for $t = T - 3$ will be $10 \times 11/2 = 55$. Some of them will no doubt be duplicates or possibly multiplicates. While the number of possible cases will explode as the number of periods increase, it is not likely to increase the richness of the model. Note that we have also carried out a computational analysis, which will be described in a forthcoming paper [6].

Another possible extension is to make $r > 0$. An analytical solution in this case is quite difficult. The computational analysis shows that we have one additional result in this case. That is, it is possible to have some case-wise utilities completely dominated – and thus not have their segments in the supremum. This result can be proved analytically for a specified value of $r \neq 0$ [6].

Finally, we note that an important extension would be to analyze the problem in the continuous-time framework. We have no conjecture regarding the effect of this change on the cuspy nature of the utility curve $J_{T-t}(W)$ with time t remaining except that the effect should be quite interesting. It appears that this problem is a mathematically difficult stochastic optimal control problem.

Appendix

Theorem 1. $J_t(W) = \sup_{i \in I(t)} J_t^i(W), \forall t \epsilon [1, T]$, where $I(t)$ denotes the index set of possible cases in period t.

Proof.   The proof is by induction. First, we observe that $I(T) = \{1, 2\}$, i.e., case 1 for $W < 1$ and case 2 for $W \geqslant 1$. By noting that $J_T^1(W) = 0$ and $J_T^2(W) = \log W$, we have

$$J_T(W) = \sup_{i \in I(T)} J_T^i(W) = \sup [0, \log W]. \tag{A1}$$

Next we assume that this property holds for some $t < T$. Thus

$$J_t(W) = \sup_{i \in I(t)} J_t^i(W). \tag{A2}$$

We then show (by contradiction) that

$$J_{t-1}(W) = \sup_{i \in I(t-1)} J_{t-1}^i(W). \tag{A3}$$

Suppose (A3) is not true for some value of W. Let the part of the supremum relevant for W be the segment of $J_{t-1}^k(W), k \in I(t-1)$. By definition

$$J_{t-1}^k(W) = J_{t-1}^k(W; c^{*k}, v^{*k}) \geqslant J_{t-1}^i(W; c^{*k}, v^{*k}), \quad \forall i \neq k. \tag{A4}$$

Since A3 is not true for this value of W, it means $J_{t-1}^k(W)$ is invalid, i.e., either A or B or both are out of range of case k. Since case $k \epsilon I(t-1)$ maps into some m, $n \epsilon I(t)$, it means $J_t^m(A)$ or $J_t^n(B)$ or both are below the supremum of $J_t^i(W), i \epsilon I(t)$ which yields $J_t(W)$ from (A2). This implies that $\exists l \epsilon I(t-1), l \neq i \ni$

$$J^l(W; c^{*k}, v^{*k}) > J^k(W; c^{*k}, v^{*k}). \tag{A5}$$

This contradicts with (A4) for $i = l$. Hence (A3) holds $\forall W \epsilon [0, \infty]$.

Theorem 2. $(1 + p_1)^{(1+p_1)/p_1}$ increases strictly with p_1 for $p_1 > 0$.

Proof.   Let $\psi(p_1) = \log(1 + p_1)^{(1+p_1)/p_1} = [(1 + p_1)/p_1] \log(1 + p_1)$. It is easy to show that

$$\frac{d\psi}{dp_1} = \frac{1}{p_1} \left[1 - \frac{\log(1 + p_1)}{p_1} \right] > 0 \quad \text{for } p_1 > 0,$$

since $\log(1 + p_1) < p_1$ for $0 < p_1$.

Theorem 3. $\underline{W} < \overline{W}$ for $0 < p_1 < 1$. Furthermore, as p_1 increases in the interval $(0, 1]$, $\underline{W}$ monotonically increases in the interval $(e/(1+r), 4/(1+r)]$, and $\overline{W}$ monotonically increases in the interval $(4/(1+r), 2e/(1+r)]$; lower and upper values in these intervals are limiting values as $p_1 \to 0$ and $p_1 \to 1$, respectively.

Proof. It is easy to show that for $0 < p_1 < 1$

$$\underline{W} < \overline{W} \Leftrightarrow (1+p_1)^{(1+p_1)/p_1} < 4.$$

From this, $\underline{W} < \overline{W}$ for $0 < p_1 < 1$ by theorem 2 and that the fact that

$$(1+p_1)^{(1+p_1)/p_1}\big|_{p_1=1} = 4.$$

It is obvious from theorem 2 that $\underline{W}$ increases with p_1 for $p_1 > 0$. Also, obvious are $\lim_{p_1 \to 0} \underline{W} = e/(1+r)$ and

$$\underline{W} = 4/(1+r) \qquad \text{for} \qquad p_1 = 1.$$

To obtain the behavior of $\overline{W}$, note that

$$(1+r)\overline{W} = \frac{2^{2/(1-p_1)}}{(1+p_1)^{(1+p_1)/(1-p_1)}} = 2\left(1 + \frac{1-p_1}{1+p_1}\right)^{(1+p_1)/(1-p_1)}$$

Obviously $\overline{W}$ increases with p_1 for $p_1 > 0$. Furthermore, $\overline{W} = 4/(1+r)$ for $p_1 = 0$ and $\lim_{p_1 \to 1} \overline{W} = 2e/(1+r)$.

Theorem 4. $\phi(q)$ increases with q for $q > 0$.

Proof. Note that $\phi(p_1)$ can be written as

$$\phi(p_1) = \underline{W}^{p_1/(1+p_1)}.$$

But $\underline{W}$ and $p_1/(1+p_1)$ increase with p_1 for $p_1 > 0$. Thus $\phi(p_1)$ increases with p_1 for $p_1 > 0$. Replacing p_1 by q completes the theorem.

Theorem 5. $q_j < q_k \Rightarrow W_{ij} < W_{ik}$ for each i. Furthermore, $q_i < q_j < q_k \Rightarrow W_{ij} < W_{jk}$.

Proof. Define $\theta(q) = (1+q)^{(1+q)}$. Then

$$q_j < q_k \Rightarrow \theta(q_j)/\theta(q_i) < \theta(q_k)/\theta(q_i)$$

$$\Rightarrow \theta(q_j)/\theta(q_i) < [\theta(q_k)/\theta(q_i)]^{(q_k - q_i)/(q_j - q_i)}$$

$$\left(\text{since } \frac{q_k - q_i}{q_j - q_i} > 1\right)$$

$$\Rightarrow [\theta(q_j)/\theta(q_i)]^{(q_j - q_i)} < [\theta(q_k)/\theta(q_i)]^{(q_k - q_i)}$$

$$\Rightarrow W_{ij} < W_{ik}.$$

To prove the second part, let us suppose that for some i, j, k such that $q_i < q_j < q_k$, we have $W_{ij} \geqslant W_{jk}$. By drawing a figure, it will be obvious that this means $W_{ij} \geqslant W_{ik}$. This leads to a contradiction with the first part of the theorem. This completes the proof.

References

[1] S.E. Dreyfus, Dynamic Programming and the Calculus of Variations, (Academic Press, New York, 1965).

[2] M. Friedman and L.J. Savage, The utility analysis of choices involving risk, The Journal of Political Economy 56 (August 1948).

[3] M. Gordon, G. Paradis and C. Rorke, Experimental evaluation of alternative portfolio decision rules, American Economic Review 62 (March 1972).

[4] R.C. Merton, Optimum consumption and portfolio rules in a continuous-time model, Journal of Economic Theory 3 (December 1971).

[5] P.A. Samuelson, Lifetime portfolio selection by dynamic stochastic programming, The Review of Economics and Statistics 51 (1969).

[6] S.P. Sethi and B. Ingham, Optimal dynamic consumption and portfolio planning in a welfare state: computational result and generalizations (in-process).

TIMS Studies in the Management Sciences 11 (1979) 197–213
© North-Holland Publishing Company

A MULTI-PERIOD PORTFOLIO THEORY MODEL
FOR COMMERCIAL BANK MANAGEMENT *

Abraham I. BRODT

University of Ottawa

1. Introduction

Portfolio theory has been one of the most active areas of research in finance in the close to one quarter century since it was first developed by Harry Markowitz. While it has been applied by some institutions, notably mutual funds, it has, to the author's knowledge, not yet been applied by the most important of the financial institutions, viz. the commercial banks.

In this paper we present a model, based on Markowitz portfolio theory, which can be used by the senior executives of a bank to manage the bank's assets and liabilities. Our model not only generates the optimal decisions but also enables one to perform a rich postoptimality analysis. The model is quite flexible and can easily be applied by bankers.

§ 2 of the paper presents the nature and scope of the bank balance-sheet management problem. § 3 briefly lists some of the previous approaches to solving the bank balance-sheet management problem and indicates their shortcomings. In § 4 we present our model, the MIN-SAD Model, for solving the bank balance-sheet management problem. In § 5 we describe some of the postoptimality analysis which can be performed with the MIN-SAD Model. The size and structure of the MIN-SAD Model is briefly discussed in § 6.

2. The bank balance-sheet management problem

One of the most difficult problems facing the senior executives of a commercial bank is the determination of the optimal size and composition of the bank's balance sheet. While the problem of finding the optimal size and composition of a balance sheet is a common problem, it is an especially difficult problem for commercial banks.

* This paper is an abridged version of the paper presented at the TIMS/ORSA meetings in Miami Beach, Florida, November, 1976. I wish to thank Dr. Kalman J. Cohen for his review of the original paper. The author assumes sole responsibility for any deficiencies remaining in this paper.

Some of the reasons why balance-sheet management is very difficult for banks are the nature of a bank's sources of funds, the legal constraints imposed on banks, and the investment policy of banks. The major reasons, however, are the countless number of possible balance-sheet adjustments, the uncertainty about future economic conditions, and the dynamic nature of the problem.

In most organizations management seeks to match the liabilities to the assets. Thus, long-lived (short-lived) assets will generally be financed with long-term (short-term) liabilities. In commercial banks however, where deposits are the major component of liabilities, management must match the assets to the liabilities. Because deposits are quite volatile and a bank must be prepared to meet any withdrawals that may occur, one of a bank's prime concerns will be the liquidity of its assets.

A commercial bank, whether operating under federal charter or under state charter, must meet various legal requirements not imposed on other organizations. Among the most important of these requirements are the legal reserve requirements and the capital adequacy requirements. Banks must maintain minimum cash reserves based on the size and composition of the bank's deposits. Banks are also expected to satisfy minimum capital requirements based on the size and composition of their assets and liabilities and on the volume of their trust operations.

Another important concern of the senior executives of a bank is the bank's ability to meet loan demand. It is common policy for banks to grant any reasonable loan requests made by depositors and/or clients. Bankers therefore wish to ensure that the bank will have sufficient liquidity to meet future loan demand.

The objective of maintaining sufficient liquidity is, however, in conflict with another prime objective of the bank, viz. the objective of maximizing profits. Those assets which are generally more profitable, are more risky and less liquid. Long-term government securities, which generally offer a greater yield than short-term government securities, will suffer a greater capital loss than will short-term government securities in the case of a rise in interest rate levels. Loans, which are generally the most profitable assets, have a risk of default and are, with the exception of Federal funds sold and loans to brokers and security dealers, completely illiquid.

What makes bank balance-sheet management especially difficult is the virtually countless number of different possible adjustments which can be made. For example, if the bank wishes to expand loans by $ 10 million and reduce securities by $ 10 million then the number of ways in which this can be done is 2^n, where n is the number of different securities which can be sold. For 25 securities, there will be over 33 million ways in which the bank can obtain the $ 10 million. Which of these is optimal?

The optimal balance-sheet adjustments would be evident if the bank could accurately forecast the future economic conditions. In the above example, if interest rates are going to increase, the optimal solution would be to sell long-term securities, as these will suffer the greatest decline in value, and shift the securities portfolios as much as possible to short-term securities.

It is, however, difficult to predict exactly what will happen in the future, even in the best of times. Thus, although the bank's economists predict a rise in interest rates, it is quite possible that interest rates will remain stable, or even decline. A solution which is the best when interest rates increase, can be the worst when interest rates decrease. Given the uncertainty about future economic conditions, it is no longer clear what is the optimal solution.

Finally, what further complicates the bank balance-sheet managment problem is that it is a multiperiod dynamic stochastic decision problem. The bank must consider the interrelationships between the possible balance-sheet adjustments in different periods.

Let BS_0 denote a bank's balance sheet at the present point in time t_0. Based on present economic conditions and forecasts of future interest rates, loan demand, and deposit flows, the bank must determine what balance sheet adjustments should be made to obtain a revised balance sheet BS_0'. At future points in time t_i, $i = 1$, 2, 3, ..., when the bank will again examine its balance sheets BS_i, economic conditions and future forecasts may be different from what they were at t_0, and the bank will again have to determine what balance sheet adjustments should be made to obtain the revised balance sheets BS_i'.

The balance-sheet adjustments that the bank makes at any point in time t_i will depend not only on forecasts of the future economic situation and opportunities but also on the balance-sheet adjustments that the bank made at points in tim t_0, t_1, t_2, ..., t_{i-1}, and the intervening random economic events. Thus, at point in time t_0, the bank must determine not only the immediate balance-sheet adjustments but also their possible future impacts and the resultant future balance-sheet adjustments.

To summarize, the balance-sheet management problem which faces the bank's senior executives is:

> To determine the optimal balance-sheet adjustments which the bank should make at t_0 and plan to make at future points in the planning horizon t_1, t_2, ... t_{H-1} contingent on the economic situations which may develop.

The bank must select the optimal solution from a countless number of possible solutions bearing in mind the bank's current condition, the economic forecasts and the degree of uncertainty associated with these, and the special legal, liquidity, and policy constraints under which the bank operates.

3. Review of the literature

Several models and approaches have been recommended for solving the bank balance-sheet management problem described in the previous section. The models range in complexity from linear programming under certainty models to the theoretically most valid Decision Theory models. Some of these models have been applied by banks. Other models are theoretically superior but have practical problems which have to date prevented their application.

Chambers and Charnes [8] presented an intertemporal linear programming model under certainty for solving the bank balance-sheet management problem. Their model was subsequently expanded by Cohen and Hammer [13,14], and Beighley [3].

Chance-constrained programming models were developed by Charnes and Thore [10] and Charnes and Littlechile [9]. Multistage programming under uncertainty models were developed by Cohen and Thore [16], Booth [4], Crane [17] and Bradley and Crane [5–7].

Wolf [36] developed a sequential decision theory model and Fried a portfolio theory model [20].

These models had at least one of the following shortcomings:

A. Only one period is examined. Decision may suffer from myopia and hence be suboptimal [20].

B. Only the bond portfolio is examined. Size of bond portfolio is not determined in conjunction with other asset decisions. Total asset allocation will likely be suboptimal [5,7,17–36].

C. Uncertainty about the future level of deposits, loan demand, and interest rates at is inadequately handled [8,10,13,14].

D. No measure of risk is given. Also, the trade-off between risk and return is unknown [3,4,8–10].

4. The MIN-SAD Model

To solve the bank balance-sheet management problem described in the second section, we developed the MIN-SAD Model. The MIN-SAD Model is a multiperiod linear programming under uncertainty model based on the models developed by Cohen and Thore [16] and Bradley and Crane [5–7] and on Markowitz portfolio theory [28].

In our model we will assume that for each point in time t_i and contingent economic situation e a bank can make decisions regarding cash (desired balance), federal funds (amount sold and/or purchased), securities (securities retained, sold, and/or purchased), loans (amount granted), and time deposits (amount bought). These decisions will affect the banks demand deposits and capital accounts as discussed later.

The majority of the constraints of the MIN-SAD Model serve to differentiate between permissible and nonpermissible balance-sheet adjustments. These will be discussed in the first part of this section. The remaining constraints and the objective function of the MIN-SAD Model serve to select from the permissible balance-sheet adjustments those adjustments which satisfy a certain criterion. This decision criterion will be presented in the second part of this section.

The constraints which determine permissible balance sheet adjustments. The constraints which serve to differentiate between permissible and nonpermissible balance–sheet adjustments can be classified into two categories — intratemporal constraints and intertemporal constraints. The intratemporal constraints are those constraints which the bank faces each time it evaluates the bank's balance sheet. The intertemporal constraints are those constraints which take into consideration the effects of the decision at point in time t_i and contingent economic situation e on the balance sheet account values and decisions at point in time t_{i+i} and contingent economic situation ϵ (which may differ from e).

Intratemporal constraints. Included in the intratemporal constraints are accounting constraints, legal constraints, market constraints, policy constraints, and behavioral constraints. We will describe each of these constraints. Each one of these constraints can easily be formulated mathematically by linear equalities and/or linear inequalities. [1]

Accounting constraints. There are four intratemporal accounting constraints. They are: (1) the revised assets equal revised liabilities constraints, (2) the security inventory balance constraints, (3) the revised cash constraints, and (4) the revised equity constraints. The first two accounting constraints serve to ensure that the decisions made are feasible and consistent with each other. The last two accounting constraints show how the bank's cash account and shareholder's equity account will be affected by the balance sheet adjustments made by the bank.

The revised assets equal revised liabilities constraints. These constraints are a set of equations formulating the fact that the only balance sheet adjustments which the bankers may consider are those where after the adjustments are made we have the necessary identity: total assets (revised) equal total liabilities (revised). Thus, for each t_{ie} (point in time t_i and contingent economic situation e) there is a linear equation which states that after the balance-sheet adjustments are made, revised cash plus Federal funds sold plus securities retained plus securities purchased plus loans outstanding plus new loans granted plus other assets are equal to federal funds bought plus revised demand deposits plus savings deposits plus time deposits outstanding plus time deposits bought plus deposits of banks and governments plus other liabilities plus debentures plus revised total shareholders' equity.

The security inventory balance constraints. These constraints ensure that the model does not consider a balance sheet adjustment requiring the bank to sell more of a security than it has, as this is impossible. For each security and each t_{ie} there will be a linear equation stating that the amount of a security retained by the bank plus the amount of a security sold by the bank must equal the amount of the security held by the bank prior to revision.

The revised cash constraints. These constraints state that at each t_{ie} the amount of cash the bank will have after the balance sheet adjustment will equal the amount

---

[1] Due to space constraints we omitted the mathematical formulation of the intratemporal and intertemporal constraints. For mathematical formulations of these constraints see Cohen and Hammer [13], Booth [3], or the author's unabridged paper.

of cash the bank held before the adjustments minus cash outflows from federal funds sold, securities purchased and loans granted plus cash inflows from securities sold, federal funds bought, and time deposits bought.

The revised total shareholders' equity constraints. For each t_{ie} there will be a linear equation which states that the total shareholders' equity will be reduced by the commission expenses on securities purchased and sold when the balance sheet is adjusted.

Legal constraints. There are three special legal requirements which must be satisfied by banks. They are: (1) the minimum cash reserve requirements, (2) the capital adequacy requirements, and (3) the pledged assets requirements. We will briefly describe each of these in turn.

The minimum cash reserves constraints. Member banks [2] are required by law to maintain a minimum amount in cash plus reserves with the Federal Reserve based on the size and composition of their deposits. The Federal Reserve may change the reserve requirements within specified limits if the economic situation warrants this. In addition to the minimum reserve requirements, the bankers may wish to maintain an additional amount as a safety margin to meet fluctuations in deposit levels. For each t_{ie} there will be a linear inequality formulating the bank's minimum cash reserve constraints.

The capital adequacy requirements. Banks are required by law to maintain a minimum amount of capital in order to protect the depositor against possible loss. A member bank of the Federal Reserve System, and banks wishing to have deposit insurance, must maintain sufficient capital in relation to the character and condition of its assets and to its deposit liabilities and other corporate responsibilities, mainly trust activities. A bank with a sufficient amount of capital will inspire sufficient confidence so that temporary losses or difficulties will not force it into costly liquidation. For each t_{ie} there will be a set of linear equalities and inequalities expressing the bank's capital adequacy constraints. [3]

The pledged assets constraints. The federal government and most states require that banks pledge securities against their holdings of government deposits. These must be deposited in advance with the Federal Reserve. For each t_{ie} there will be a linear inequality which states that the amount of pledged assets in the bank's portfolio equal or exceed a given percentage (usually greater than 100%) of the bank's government deposits.

Market constraints. Market constraints will limit the balance sheet adjustments which the bank can make. Thus, the amount of a security that the bank can sell or purchase at a given point in time is limited by the marketability of that particular issue. Similarly, the amount of Federal funds which the bank can sell or purchase will be limited by market conditions. New loans granted cannot exceed the demand

---

[2] The reserve requirements for nonmember banks are essentially similar.
[3] For a very good presentation of the mathematical formulation of the capital adequacy requirements see Beazer [2, pp. 55–61] and Cohen and Hammer [14, pp. 395–402].

for new loans. Finally, there will be a maximum amount of time deposits which the bank can buy at a given interest rate. For each t_{ie} there will be a set of linear inequalities giving the upper and/or lower bounds for the affected decision variables.

Policy constraints. Bankers may establish lower and/or upper bounds to ratios which they feel are being watched by the banks' depositors, borrowers or other interested parties. Thus, for example, the bank may require that the governments to total assets ratio exceed a certain minimum and that the loans to deposits ratios not exceed a certain maximum. Another policy which the bank may have is to accept a minimum percentage of new loans demanded. Such policy constraints are expressed by a set of linear inequalities for each t_{ie}.

Behavioral constraint. We assume in the MIN-SAD Model that when a bank grants a loan of \$ X to a customer, i.e., increases his demand deposits by \$ X, he will use this amount to make various payments. Of these payments a certain percentage, assumed to equal the bank's share of deposits, BSD_{ie}, will go to other depositors of the bank and the remainder $(1 - \mathrm{BSD}_{ie})$ to outsiders. Therefore, the effects of granting a loan of \$ X are assumed to be a net increase in demand deposits of $(\mathrm{BSD}_{ie})X$ and a net reduction in cash of $(1 - \mathrm{BSD}_{ie})X$. This is reflected in a loan-demand deposit constraint (a linear equality) and in the revised cash constraint (presented earlier) for each t_{ie}.

Intertemporal constraints. The balance sheet which the bankers will have to evaluate and revise at point in time t_{i+1} will depend on two factors. It will depend on the decisions the bankers took at point in time t_i and it will depend on the economic situation which develops after the balance-sheet adjustments are made at t_i.

The intertemporal initial cash constraints. The initial amount of cash at the start of period t_{i+1}, for economic situation ϵ, before any adjustments are made, will equal the amount of cash after the balance-sheet adjustments at t_{ie} increased by coupons received from securities plus the face amount of securities maturing plus interest received on loans plus principal repaid on loans plus the net change in deposits minus the interest paid on deposits minus taxes minus miscellaneous items (wages, etc.). These constraints will be expressed by a linear equality for each $t_{i+1,e}$.

The intertemporal securities inventory balance constraints. The initial number of securities of a given type that the bank will have in its portfolio at $t_{i+1,e}$ before any balance-sheet adjustments will be either the amount it held after balance-sheet adjustments at t_{ie} or 0 (if the security matures at $t_{i+1,e}$). For each security and each $t_{i+1,e}$ there will be a linear equality stating that the amount of the security on hand after balance-sheet adjustments at t_{ie} will equal either the amount retained plus the amount sold at $t_{i+1,e}$ (for nonmaturing securities) or the amount sold at $t_{i+1,e}$ (for maturing securities).

The intertemporal initial loans outstanding constraints. The initial loan balance outstanding at $t_{i+1,e}$, before any new loans are made, is equal to the sum of the loans balance outstanding at $t_{i+1,e}$ of the original loans outstanding at t_{ie} plus the loans balance outstanding on new loans granted at t_{ie}. These constraints are expressed by a linear equality for each $t_{i+1,e}$. We assume that loans to brokers, to finance dealers, and for purchase of securities, Federal funds sold and/or purchased are fully repaid at the start of each period, and therefore, the initial balance outstanding for each of these is 0.

The intertemporal initial demand deposits constraint. Based on our earlier assumption, we assume that the initial amount of demand deposits outstanding at $t_{i+1,\epsilon}$ is a function of the amount of loans then outstanding. This assumption is expressed by a linear equality for each $t_{i+1,e}$

The intertemporal initial time deposits constraint. The initial amount of time deposits outstanding at $t_{i+1,\epsilon}$, before any additional amount is bought will equal the amount of time deposits after the balance sheet adjustments at t_{ie} minus maturing time deposits minus time deposits preredeemed. For each $t_{i+1,\epsilon}$ there is a linear equality which expresses this.

The intertemporal initial total shareholders' equity constraints. The initial total shareholders' equity at $t_{i+1,\epsilon}$ is assumed to equal the total shareholders' equity at t_{ie} increased by profits net of taxes [4] at $t_{i+1,\epsilon}$. Profits net of taxes at $t_{i+1,\epsilon}$, $PNT_{i+1,\epsilon}$, is equal to income generated from federal funds sold, securities (including capital gains/losses), loans, and other assets minus the interest expense on federal funds bought, deposits, and other liabilities plus other revenues minus other expenses. For each $t_{i+1,\epsilon}$ there will be one linear equality for the value of $PNT_{i+1,\epsilon}$ and one linear equality for the value of the initial total shareholders' equity.

The remaining balance-sheet items are determined exogenously. They therefore do not require any equations. Their values will be specified in the model.

The aforementioned constraints serve to differentiate the permissible balance-sheet adjustments from the nonpermissible balance-sheet adjustments. The set of permissible balance sheet adjustments may also contain a countless number of elements. We now present our decision criterion for selecting balance-sheet adjustments from the set of permissible balance-sheet adjustments.

The decision criterion. For selecting desirable balance sheet adjustments from the set of permissible balance-sheet adjustments, the MIN-SAD Model uses the following criterion:

> If there are several balance-sheet adjustments which yield the same expected "profits", the bank should select that balance sheet adjustment which involves the minimum amount of "risk".

This criterion can be stated in the following equivalent way:

> If there are several balance-sheet adjustments which involve an equal amount or "risk," the bank should select that balance-sheet adjustment which yields the highest expected "profits."

A balance-sheet adjustment decision will be called an optimal, or efficient, decision if there is no other balance-sheet adjustment decision which gives a higher expected profit for the same amount of risk or less risk for the same amount of expected profits.

---

[4] For simplicity, we abstract from the dividend policy problem by assuming that all earnings are reinvested.

Our decision criterion is essentially the one used by Markowitz in his development of modern portfolio theory. The measure of risk used in the MIN-SAD Model, however, is not the same as the one used in Markowitz portfolio theory where risk is measured by the variance of returns. Before describing our measure of risk, we will first define our "profits" and expected "profits" terms.

Definition of profits. We are considering what balance-sheet adjustments the bank should make at point in time t_0 and should plan to make at points in time $t_1, t_2, \dots t_{H-1}$ for each of the possible economic situations at these points in time. For any decision, d, we define our measure of profits as the present value (discounted at the risk free rates for each period) of the profits net of taxes realized at the end of each period over the planning horizon. Thus, if at the horizon the economic situation which unfolded was $H\epsilon$ then the profits realized from a given decision d, $\mathrm{PROF}(d)_{H\epsilon}$, is equal to:

$$\mathrm{PROF(d)}_{H\epsilon} = \sum_{j=1}^{H} [\mathrm{PNT(d)}_{j\epsilon}/\prod_{k=0}^{j-1} (1 + i_{k\epsilon})].$$

Our expected profits at point in time t_0 for a given decision d is the expected value of the possible profits:

$$E\,\mathrm{PROF(d)}_H = \sum_{\epsilon} [(\mathrm{PROB}\,H\epsilon)(\mathrm{PROF(d)}_{H\epsilon})]$$

where RPOB $H\epsilon$ is the probability of obtaining profits $\mathrm{PROF}(d)_{H\epsilon}$.

We will let the expected profits at point in time t_0 be a parameter. For a given value of the parameter, i.e., a given expected profits goals, we will find the decision which satisfies all the constraints and which yields our desired expected profits with the minimum amount of risk.

A risk measure: SAD (Semi-Absolute Deviations). The profits that will result from a given set of decisions cannot be predicted in advance by the bank. These profits will depend on the economic situation that will develop in the future. If the forecasters can, however, tell us what are the different possible future economic situations and give us the associated probabilities, then, for any given set of decisions, we can obtain a distribution of possible profits with their associated probabilities.

In evaluating a probability distribution of profits the bankers will be interested mainly in the expected profits and in the amount and nature of the variability of profits. We assume that bankers, when faced with a choice between two alternative decisions for the bank which yield the same expected profits, will prefer the alternative which has less variability.

In Markowitz portfolio theory it is assumed that an individual's preferences are a function of expected return and variance of returns only. For any given expected return on a portfolio, the portfolio with the smallest variance is preferred to all others; for any given portfolio variance, the portfolio with the maximum expected return is preferred to all others. This criterion requires that either the distribution of returns is normal or that the individual's utility function for returns is quadratic.

We will assume that an individual's preferences are a function of expected return and the semi-absolute deviations (SAD) of returns only. For any given expected return on a portfolio, the portfolio with the smallest SAD is preferred to all others; for any given portfolio SAD, the portfolio with the maximum expected return is preferred to all others.

There are both practical and theoretical reasons why we use the semi-absolute deviations of returns rather than variance of returns as our measure of risk. The practical reason for using semi-absolute deviations of returns as our measure of risk is that we can use standard linear programming techniques to find the set of efficient portfolios. The use of variance of returns as the risk measure requires the use of quadratic programming techniques to find the set of efficient portfolios. The size of our problem is, as is shown later in the paper, too large to be solved by quadratic programming. In addition, even for problems which are small enough to be solved by quadratic programming, linear programming allows one to perform a richer analysis of the optimal solution than does quadratic programming.

There are several theoretical reasons too for using SAD. First, if the distribution of returns, X, is normal, then the sets of efficient portfolios generated by the two criteria will be identical. The reason for this is that for a normal distribution we have the following relationship between its semi absolute deviation and its variance. [5]

$$\text{SAD}(x) = \sqrt{\text{var}(x)/2\pi}$$

[5] This result follows from the definition of SAD and straight integration:

$$\text{SAD}(x) = \frac{1}{\sqrt{2\pi}\sigma} \int_{-\infty}^{u} |(x-u)| \exp(-\tfrac{1}{2}((x-u)/\sigma)^2)\, \mathrm{d}x$$

$$= \frac{1}{\sqrt{2\pi}\sigma} \int_{u}^{\infty} (x-u) \exp(-\tfrac{1}{2}((x-u)/\sigma)^2)\, \mathrm{d}x$$

$$= \frac{\sigma^2}{\sqrt{2\pi}} \int_{u}^{\infty} \exp(-\tfrac{1}{2}((x-u)/\sigma)^2)\, \mathrm{d}(\tfrac{1}{2}((x-u)/\sigma)^2)$$

$$= \frac{\sigma}{\sqrt{2\pi}} [-\exp(-\tfrac{1}{2}((x-u)/\sigma)^2)|_{u}^{\infty}]$$

$$= \left(\frac{\sigma^2}{2\pi}\right)^{1/2} \quad [1].$$

Thus, the portfolio which has the smallest variance of returns for a given expected profits also has the smallest semi-absolute deviations of returns.

Second, if the distribution of returns is not normal but rather, as has been suggested by Mandelbrot [26] and others, Stable Paretian, then the variance does not exist — it is infinite — and one cannot then attempt to find a portfolio with minimum variance. The semi-absolute deviation of returns, however, does exist for Stable Paretian distributions and one can therefore look for the portfolio which minimizes SAD for a given expected return.

For a probability distribution of profits which is neither normal nor Stable Paretian and which has a finite variance, there is no a priori reason for preferring the variance to the semi-absolute deviations as a measure of risk, [6] unless one's utility function for returns is quadratic. Even for the case of an individual with a quadratic utility function, [7] we will use SAD instead of variance because of the aforementioned practical reason. Finally, absolute deviation is the measure of dispersion recommended by the Bank Administration Institute [1].

To summarize, we assume that the bankers' utility function is that $E[U(X)] = f[E(X), \text{SAD}(X)]$ with the properties:

$$\partial E[U(X)]/\partial E(X) \geqslant 0 \qquad (1)$$

and

$$\partial E[U(X)]/\partial \text{SAD}(X) \leqslant 0. \qquad (2)$$

The H-period MIN-SAD Model. We propose the following model to aid a bank's senior executives to determine the optimal decision: (i.e., the balance sheet adjustments for point in time t_0 and the expected balance sheet adjustments for $t_i, \ldots t_{H-1}$ contingent on the economic situations prevailing at those times).

$$\text{Minimize SAD(d)} = \sum_{\epsilon} (\text{PROB } H\epsilon)(\text{SAD}[|\text{PROF(d)}_{H\epsilon} - \text{EPG}_a|]),$$

Subject to:

(1) $E \text{ PROF(d)}_H = \text{EPG}_a$,
(2) the intratemporal constraints,
(3) the intertemporal constraints,

---

[6] For a discussion of the relative merits of SAD vs. variance, see M. Padberg and J. Wiginton [29].
[7] The quadratic utility function, as is well known, has two unsatisfactory implications: (1) marginal utility of wealth becomes negative at some point; and (2) absolute risk aversion increases with wealth. We would thus not expect a banker to have a quadratic utility function.

and

(4) all decision variables $\geqslant 0$.

While the constraints in the above model are linear functions, the objective function is nonlinear. The solution to the above nonlinear model is found by solving an equivalent linear model.

Let $\mathrm{PROF}(d)^+_{H\epsilon}$ and $\mathrm{PROF}(d)^-_{H\epsilon}$ denote the positive and negative deviations, respectively. That is,

if $\qquad\mathrm{PROF(d)}_{H\epsilon} \geqslant \mathrm{EPG}_a$
then $\qquad\mathrm{PROF(d)}^+_{H\epsilon} = \mathrm{PROF(d)}_{H\epsilon} - \mathrm{EPG}_a$
and $\qquad\mathrm{PROF(d)}^-_{H\epsilon} = 0$
and if $\quad\;\mathrm{PROF(d)}_{H\epsilon} < \mathrm{EPG}_a$
then $\qquad\mathrm{PROF(d)}^+_{H\epsilon} = 0$
and $\qquad\mathrm{PROF(d)}^-_{H\epsilon} = |\mathrm{PROF(d)}_{H\epsilon} - \mathrm{EPG}_a|$
in any case $\;|\mathrm{PROF(d)}_{H\epsilon} - \mathrm{EPG}_a| = \mathrm{PROF(d)}^+_{H\epsilon} + \mathrm{PROF(d)}^-_{H\epsilon}$

The solution to the above MIN-SAD problem is obtained by solving the following equivalent linear programming problem:

Find the balance sheet adjustment decisions for point in time t_0 and points in time t_i contingent on the economic situation at t_i, $1 \leqslant i \leqslant H-1$, such that we obtain values from $\mathrm{PROF}(d)^-_{H\epsilon}$ which will:

$$\text{Minimize } \sum_\epsilon [(\mathrm{PROB}\ H\epsilon)(\mathrm{PROF(d)}^-_{H\epsilon})]$$

subject to:

(1) $E\ \mathrm{PROF(d)}_{H\epsilon} = \mathrm{EPG}_a$,
(2) the intra-temporal constraints,
(3) the inter-temporal constraints,
(4) $(\mathrm{PROF(d)}_{H\epsilon} - \mathrm{EPG}_a) - \mathrm{PROF(d)}^+_{H\epsilon} + \mathrm{PROF(d)}^-_{H\epsilon} = 0\ \forall \epsilon$,
(5) all decision variables $\geqslant 0$.

The two problems are equivalent since by linear programming theory the constraint types (4) can have at most one of $\mathrm{PROF}(d)^+_{H\epsilon}$ and $\mathrm{PROF}(d)^-_{H\epsilon}$ positive if they are not both zero. Hence we have $|\mathrm{PROF}(d)_{H\epsilon} - \mathrm{EPG}_a| = \mathrm{PROF}(d)^+_{H\epsilon} + \mathrm{PROF}(d)^-_{H\epsilon}$, and hence the models have the same objective function.

The efficient set. By varying the expected profits goal, we will come up with different optimal decisions. This set of optimal decisions is called the efficient set. We can present graphically the expected returns and risks of the efficient set as shown in figure 1.

The bankers can then examine the set of efficient decisions and select the deci-

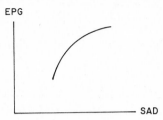

Figure 1. The efficient frontier.

sion which best satisfies them, i.e., has the highest expected utility of returns. No other decision outside the efficient set will give the bankers either less risk for the same return or greater return for the same risk.

Also, the other decisions in the efficient set are such that the bankers feel they either have to take on too much additional risk for the additional expected profits obtainable or that they have to reduce their expected profits by too large an amount for the amount of risk reduction that can be achieved.

5. Post-optimality analysis with the MIN-SAD Model

The MIN-SAD Model not only solves the bank balance sheet management problem but also offers some important fringe benefits. In this section, we will describe how the MIN-SAD Model can be used to examine the bank's economic forecasts and policy constraints.

Examination of the economic forecasts. One of the major inputs required for the MIN-SAD model is the bank's forecasts of the possible future economic conditions and their associated probabilities of occurrence. It may well be that different forecasters will assign different probabilities to the possible future economic situations. An important question that the bankers will then wish to answer is waht are the consequences of using a different set of economic forecasts. The MIN-SAD Model can help answer this question.

First the bank runs the MIN-SAD Model for each set of economic forecasts obtaining two efficient frontiers (see figures 2a and 2b). From each efficient set, the bankers choose an optimal solution — point A in figure 2a and point B in figure 2b.

One then compares the immediate balance sheet adjustments required under optimal solution *A* and *B*. Such an analysis may reveal a good deal of commonality between the two solutions. For example, both solutions *A* and *B* may call for the bank to sell $ 10 million of the bank's long-term bonds. If there is a lot of commonality between the two solutions then the disagreement about the economic forecasts is not significant.

If there is little commonality between the two solutions, then one can calculate

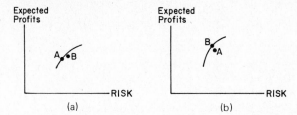

Figure 2. (a) Economic forecast I. (b) Economic forecast II.

the risk and return of each optimal solution under the alternate set of economic forecasts. If the risk and return of the optimal solution under the alternate set of economic forecasts are relatively close in value to the risk and return of the optimal solution for one's own economic forecasts (see figures 2a and 2b) then the disagreement in the economic forecasts is not significant. If they are not relatively close in value, then the disagreement in the economic forecasts is significant and must be ironed out.

Evaluation of a policy constraint. As pointed out earlier in the paper, bankers may have certain policy constraints such as investing a minimum percentage of deposits in government securities. A question which the bankers may wish to examine is what would be the consequence of changing one or more of their policy constraints. This question too can be answered with the help of the MIN-SAD Model.

After one has obtained the optimal solution for the first set of policy constraints, one runs the model again for the modified set of policy constraints. Figure 3 shows the efficient sets for the two sets of policy constraints. (We are assuming that the modifications are a relaxation of one or more constraints.)

Point *A* represents the optimal solution on the first efficient set. The points on the *BC* section of the new efficient set show by how much risk and/or return can be improved by relaxing some of the policy constraints. If the increase in utility obtained from the optimal solution *D* (which need not be in section *BC*) on the new efficient set is greater than the decrease in utility (as a result of lower liquidity, for

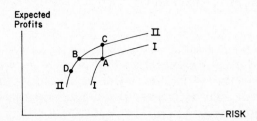

Figure 3. The efficient sets for alternative policy constraints.

example) due to the changes in the policy constraints, then the bank should make the changes. If net utility does not increase, then the bank should maintain its existing policies.

6. The size and structure of the MIN-SAD Model

The size and structure of the MIN-SAD Model are such that it can easily and quickly be solved with existing LP packages such as IBM's MPSX program which can handle as many as 16,383 rows and an unlimited number of columns. The size of the MIN-SAD Model will be a function of the degree of detail the bank uses in its planning. In general, the size of the model will be a function of the number of periods (H) in the planning horizon, the number of different economic situations possible at each t_i (N_{ie}), the number of different possible securities (NS), loan categories (NL), time deposits (NDT), and the number of policty constraints (NP) at each t_i. The number of rows, NR, in the MIN-SAD Model will approximately equal:

$$NR = \sum_{i=0}^{H-1} [(N_{ie})(22 + 4NS_i + 2NL + 2NDT + NP_{ie})]$$

$$- NSo - NLo - NDTo + 2N_{He} - 3$$

and the number of columns, NC, in the MIN-SAD Model will approximately equal:

$$NC = \sum_{i=0}^{H-1} [(N_{ie})(14 + 3NS + 2NL + 2NDT)] + 3N_{He}.$$

The MIN-SAD Model will also have a special structure. Figure 4 illustrates the

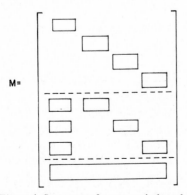

$$M =$$

Figure 4. Structure of a two period model.

structure for a two-period model with three possible economic situations at the start of the second period.

The top part of the matrix contains the intratemporal constraints. The middle part of the matrix contains the intertemporal constraints. The bottom part of the matrix contains the profit constraints. All the numbers not in any rectangle, and also a good portion of the numbers within the rectangles, are zeros. The density of the matrix will thus be quite low and the solution time consequently quite rapid.

6. Summary

The MIN-SAD Model can be a valuable tool to senior executives of a commercial bank in solving the bank balance-sheet management problems. The model incorporates the multiperiod dynamic nature of the problem. It finds the risk-return efficient set of solutions, as in Markowitz portfolio theory, from which the bankers can choose an optimal solution. The model can be used to perform a rich postoptimality analysis. It can easily and inexpensively be solved with existing computer packages.

References

[1] Bank Administration Institute, Measuring the Investment Performance of Pension Funds, (BAI, Park Ridge, Ill., 1968).

[2] William F. Beazer, Optimization of Bank Portfolios (D.C. Heath and Co., Lexington, Mass., 1975).

[3] H.P. Beighley, An Application of Linear Programming to Commercial Bank Asset Management under Certainty and Uncertainty, unpublished Ph.D. dissertation, Purdue University (1970).

[4] G.G. Booth, Programming bank portfolios under uncertainty: An extension, Journal of Bank Research 2 (Winter 1972).

[5] S.P. Bradley and D.B. Crane, A dynamic model for bond portfolio management, Management Science 19 (October 1972).

[6] S.P. Bradley and D.B. Crane, Simulation of bond portfolio strategies, Journal of Bank Research 6 (Summer 1975).

[7] S.P. Bradley and D.B. Crane, Management of Bank Portfolio (John Wiley and Sons, New York, 1975).

[8] D. Chambers and A. Charnes, Intertemporal portfolio analysis and optimization of bank portfolios, Management Science (July 1961).

[9] A. Charnes and S.C. Littlechild, Intertemporal bank asset choice with stochastic dependence, unpublished manuscript.

[10] A. Charnes and S. Thore, Planning for liquidity in financial institutions: the chance-constrained method, Journal of Finance 32 (Dec. 1966).

[11] A.H.Y. Chen, F.C. Jen and S. Zionts, The optimal portfolio revision policy, Journal of Business.

[12] Kalman J. Cohen and Frederick S. Hammer, eds., Analytical Methods in Banking (Richard D. Irwin, Homewood, Ill., 1966).

[13] K.J. Cohen and F.S. Hammer, Linear programming and optimal bank asset management decisions, Journal of Finance 23 (May 1967).

[14] K.J. Cohen and F.S. Hammer, Linear programming models for optimal bank dynamic balance sheet management, in Mathematical Methods in Investments and Finance, G.P. Szego and K. Shell, eds. (North-Holland, Amsterdam, 1972).

[15] K.J. Cohen and D.P. Rutenberg, Toward a comprehensive framework for bank financial planning, Journal of Bank Research 1 (Winter 1971).

[16] K.J. Cohen and Sten Thore, Programming bank portfolio under uncertainty, Journal of Bank Research 1 (Spring 1970).

[17] D.B. Crane, A stochastic programming model for commercial bank portfolio management, Journal of Financial and Quantitative Analysis (June 1971).

[18] Howard D. Crosse and George H. Hempel, Management Policies for Commercial Banks, 2nd ed. (Prentice Hall, Inc., Englewood Cliffs, New Jersey 1973).

[19] W.B. Davis, IBM-McKinsey bank management simulation, in Analytical Methods in Banking, K.J. Cohen and F.S. Hammer, eds. (Richard D. Irwin, Homewood, Ill., 1966).

[20] J. Fried, Bank portfolio selection, Journal of Financial and Quantitative Analysis 5 (June 1970).

[21] K.B. Gray, Managing the balance sheet: A mathematical approach to decision making, Journal of Bank Research 1 (Spring 1970).

[22] Frederick S. Hillier and Gerald J. Lieberman, Introduction to Operations Research, 2nd ed. (Holden-Day, Inc., San Francisco, 1974).

[23] Donald R. Hodgman, Commercial Bank Loan and Investment Policy (University of Illinois, Champaign, Ill., 1963).

[24] I.B.M., Mathematical programming system – extended (MPSX) and generalized upper bounding (GUB): program description, Manual No. SH 20-0968-1 (International Business Machines Corporation, White Plains, N.Y., 1972).

[25] R.I. Komar, Developing a liquidity management model, Journal of Bank Research, 2 (Spring 1971).

[26] Haim Levy and Marshall Sarnat, Investment and Portfolio Analysis (John Wiley and Sons, New York, 1972).

[27] B. Mandelbrot, The Variation of Certain Speculative Prices, Journal of Business 36 (July 1963).

[28] H. Markowitz, Portfolio Selection: Efficient Diversification of Investments (John Wiley and Sons, New York, 1959).

[29] B. Naslund and O. Whinston, A model of multiperiod investment under uncertainty, Management Science 8 (January 1962).

[30] M. Padberg and J. Wiginton, Efficient computation with MSAE regression, unpublished manuscript.

[31] G.A. Pogue, An intertemporal model for investment management, Journal of Bank Research 1 (Spring 1970).

[32] Roland I. Robinson, The Management of Bank Funds, 2nd ed. (McGraw-Hill, New York, 1962).

[33] G.P. Szego and K. Shell, eds., Mathematical Methods in Investments and Finance (North-Holland, Amsterdam, 1972).

[34] Harvey M. Wagner, Principles of Operations Research: With Applications to Managerial Decisions (Prentice-Hall, Inc., Englewood Cliffs, New Jersey, 1969).

[35] R.D. Watson, Tests of maturity structures of government securities portfolios: A simulation approach, Journal of Bank Research 3 (Spring 1972).

[36] C. Wolf, A model for selecting commercial bank government security portfolio, Review of Economics and Statistics 51 (February 1969).

TIMS Studies in the Management Sciences 11 (1979) 215–232
© North-Holland Publishing Company

A GENERALIZED CAPITAL ASSET PRICING MODEL

Scott F. RICHARD

Carnegie–Mellon University

1. Introduction

In a seminal paper Harry Markowitz [13] founded modern portfolio theory. In a two-period model Markowitz characterizes the efficient portfolios of risky securities as those with the highest expected return for any given level of variance of return. Tobin [23] introduced into the analysis a riskless asset and thus derived a separation theorem. This theorem shows that each investor holds only two portfolios: an efficient risky portfolio and the riskless asset. The composition of the risky portfolio is independent of the investor's preferences and depends only upon the expected returns and covariances of returns among securities.

The theory as developed by Markowitz and Tobin could not be implemented because it required the inversion of the covariance matrix of the returns among all securities under consideration — an impossible task at the time. In order to overcome this practical obstacle, Sharpe [21] suggested an index model. Sharpe shows that if an index can be identified such that all comovements in security returns are through the movement of the index, then only the covariances between the return on the index and each of the securities are required to find the efficient portfolios.

In their now famous papers, Sharpe [22], Lintner [11] and Mossin [17] each require market equilibrium and thus identify the index portfolio as the value weighted market portfolio. They independently derive a two-period, stationary opportunity set, capital asset pricing model (CAPM) relating the expected return on a security to the covariance of the security return with the market portfolio. Unfortunately, their model, as extended and tested by Black, Jensen and Scholes [2], is not empirically supported by New York Stock Exchange data.

Besides the empirical objections to the Sharpe–Lintner–Mossin model there are theoretical objections. In a seminal paper Merton [14] observed that the opportunity set is changing intertemporally since the short-term interest rate is changing stochastically. Merton shows in a continuous time model that in the presence of a stochastic short-term interest rate, the two-fund separation theorem is not valid and must be replaced by a three-fund separation theorem. The third fund is a security which is perfectly negatively correlated with the movement of the short-term interest rate. Furthermore, Merton shows that the Sharpe-Lintner-Mossin CAPM must be modified — an extra term is added — due to the stochastic nature of the short-term interest rate. Long [12] extends Merton's model in a discrete time, multiperiod model to include stochastic prices of consumption goods and long-term interest rates. [1]

In this paper we show Merton's model can be extended to cover *any* sources of environmental uncertainty in the opportunity set. [2] The only restriction we place on the sources of environmental uncertainty is that it be possible to model them as state variablles that follow Markov diffusion processes. In general, the state variables include anything that materially affects the production opportunity set. For example the state variables might include the prices of industrial goods, wage rates, or aggregate economic indicies, such as disposable per capital income or the rate of growth of the money supply.

Besides allowing for any sources of environmental uncertainty, in § 2 we extend Merton's continuous-time model of individual consumption—investment decision making to include a stochastic wage earnings stream and progressive income taxation. Furthermore, we allow investors to have state dependent utility functions.

We prove a general separation theorem in § 3. If there are N sources of environmental uncertainty, then each investor is indifferent between selecting from a set of $N + 2$ mutual funds. The mutual funds include N "hedging funds," which serve to hedge against movements in the opportunity set.

In § 4 we derive a general CAPM. This result is based on the investor demand functions derived in § 2 and the assumption that the security market is continuously in equilibrium. In § 3 we develop an empirically estimable version of the CAPM found in § 4. The final section contains some concluding remarks.

2. The economic environment and the investor's optimal consumption-investment decision

The unit of our analysis is a rational certain lived [3] investor who maximizes his lifetime expected utility of consumption and legacy. There are a fixed number K of such investors at all times. At time t individual k has wealth $W^k(t)$, denominated in dollars, which he continuously allocates to consumption goods and capital assets. The capital assets have stochastic rates of return which depend upon the state of the economy. The state of the economy is summarized by a vector, $\phi(t)$, of N state variables, which we discuss further below.

---

[1] Ross [20] develops a multi-factor CAPM using an arbitrage argument. His assumption is that the random return on each security is a linear combination of the returns on a set of factors plus an independent error.

[2] Not surprisingly, Merton [16] seems to have independently derived the general CAPM developed in this paper, since he alludes to the result in his speech before the Western Finance Association in 1975. Apparently he has not published the derivation.

[3] The analysis can easily be extended to uncertain lived investors with an arbitrary distribution of lifetime. See Richard [19].

There are n capital assets which are continuously traded in perfect frictionless markets. The dollar price, $P_i(t)$, of asset i at time t has dynamics given by the stochastic differential equation [4]

$$\frac{dP_i(t)}{P_i(t)} = \alpha_i(\phi, t)\, dt + \sigma_i(\phi, t)\, dZ_i(t) \quad \text{for } i = 1, ..., n, \tag{1}$$

where α_i is the expected instantaneous rate of return, σ_i is the instantaneous variance of return and $Z_i(t)$ is a standard Wiener process. The processes $\{Z_i(t)\}$ are correlated so that the rates of return have an instantaneous covariance matrix [5]

$$\Omega_{11} = [\sigma_{ij}(\phi, t)], \qquad i, j = 1, ..., n, \tag{2}$$

where by Ito's Theorem

$$\frac{dP_i}{P_i} \cdot \frac{dP_j}{P_j} \equiv \sigma_{ij}(\phi, t)\, dt. \tag{3}$$

We assume that Ω_{11} is of rank n.

In addition to the n risky assets, there is an instantaneously riskless asset which all investors may buy or sell (short) in any quantities. The price of the riskless asset is $P_0(t)$ and has an instantaneous rate of return

$$\frac{dP_0(t)}{P_0(t)} = r(\phi)\, dt, \tag{4}$$

where $r(\phi)$ is the nominal instantaneous riskless rate of return.

The economy is characterized by N state variables $\phi(t) = \{\phi_i(t)\}$. The state variables have dynamics given by the stochastic differential equations

$$d\phi_i = \mu_i(\phi, t)\, dt + \eta_i(\phi, t)\, dX_i(t), \quad \text{for } i = 1, ..., N. \tag{5}$$

In general the movements of the state variables are correlated with instantaneous

---

[4] For a detailed explanation of stochastic differential equations see Arnold [1] or Gihman and Skorohod [8].

[5] To guarantee the existence of a solution to (1), assume there exist constants $K_i > 0$ such that for all $i = 1, ..., n$

$$|\alpha_i(\phi^1, t) - \alpha_i(\phi^2, t)| + |\sigma_i(\phi^1, t) - \sigma_i(\phi^2, t)| \leqslant K_i|\phi^1 - \phi^2|$$

and

$$|\alpha_i(\phi, t)|^2 + |\sigma_i(\phi, t)|^2 \leqslant K_i^2(1 + |\phi|)^2.$$

We make similar assumptions regarding μ_i and η_i in (5). Furthermore we assume that α_i, σ_i and μ_i, η_i are continuous functions of (ϕ, t). For a detailed discussion of the existence of solutions see Arnold [1]. In general we are not concerned with the regularity properties of functions and simply assume enough smoothness to justify the theorems used.

covariance matrix

$$\Omega_{22} = [\eta_{ij}(\phi, t)], \qquad i, j = 1, ..., N, \tag{6}$$

where by Ito's Theorem

$$d\phi_i \, d\phi_j \equiv \eta_{ij}(\phi, t) \, dt. \tag{7}$$

More importantly the movement of the state variables and the returns on securities are correlated with an $(n \times N)$ covariance matrix

$$\Omega_{12} = [\gamma_{ij}(\phi, t)], \qquad i = 1, ..., n \text{ and } j = 1, ..., N, \tag{8}$$

where again by Ito's Theorem

$$dP_i/P_i \cdot d\phi_j \equiv \gamma_{ij}(\phi, t) \, dt. \tag{9}$$

The entire covariance matrix is

$$\Omega(\phi, t) = \begin{bmatrix} \Omega_{11} & \Omega_{12} \\ \Omega'_{12} & \Omega_{22} \end{bmatrix}, \tag{10}$$

which we assume is nonsingular.

The state variables include anything that materially affects the production opportunity set. In a general equilibrium analysis (instead of the partial equilibrium done here) uncertainty enters the model through stochastic production of real goods and services. The stochastic processes governing production of real goods and services are reflected in the equilibrium prices of capital assets, which we assume as the starting point of our model. Therefore any quantities that might be considered important by managers in making production decisions in various industries may be included as state variables. Examples of possible state variables are prices of industrial goods such as steel or oil; wage rates in various industries or even average wage rates; aggregate economies indices such as disposable per capital income, size of the Federal Government's deficit, unemployment or employment rate, or rate of growth in the money supply; the interest rate, $r(\phi)$;[6] prices of consumption goods and the overall price level; and, finally, states of nature such as rainfall or crop yields.

---

[6] We have shown elsewhere, Richard [19], that long-term bonds are derivative securities with prices that depend on the instantaneous interest rate r and the anticipated rate of inflation.

We assume throughout that all investors agree on the set of state variables, $\phi(t)$, their dynamics, (5), and the dynamics of security prices, (1).

Each investor continuously allocates his wealth to the purchase of the n risky securities, the riskless security and m consumption goods. Let $w_i(t)$ be the fraction of his wealth, W, the individual chooses to invest in security i, so that

$$\sum_{0}^{n} w_i \equiv 1 \qquad (11)$$

for all t. (We have omitted the superscript k during the remainder of this section for notational simplicity.) Assume the investor chooses to consume good i at the rate $C_i(t)$ for $i = 1, ..., m$; has wage earnings of $Y(\phi, t)$ [7], and has an income tax rate [8] of $\theta(W,Y,\phi,t) \in [0, 1)$. The the investor's wealth at time t is the sum of his initial wealth and his after tax earnings from both labor and capital less his expenditures for consumption:

$$W(t) = W(0) + \int_0^t Y(\phi, s)(1 - \theta)\, ds$$

$$+ \sum_{i=0}^{n} \int_0^t W(s)w_i(s)(1 - \theta)\frac{dP_i(s)}{P_i(s)} - \sum_{i=1}^{m} \int_0^t C_i(s)\, ds. \qquad (12)$$

Substituting (1), (4) and $w_0 = 1 - \Sigma_{i=1}^n w_i$ into (12) and differentiating gives the wealth dynamics,

$$dW = [(1 - \theta)W(r + \sum_{i=1}^{n}(\alpha - r)) + (1 - \theta)Y - \sum_{i=1}^{m} C_i]\, dt$$

$$+ (1 - \theta)W \sum_{i=1}^{n} w_i \sigma_i\, dZ_i(t). \qquad (13)$$

---

[7] More generally the wage income for the kth individual, $dy^k(t)$, could be modeled as satisfying

$$dy^k(t) = Y^k(\phi, t)\, dt + \sigma_y^k(\phi, t)\, dZ_y^k(t).$$

In this more general case, however, it is not possible to aggregate demand across individuals (as we do in § 4 below) and achieve a capital asset pricing model. This is because there are market imperfections (caused by legal restrictions) which prevent individuals from selling shares in their future wage earnings. Instead we assume that $\sigma_y^k \equiv 0$ for all individuals and attribute all uncertainties about future wages to the randomness in the indexes ϕ. Intuitively this means that for the next decision period the investor considers his wage rate $Y(\phi, t)$ known and certain, but that wage rates in subsequent periods are uncertain and depend upon the state of the economy.

[8] We make no allowance for different tax rates on "ordinary" and capital gain income. As an approximation to progressive taxation, the tax rate depends upon wealth W, the state variables ϕ and time t as well as earnings Y. The parameters of the income tax system may be among the state variables.

The investor values the real goods and services his consumption dollar brings. Therefore the utility of the consumption vector $C(t) = [C_1(t), ..., c_m(t)]'$ is dependent upon the prices of consumption goods, which are included in the state variables. Hence the investor's utility function for consumption at time t, $U(C(t), \phi(t), t)$, is state dependent. Similarly, when the investor dies at time T, he leaves wealth $W(T)$, which is valued for its purchasing power. Assuming the investor's estate must pay taxes at the rate of $\psi(W, \phi, T) \in (0,1)$, he will leave a legacy of $L(T) = W(T)(1 - \psi)$. The utility of $L(T)$ depends upon the price level at time T, which is among the state variables. Therefore the investor's utility for bequest function, $B(L(T), \phi(T), T)$ is also state dependent. Finally, we assume that both U and B are strictly concave in C and L, respectively.

The investor seeks to maximize his lifetime expected utility by choosing optimal consumption, $C(t)$, and investments, $w(t) = [w_0(t), ..., w_n(t)]'$:

$$\max_{\{C,w\}} E_0[\int_0^T U(C(t), \phi(t), t)\, \mathrm{d}t + B(L(T), \phi(T), T)], \qquad (14)$$

where E_0 is the expectation operator conditions on $W(0)$ and $\phi(0)$. His actions are subject to the budget constraint, (13), and the state dynamics, (1), (4) and (5). This completely specifies the investor's optimal control problem.

In the usual manner of stochastic dynamic programming, Fleming and Rishel [6, p. 157], we define the value function $V(W, \phi, t)$ by

$$V(W, \phi, t) = \max_{\{C,w\}} E_t[\int_t^T U(C, \phi, s)\, \mathrm{d}s + B(L(T), \phi(T), T)], \qquad (15)$$

where E_t is the expectation operator conditional on the states $W(t)$ and $\phi(t)$. The value function equals the expected lifetime utility of having wealth W and states of the economy ϕ at time t and proceeding optimally into the future. Hence the value function is the inputed utility of wealth.

A sufficient condition [9], Fleming and Rishel [6, p. 159], for the investor's optimal controls is the Bellman equation [10]

[9] A fundamental difficulty is the lack of proof for the existence of an optimal control C, w and hence of $V(w, \phi, t)$. In Merton [15], Kushner [10], chapter IV, theorem 7] is cited for the proof of Merton's Theorem I, which states that optimal controls exist and gives conditions these controls must satisfy. Kushner's theorem states nothing about existence, however, giving only sufficient conditions for optimal control of a strong diffusion process. (Our assumptions in footnote 4 guarantee that all processes P_i, ϕ_i are strong diffusions.) We repeat Merton's error concerning the existence of optimal controls in Richard [16].

While it is intuitively clear that optimal controls will exist for "well-behaved" U and B functions (in fact they have been explicitly found in the case where there are no indexes and for HARA class utilities in Merton [15]); it remains a somewhat bothersome mathematical technicality to define exactly what is "well behaved."

[10] Readers unfamilar with stochastic dynamic programming may find the Bellman equation puzzling. A heuristic derivation of stochastic dynamic programming is in Dreyfus [5].

$$0 = \max_{\{C,\,w\}} \left\{ U(C,\,\phi,\,t) + V_t + V_w \left[(1-\theta)W(r + \sum_{i=1}^{n} w_i(\alpha_i - r)) \right. \right.$$

$$+ (1-\theta)Y - \sum_{i=1}^{m} C_i \right] + \sum_{i=1}^{N} \mu_i V_i$$

$$+ \tfrac{1}{2}(1-\theta)^2 W^2 V_{WW} \sum_{i=1}^{n} \sum_{j=1}^{n} w_i w_j \sigma_{ij}$$

$$+ (1-\theta)W \sum_{j=1}^{N} \sum_{i=1}^{n} V_{jW} w_i \gamma_{ij} + \tfrac{1}{2} \sum_{i=1}^{N} \sum_{j=1}^{N} V_{ij} \eta_{ij} \Big\} ; \qquad (16)$$

with boundary condition

$$V(W(T),\,\phi(T),\,T) = B(L(T),\,\phi(T),\,T). \qquad (17)$$

In (16) $V_t = \partial V/\partial t$, $V_W = \partial V/\partial W$, $V_i = \partial V/\partial \phi_i$, etc.

The first order conditions for the optimal consumption rates are

$$0 = U_{C_i}(C,\,\phi,\,t) - V_W, \qquad i = 1, ..., m; \qquad (18)$$

and for the optimal investments are

$$0 = (1-\theta)WV_W(\alpha_i - r) + (1-\theta)^2 W^2 V_{WW} \sum_{j=1}^{n} w_j \sigma_{ij}$$

$$+ (1-\theta)W \sum_{j=1}^{N} V_{jW} \gamma_{ij}, \qquad i = 1, ..., n. \qquad (19)$$

The second order conditions to ensure an interior maximum are $[U_{C_i C_j}]$ negative definite, which follows from the concavity of U, and $V_{WW}\Omega_{11}$ negative definite. Since Ω_{11} is positive definite by assumption, we must show that $V_{WW} < 0$, $i.e.$, V is concave in W.

If income and estate taxes are not regressive in wealth then we can show that $V_{WW} < 0$. To see this consider an investor with two distinct wealth levels at time t, $W^1(t)$ and $W^2(t)$ with corresponding optimal consumption, C^1 and C^2, and investments, w^1 and w^2. Now consider the same investor with wealth $W^a = aW^1 + (1 - a)W^2$ where $a \epsilon$ (0, 1). Assume that θ is convex in W so that income taxes are not regressive in wealth. Then the budget constraint (13) is linear in C and w and convex in W. Hence it is feasible for the investor with wealth W^a to follow the control $w^a = aw^1 + (1 - a)w^2$ and maintain his wealth at $W^a(s) = aW^1(s) + (1 - a)W^2(s)$ for all $s \geq t$ by consuming $C^a(s) \geq aC^1(s) + (1 - a)C^2(s)$ for $s \geq t$. Similarly if estate taxes are not regressive, ψ in convex in W, then the investor leaves a legacy $L^a(T) \geq aL^1(T) + (1 - a)L^2(T)$. Therefore

$$V(W^a, \phi, t) \geq E_t[\int_t^T U(C^a, \phi, s)\, ds + B(L^a(T), \phi(T), T)]$$

$$\geq E_t[\int_t^T U(aC^1 + (1 - a)C^2, \phi, s)\, ds$$

$$+ B(aL^1 + (1 - a)L^2, \phi, T)]$$

$$> aV(W^1, \phi, t) + (1 - a)V(W^2, \phi, t), \qquad (20)$$

where the last inequality follows from the concavity of U and B. This establishes that $V_{WW} < 0$.

3. Generalized separation: an $N + 2$-fund theorem

In this section we show that an investor will be indifferent between investing in all n available securities or investing in $N + 2$ "mutual funds." This result generalizes Merton's Three Fund Theorem [14, theorem 2].

Preparatory to this result rewrite (19) for the kth investor as

$$W^k \sum_{j=1}^n w_j^k \sigma_{ij} = H_{N+1}^k(\alpha_i - r) + \sum_{j=1}^N H_j^k \gamma_{ij}, \qquad i = 1, ..., n, \qquad (21)$$

where $H_{N+1}^k = -V_W^k/V_{WW}^k(1 - \theta^k)$ and $H_j^k = -V_{jW}^k/V_{WW}^k(1 - \theta^k)$ for $j = 1, ..., N$. Denoting $\Omega_{11}^{-1} \equiv [\nu_{ij}]$, solve (21) for the demands

$$d_i^k \equiv w_i^k W^k = H_{N+1}^k \sum_{j=1}^n \nu_{ij}(\alpha_j - r) + \sum_{j=1}^N H_j^k \sum_{l=1}^n \nu_{il}\gamma_{lj}, \qquad i = 1, ..., n,$$

$$(22)$$

and

$$d_0^k \equiv W_0^k W^k = W^k - \sum_{i=1}^n d_i^k. \qquad (23)$$

Clearly relative demands depend upon preferences and only generalized separation, Cass and Stiglitz [3], obtains:

Theorem 1.   Given the n risky assets, and a riskfree asset, then there are $N + 2$ portfolios (mutual funds) such that (a) all utility maximizing risk-averse investors will be indifferent between choosing portfolios from among the original $n + 1$ assets or from these $N + 2$ funds; (b) the proportions of each fund invested in the individual assets depends only upon the parameters $\{r, \alpha_i, \sigma_{ij}, \gamma_{ij}\}$ and not on investor preference; and (c) the investor's demand for the funds does not require knowledge of the investment opportunity set for each asset or of the asset proportions held by the funds.

Proof.   To prove part (a) we explicitly find the composition of the $N + 2$ portfolios. To form portfolio j, $j = 1, ..., N$, note that there exists a unique solution x^j to

$$\Omega_{11}\begin{bmatrix} x_1^j \\ \vdots \\ x_n^j \end{bmatrix} = \begin{bmatrix} \gamma_{1j} \\ \vdots \\ \gamma_{nj} \end{bmatrix}, \tag{24}$$

because Ω_{11}^{-1} is assumed to exist. This solution is

$$x_i^j = \sum_{l=1}^n v_{il}\gamma_{lj}, \qquad i = 1, ..., n, \tag{25}$$

and

$$x_0^j = 1 - \sum_{i=1}^n x_i^j. \tag{26}$$

The $N + 1$st fund has weights

$$x_i^{N+1} = \sum_{j=1}^n v_{ij}(\alpha_j - r), \qquad i = 1, ..., n, \tag{27}$$

and

$$x_0^{N+1} = 1 - \sum_{i=1}^n x_i^{N+1}. \tag{28}$$

Fund zero contains only the riskless asset. Investor k can duplicate his demand for assets (22) if he puts a fraction ξ_i^k of his wealth in fund i where

$$\xi_i^k = \frac{H_i^k}{W^k}, \qquad i = 1, ..., N + 1, \tag{29}$$

and

$$\xi_0^k = 1 - \sum_{i=1}^{N+1} \xi_i^k. \tag{30}$$

Clearly the composition of each fund depends only upon the market parameters, establishing part (b).

It is left to the reader to verify part (c) by showing that the investor would choose $\{\xi_i^k\}$ as given in (29) and (30) if the only investment opportunities available to him were the $N + 2$ mutual funds.   Q.E.D.

The point of theorem 1 is that as extra state variables are introduced to increase the reality of the portfolio allocation model, a price must be paid in terms of the complexity of the corresponding mutual fund theorem. For each new state variable introduced a new mutual fund must be created to hedge against movements in the opportunity set caused by movements of that state variable.

Note that none of these mutual funds is the "market portfolio," composed of relative equilibrium market value weightings of all outstanding securities. This is because the market value weightings in general depend upon preferences as can be seen by aggregating (22) and (23) across investors and hence do not conform to part (b) of theorem 1. (We show in a corollary in § 4 that in equilibrium the market portfolio may be substituted for the $N + 1$st portfolio, but that the weights depend upon preferences.) Furthermore, the mutual funds are not unique since fund j for $j = 0, 1, ..., N + 1$ could be replaced by a convex combination of all the funds, where the weight for fund j is nonzero. For convenience we refer to mutual funds 1 through N as the "hedging funds" in that they are required by the investor to hedge against changes in the opportunity set brought about by changes in the state variables.

4. Market equilibrium: a generalized capital asset pricing model

In this section we derive a CAPM by assuming that the capital market is always in equilibrium. The plan of attack is to show that the demand equation (21) can be aggregated into n equations containing $N + 1$ unknowns. We then show that the $N + 1$ unknowns can be found in terms of the expected rates of return and covariances of the market portfolio and the hedging funds.

To begin, sum (21) for $k = 1, ..., K$ to find

$$\sum_{j=1}^{n} D_j \sigma_{ij} = H_{N+1}(\alpha_i - r) + \sum_{j=1}^{N} H_j \gamma_{ij} \quad \text{for} \quad i = 1, ..., n \tag{31}$$

where $D_i = \Sigma_{k=1}^{K} w_j^k W^k$ is the equilibrium demand for asset j, and $H_j = \Sigma_{k=1}^{K} H_j^k$ for ·

$j = 1, ..., N + 1$. Now if the market is always in equilibrium then the aggregate value of the market $M = \Sigma_{j=0}^{n} D_j$. Define $w_i \equiv D_i/M$, the percentage contribution of the ith asset to total market value. Then from (31)

$$\alpha_i - r = \frac{M}{H_{N+1}} \sum_{j=1}^{n} w_j \sigma_{ij} - \sum_{j=1}^{N} \frac{H_j}{H_{N+1}} \gamma_{ij}, \qquad i = 1, ..., n. \tag{32}$$

These are n equations containing the $N + 1$ unknowns, M/H_{N+1}, $-H_1/H_{N+1}$, ..., $-H_N/H_{N+1}$.

Merton [14] has shown that in equilibrium the market portfolio has dynamics

$$\frac{dP_M}{P_M} = [\sum_{1}^{n} w_j(\alpha_j - r) + r] \, dt + \sum_{1}^{n} w_j \sigma_j \, dZ_j. \tag{33}$$

The instantaneous expected rate of return on the market portfolio is $\alpha_M = r + \Sigma_{j=1}^{n} w_j(\alpha_j - r)$. The instantaneous covariance of the market portfolio return with the return on the ith asset is $\sigma_{iM} = \Sigma_{j=1}^{n} w_j \sigma_{ij}$ for $i = 1, ..., n$ and with the jth state variable is $\gamma_{Mj} = \Sigma_{i=1}^{n} w_i \gamma_{ij}$ for $j = 1, ..., N$. The instantaneous variance of the market portfolio's return is $\sigma_{MM} = \Sigma_{i=1}^{n} w_i \sigma_{iM}$.

Now consider the N hedging funds defined in the last section. Denote the price of fund j by P_{n+j}. The return on fund j is

$$\frac{dP_{n+j}}{P_{n+j}} = \sum_{i=0}^{n} x_i^j \frac{dP_i}{P_i} \tag{34}$$

$$= [\sum_{i=1}^{n} x_i^j(\alpha_i - r) + r] \, dt + \sum_{i=1}^{n} x_i^j \sigma_i \, dZ_i, \qquad j = 1, ..., N.$$

Hence the instantaneous expected rate of return on fund j is

$$\alpha_{n+j} \equiv \sum_{i=1}^{n} x_i^j(\alpha_i - r) + r, \qquad j = 1, ..., N. \tag{35}$$

The instantaneous covariance, $\sigma_{i,n+j}$, between security i and fund j is found by using Ito's Theorem:

$$\sigma_{i,n+j} \, dt \equiv \frac{dP_i}{P_i} \cdot \frac{dP_{n+j}}{P_{n+j}} = \sum_{k=1}^{n} x_k^j \sigma_{ki} \, dt \tag{36}$$

$$= \sum_{k=1}^{n} (\sum_{l=1}^{n} v_{kl} \gamma_{lj}) \sigma_{ki} \, dt = \gamma_{ij} \, dt.$$

The last equality follows from the fact that $\Omega_{11}^{-1} = [\nu_{kl}]$ and $\Omega_{11} = [\sigma_{ki}]$. Therefore,

$$\Omega_{12} \equiv [\gamma_{ij}] = [\sigma_{i,n+j}], \tag{37}$$

or in words, the covariances between the state variables and the securities are identical to the covariances between the hedging funds and the securities. Furthermore the covariance between the market portfolio and fund j is equal to the covariance between the market portfolio and state variable j:

$$\sigma_{M,n+j} = \sum_{i=1}^{n} w_i \sigma_{i,n+j} = \sum_{i=1}^{n} w_i \gamma_{ij} = \gamma_{Mj}. \tag{38}$$

As the next step in deriving the CAPM, we must find the covariances among the hedging funds. The covariance between fund i and fund j is

$$\sigma_{n+i,\, n+j} = \sum_{k=1}^{n} x_k^i \sigma_{k,n+j}, \qquad i, j = 1, ..., N. \tag{39}$$

The entire covariance matrix of the market portfolio and the hedging funds is

$$\Sigma = \begin{bmatrix} \sigma_{MM} & \sigma_{M,n+1} & \cdots & \sigma_{M,n+N} \\ \sigma_{n+1,M} & \sigma_{n+1,n+1} & \cdots & \sigma_{n+1,n+N} \\ \vdots & \vdots & & \vdots \\ \sigma_{n+N,M} & \sigma_{n+N,n+1} & \cdots & \sigma_{n+N,n+N} \end{bmatrix} \tag{40}$$

Now substitute σ_{iM} and $\sigma_{i,n+j}$ into (32) to get

$$\alpha_i - r = \frac{M}{H_{N+1}} \sigma_{iM} - \sum_{j=1}^{N} \frac{H_j}{H_{N+1}} \sigma_{i,n+j}, \qquad i = 1, ..., n. \tag{41}$$

Multiply (41) by w_i, sum over $i = 1, ..., n$ and substitute α_M, σ_{MM} and $\sigma_{M,n+j}$ into the result to find that

$$\alpha_M - r = \frac{M}{H_{N+1}} \sigma_{MM} - \sum_{j=1}^{N} \frac{H_j}{H_{N+1}} \sigma_{M,n+j}. \tag{42}$$

Finally multiply (41) by x_i^j, sum over $i = 1, ..., n$ and substitute (35) and (39) into the result to get that

$$\alpha_{n+i} - r = \frac{M}{H_{N+1}} \sigma_{M,n+1} - \sum_{j=1}^{N} \frac{H_j}{H_{N+1}} \sigma_{n+i,\, n+j}, \qquad i = 1, ..., N. \tag{43}$$

(42) and (43) are a system of $N + 1$ equations in the $N + 1$ unknowns M/H_{N+1}, $-H_N/H_{M+1}$, ..., $-H_N/H_{N+1}$.

To find the CAPM, solve the $N + 1$ equations (42) and (43) for M/H_{N+1}, $-H_1/H_{N+1}$, ..., $-H_N/H_{N+1}$ and substitute the result into (41) to find that

$$\alpha_i - r = [\sigma_{iM}, \sigma_{i,n+1}, ..., \sigma_{i,n+N}] \, \Sigma^{-1} \begin{pmatrix} \alpha_M - r \\ \alpha_{n+1} - r \\ \vdots \\ \alpha_{n+N} - r \end{pmatrix}, \qquad i = 1, ..., n,$$

(44)

where Σ is given by (40). Because of the particular choice of the market portfolio and the hedging portfolios, the coefficients in (44) are multiple regression coefficients.

Theorem 2.   (A generalized CAPM.) In equilibrium

$$\alpha_i - r = \beta_i^M(\alpha_M - r) + \sum_{j=1}^{N} \beta_i^j(\alpha_{n+j} - r), \qquad i = 1, ..., n,$$

(45)

where $\{\beta_i\}$ are the instantaneous multiple regression coefficients of dP_i/P_i on dP_M/P_M and $dP_{n+i}/P_{n+i}, j = 1, ..., N$. (45) is a security market hyperplane and is a natural generalization of the security market line.

Another way of looking at the generalized CAPM (44) is to define the vector

$$\Lambda = \begin{pmatrix} \lambda_M \\ \lambda_1 \\ \vdots \\ \lambda_N \end{pmatrix} = \Sigma^{-1} \begin{pmatrix} \alpha_m - r \\ \alpha_{n+1} - r \\ \vdots \\ \alpha_{n+N} - r \end{pmatrix}.$$

(46)

Then rewrite (44) as

$$\alpha_i - r = \sigma_{iM}\lambda_M + \sum_{j=1}^{N} \sigma_{i,n+j}\lambda_j = \sigma_{iM}\lambda_M + \sum_{j=1}^{N} \gamma_{ij}\lambda_j.$$

(47)

(47) indicates how the market compensates investors, in terms of expected return, for bearing the market risk and the state variable risks, as measured by the covariances. In this context the λ's are interpreted as the market "prices" for the compensated risks of market changes and changes in the opportunity set. (Actually the λ's are not prices because they are dimensionless. Perhaps they should be called "market risk factors.") If the risk borne by security i with respect to index j is mea-

sured by γ_{ij}, then $\gamma_{ij}\lambda_j$ is the excess expected return received (over the riskless rate) for bearing that risk. Lastly, if $\sigma_{iM} = 0$ then $\alpha_i \neq r$ in general, i.e., the "zero beta" portfolio does not have the same expected return as the riskless security.

We now return to the issue raised at the end of § 3 and show that in equilibrium each investor is indifferent between holding all $n + 1$ securities and holding $N + 2$ mutual funds, one of which is the market portfolio. This follows easily as a corollary to theorem 1.

Corollary. In equilibrium each investor behaves as if he allocates his wealth to:
(a) the riskless asset (fund 0);
(b) the N hedging funds (funds $1, ..., N$); and
(c) the market portfolio (fund $N + 1$).

Proof. As we remarked following Theorem 1, any of the $N + 2$ funds can be replaced by a nonsingular linear combination of the $N + 2$ funds. This is true because investors can simply undo a *linear* recombination of the funds by changing their personal allocations of wealth among the funds. Hence we need only show that the market portfolio is a linear combination of the $N + 2$ funds in theorem 1. From (31) we find by matrix inversion that

$$w_i \equiv \frac{D_i}{M} = \frac{H_{N+1}}{M} \sum_{j=1}^{n} v_{ij}(\alpha_j - r) + \sum_{j=1}^{N} \frac{H_j}{M} \sum_{l=1}^{n} v_{il}\gamma_{lj}, \qquad i = 1, ..., n, \quad (48)$$

are the equilibrium proportions of the market portfolio invested in the n risky assets. Substituting (25) and (27) into (48) gives

$$w_i = \frac{H_{N+1}}{M} x_i^{N+1} + \sum_{j=1}^{N} \frac{H_j}{M} x_i^j, \qquad i = 1, ..., n. \tag{49}$$

Therefore the weights of the market portfolio are linear combinations of the weights of the N hedging funds and the $N + 1$st fund of Theorem 1.   Q.E.D.

5. Empirical implications

In this section we develop an empirically estimable equation consistent with the CAPM of section 4. The equation we derive contains no unobservable quantities and can in theory be estimated with currently available data.

First we substitute (1), (33) and (34) into (45) to find that for $i = 1, ..., n$

$$\frac{dP_i}{P_i} - r\,dt = \sum_{j=1}^{N+1} \beta_i^j \left(\frac{dP_{n+j}}{P_{n+j}} - r\,dt\right) + \sigma_i\,dZ_i - \sum_{j=1}^{N+1} \beta_i^j \sigma_{n+j}\,dZ_{n+j}. \tag{50}$$

For convenience in (50) we have denoted the market portfolio as the $N+1$st hedging portfolio so that

$$\alpha_{n+N+1} \equiv \alpha_M \tag{51}$$

and

$$\sigma_{n+N+1}\, dZ_{n+N+1} \equiv \sum_1^n w_j \sigma_j\, dZ_j. \tag{52}$$

Now by Ito's Theorem

$$d \ln P_i = \frac{dP_i}{P_i} - \tfrac{1}{2}\sigma_i^2\, dt, \qquad i = 0, ..., n+N+1. \tag{53}$$

Substitute (53) into (50) to find

$$d \ln P_i - d \ln P_0 = a_i\, dt + \sum_{j=1}^{N+1} \beta_i^j\, (d \ln P_{n+j} - d \ln P_0) + \sigma_i\, dZ_i$$

$$- \sum_{j=1}^{N+1} \beta_i^j \sigma_{n+j}\, dZ_{n+j}, \tag{54}$$

where

$$a_i \equiv \tfrac{1}{2}[-\sigma_i^2 + \sum_{j=1}^{N+1} \beta_i^j \sigma_{n+j}^2]. \tag{55}$$

To get an empirically estimable equation we must integrate (54) across the measurement period, which we assume has a length of one unit of time. In order to have this integration result in *observable* variables we must make two assumptions. We assume that the covariance matrix, Ω, is stationary which implies that Σ is also stationary. [11] This in turn implies that $\{\beta_i^j\}$ are stationary. The changing opportu-

---

[11] This is not as restrive as it might at first seem to be. If one (or more) of the state variables have dynamics such that for η_i constant
$$d\phi_i = \mu_i \phi_i\, dt + \eta_i \phi_i\, dX_i,$$
then use $\ln \phi_i$ as a substitute state variable and
$$d \ln \phi_i \equiv (\phi_i - \tfrac{1}{2}\eta_i^2)\, dt + \eta_i\, dX_i,$$
which has a constant variance term. Thus the hedging portfolio for state variable $\ln\phi_i$ would have a constant covariance with the other securities.

nity set is manifest only through changes in the expected rates of return. Second, we assume that

$$\ln P_0(t+1) - \ln P_0(t) \approx R_{Ft} \tag{56}$$

where R_{Ft} is the continuously compounded rate of return on a nominally riskless discount bond maturing at $t+1$.

Integrating (54) and substituting (56) into the result we find the linear regression equation

$$R_{it} - R_{Ft} = a_i + \sum_{j=1}^{N+1} \beta_i^j (R_{n+j,t} - R_{Ft}) + \epsilon_{it}, \qquad i = 1, ..., n, \tag{57}$$

where

$$R_{it} \equiv \ln P_i(t+1) - \ln P_i(t) \tag{58}$$

and

$$\epsilon_{it} \equiv \sigma_i [Z_i(t+1) - Z_i(t)] - \sum_{j=1}^{N+1} \beta_i^j \sigma_{n+j} [Z_{n+j}(t+1) - Z_{n+j}(t)]. \tag{59}$$

An ordinary least squares time series regression gives consistent unbiased estimators of the coefficients in (57) if the assumptions of the model are met. The "errors" ϵ_{it} are normally distributed with the properties shown below following as consequences of the properties of the Wiener process:

$$E\epsilon_{it} = 0, \qquad i = 1, ..., n; \tag{60}$$

$$E\epsilon_{it}\epsilon_{j\tau} = 0, \qquad t \neq \tau; \tag{61}$$

$$E\epsilon_{it}\epsilon_{kt} = \sigma_{ik} - \sum_{j=1}^{N+1} \beta_i^j \sigma_{k,n+j} - \sum_{j=1}^{N+1} \beta_k^j \sigma_{i,n+j} + \sum_{j=1}^{N+1} \beta_i^j \sigma_{k,n+j}$$

$$= \sigma_{ik} - \sum_{j=1}^{N+1} \beta_{kt}^j \sigma_{i,n+j}; \tag{62}$$

and

$$ER_{n+j,t}\,\epsilon_{it} = E[\sigma_{n+j}(Z_{n+j}(t+1) - Z_{n+j}(t))\epsilon_{it}]$$

$$= \sigma_{i,n+j} - \sum_{l=1}^{N+1} \beta_i^l \sigma_{n+j,n+l} = \sigma_{i,n+j} - \sigma_{i,n+j}$$

$$= 0, \qquad j = 1, ..., N+1. \tag{63}$$

(63) shows that $R_{n+j,t}$ and ϵ_{it} are independent since they are orthogonal and jointly normally distributed.

There is, however, a difficult econometric problem involved in estimating (57). This problem is finding the hedging funds, which have rates of return that are required data in (57). In theory this is an easy task since we have shown in (25) how to find the composition of the hedging portfolios by inverting the covariance matrix, Ω_{11}, for security returns. In practice the matrix Ω_{11} is typically very large and its estimation – let alone inversion – is a difficult, if not impossible task. In a sense we have come full circle: we face the same difficulty in implementing our theory that Markowitz [13] faced in implementing his.

6. Conclusions

The CAPM (57) that we have derived can be used to identify the economic risks that are being borne by investors. It seems that the corrected specification of the state variables is largely an empirical question. We have shown that *any* factors that can be modeled by (5) can be considered state variables. Many different and reasonable models can be built conjecturing what those state variables are. (In particular, there has been much recent interest in the price level or changes in the price level as a possible state variable. [12]) The most reasonable way to distinguish which models capture more economic behavior is, we think, now largely an empirical issue to be decided by testing (57) using alternative sets of state variables.

References

[1] Ludwig Arnold, Stochastic Differential Equations (Wiley, New York, 1974).
[2] F. Black, M.C. Jensen and M. Scholes, The capital asset pricing model: some empirical tests, in Studies in the Theory of Capital Markets, M.C. Jensen, ed. (Praeger Publishers, New York, 1972).
[3] D. Cass and J.E. Stiglitz, The structure of investor preferences and asset returns, and separability in portfolio allocation: a contribution to the pure theory of mutual funds, Journal of Economic Theory 2 (1970).
[4] A.H. Chen and A.J. Boness, Effects of uncertain inflation on the investment and financing decision of a firm, The Journal of Finance (May 1975).
[5] S.L. Dreyfus, Dynamic Programming and the Calculus of Variations (Academic Press, New York, 1965).
[6] Wendell H. Fleming and Raymond W. Rishel, Deterministic and Stochastic Optimal Control (Springer–Verlag, New York, 1975).
[7] Irwin Friend, Yoram Landskroner and Etienne Losq, The demand for risky assets under uncertain inflation, The Journal of Finance 31 (December 1976).

[12] For example, Chen and Boness [4], Hagerman and Kim [9] and Friend, Landskroner and Losq [7].

[8] I.I. Gihman and A.V. Skorohod, Stochastic Differential Equations (Springer–Verlag, New York, 1972).

[9] R.L. Hagerman and E.H. Kim, Capital asset pricing with price level changes, Journal of Financial and Quantitative Analysis 11 (Sept. 1976).

[10] H.J. Kushner, Stochastic Stability and Control (Academic Press, New York, 1967).

[11] J. Lintner, The valuation of risk assets and the selection of risky investments in stock portfolios and capital budgets, Review of Economics and Statistics 47 (1965).

[12] J.B. Long, Jr., Stock prices, inflation and the term structure of interest rates, Journal of Financial Economics 1 (1974).

[13] H. Markowitz, Portfolio selection, The Journal of Finance (March 1952).

[14] R.C. Merton, An intertemporal capital asset pricing model, Econometrica 41 (Sept. 1973).

[15] R.C. Merton, Optimal consumption and portfolio rules in a continuous-time model, Journal of Economic Theory 3 (Dec. 1971).

[16] R.C. Merton, Theory of Finance from the perspective of continuous time, Journal of Financial and Quantitative Analysis 10 (November 1975).

[17] J. Mossin, Equilibrium in a capital asset market, Econometrica 34 (1966).

[18] S.F. Richard, Optimal consumption, portfolio and life-insurance rules for an uncertain lived individual in a continuous time model, Journal of Financial Economics 2 (June 1975).

[19] S.F. Richard, An analytical model of the term structure of interest rates, Carnegie-Mellon University, GSIA, W.P. # 19-76–77 (1976).

[20] Stephen A. Ross, The arbitrage theory of capital asset pricing, Journal of Economic Theory 13 (December 1976).

[21] W.F. Sharpe, Capital Asset Prices: A Theory of Market Equilibrium under Conditions of Risk, Journal of Finance 19 (1964).

[22] W.F. Sharpe, A simplified model for portfolio analysis, Management Science 9 (January 1963).

[23] James Tobin, Liquidity preference as behavior towards risk, Review of Economic Studies 25 (February 1958).

TIMS Studies in the Management Sciences 11 (1979) 233–248

MULTIPERIOD EQUILIBRIUM: SOME IMPLICATIONS FOR CAPITAL BUDGETING

R.C. STAPLETON * and M.G. SUBRAHMANYAM **

The principal normative purpose of developing valuation models of the firm is to derive capital budgeting decision rules for wealth maximizing firms. In a previous paper, Stapleton and Subrahmanyam [16] presented a multiperiod equilibrium asset pricing model which related the value of the firm to its future, stochastic cash flows. The present paper will derive the implications of that model for the wealth maximizing firm's investment decision.

In perfect capital markets it can be shown that the value of a sum of cash flows is equal to the sum of the market values of the individual flows. This allows cash flows from individual projects to be valued separately. The capital budgeting problem is then to estimate the value of the cash flows from the project and compare them with the cost of the project. To capture the essence of the multiperiod problem it is sufficient to consider projects with cash inflows arising in just two periods. We will derive the value of project j's cash flows in a two period model where the cash flows of all other projects and firms also arise in periods 1 and 2.

1. Problems in applying the single period capital asset pricing model

A number of authors (Lintner [7], Stevens [17], Hamada [5], Bogue and Roll [2], Myers and Turnbull [13], Bierman and Smidt [1], and Fama [4]) have suggested applying the single period model stage by stage to value multiperiod projects. To varying degrees these papers ignore the single period limitations of the Sharpe [15], Lintner [7], Mossin [12] [SLM] capital asset pricing model or make arbitrary assumptions about the parameters of the model. The kind of problems that arise can be appreciated by trying to apply the SLM model to the valuation of X_1^j and X_2^j the cash flows of project j at $t = 1$ and $t = 2$.

If $P_{1,2}^j$ represents the market value at $t = 1$ of X_2^j, the SLM model predicts that the value, contingent on the state of the world at $t = 1$, is

$$P_{1,2}^j | \phi_1 = \frac{1}{r_2} [E(X_2^j | \phi_1) - \lambda_2 \, \text{cov}(X_2^j X_2^M | \phi_1)] \tag{1}$$

where $X_2^M = \Sigma_k X_2^k$ summed over all projects in the economy, where r_2 is (one plus)

* Manchester Business School and New York Univeristy.
** Indian Institute of Management and New York University.

the risk free rate over the second period and λ_2 is the market price of risk and expected cash flow and covariance of the cash flow are conditional on the state of the world ϕ_1.

Having derived the future price of X_2^j the single period model can be applied again to find P_{02}^j and P_{01}^j the values at $t = 0$ of X_2^j and X_1^j. Assuming that the cash flows X_1^k are paid out as dividends, the returns on the market portfolio at $t = 1$ are $X_1^M + P_{12}^M$ where P_{12}^M is the value of the market portfolio (of the X_2^k) at $t = 1$. Hence

$$P_{02}^j = \frac{1}{r_1}[E[P_{12}^j] - \lambda_1 \, \text{cov}(P_{12}^j, X_1^M + P_{12}^M)], \qquad (2)$$

$$P_{01}^j = \frac{1}{r_1}[E(X_1^j) - \lambda_1 \, \text{cov}(X_1^j, X_1^M + P_{12}^M)]$$

where $\text{cov}(P_{12}^j, X_1^M + P_{12}^M)$ and $\text{cov}(X_1^j, X_1^M + P_{12}^M)$ are covariances between the return on the asset and the market, where the market return is a set of cash flows paid out as dividends plus a set of values of future flows. The value of a project yielding X_1^j and X_2^j is then the sum of the values P_{01}^j and P_{02}^j.

All the papers mentioned above suggest essentially the same analysis although they normally use the Sharpe–Lintner rate of return version of the SLM model rather than the more explicit Mossin version used here. They then proceed to simplify the substitution of the expected value of (1) in (2) by assuming something about the relationship of λ_2 to λ_1, r_2 to r_1, and about the process by which expectations regarding X_2^j develop over time (see Myers and Turnbull [13]). The assumptions are made in order that the single period model can be applied period by period, and in some cases to simplify the analysis.

The problems that arise in the period by period approach can be summarized as follows:

(1) The earlier papers (Lintner [7], Stevens [17], Bogue and Roll [2]) failed to check whether the Fama [3] conditions for the validity of the single period model in a multiperiod world were fulfilled. One of the Fama conditions is nonstate dependence of the future opportunity set, and this will be violated if, in the example above, r_2 is stochastic and dependent on the outcomes of X_1^k. If this were the case the normal single period model would not hold over the first period. [1]

(2) The future risk free interest rate is taken to be nonstochastic in the later papers on the period by period approach. Also, the future market price of risk, λ_2, is taken as known and in order to simplify the analysis in a specific relation to λ_1. For example, Myers and Turnbull [13] define the market price of risk as $\lambda_t^* = \lambda_t P_t^M$ and arbitrarily assume that it is (a) nonstochastic and (b) constant over time. Fama [4] defines the market price of risk in a similar manner and again assumes that it is certain and constant. [2]

---

[1] As Merton [10] and Long [9] have shown, a three rather than a two factor model is required in this case.

[2] Note that it is Fama's ϕ that he assumes is constant and certain and this is the same as Myers and Turnbull's λ. Both these notations are different from that used here.

While it seems reasonable to take the future risk free rates as exogenous in a multiperiod model as the single period model takes the one period rate as given, the same is not true of the future market price of risk. In the single period model the λ is endogenous and a genuine multiperiod model should derive future as well as the current λs. The danger in imposing an arbitrary relationship on the λs is that it might be inconsistent with other assumptions in the model. For example, it appears to be extreme to assume that λ'_t is nonstochastic when the value of the market, P^M, clearly is and that λ'_t is constant when P^M is likely to grow over time. A theory of the relationship between the λs is derived in Stapleton and Subrahmanyam [16] and it does not imply the assumptions made by Myers and Turnbull [13] and Fama [4].

(3) The SLM single period model assumes either quadratic utility or concave utility and normality of the exogenously given end of period returns. In a multiperiod model quadratic utility is ruled out since it would induce state dependence in λ which is excluded by the Fama [3] conditions. It is natural to assume joint normality of the X_t^k. However, when we move back to valuation at $t = 0$ normality of the $P^j_{1,2}$ is required and this is a variable endogenous to the model which may or may not be normally distributed. In Stapleton and Subrahmanyam [16] it is shown that $P^j_{1,2}$ is normal if the X_2^k are normal and it is assumed that investors have exponential utility and firms do not have limited liability.

(4) In order to provide neat solutions to the multiperiod valuation problem, Myers and Turnbull [13] assume that expectations of the project's cash flow are generated by a single index model. Fama [4] on the other hand assumes that future conditional covariance matrices are known at $t = 0$. There seems to be little justification for making the simplification that Myers and Turnbull make in a capital budgeting model just as there would be little justification for using Sharpe's diagonal model in a theory of equilibrium prices. One reasonable simplification, which can be made without too much loss of generality, is to assume that the characteristics of the state of the world ϕ_1 relevant for expectations of the X_2^k are sufficiently described by the outcome of the vector of each cash returns at $t = 1$ on all the firms in the market. This allows us to write

$$X_1 = \begin{bmatrix} X_1^1 \\ X_1^2 \\ \vdots \\ X_1^n \end{bmatrix},$$

$$P^j_{12} | X_1 = \frac{1}{r_2} \left[E(X_2^j | X_1) - \lambda_2 \operatorname{cov}(X_2^j X_2^M | X_1) \right]. \tag{3}$$

Fama [4] on the other hand makes two assumptions to make the multiperiod problem manageable. First, he makes an assumption which is designed to exclude any stochastic future discount rates and guarantee that the single period model will hold period by period. The second assumption guarantees that the cost of capital is equal in each period. Like Myers and Turnbull's single index model assumption, this second one restricts the applicability of Fama's results. However, in principle the first assumption is more objectionable. The use of nonstochastic discount rates is a sufficient but nonnecessary condition for the period by period model to hold. As we will show later, necessary conditions are that the market parameters r_2 and λ_2 in (3) are nonstochastic and that the conditional covariance matrix whose elements are $\text{cov}(X_2^k \, X_2^M | X_1)$ is also nonstochastic. Joint normality of the X_t^k guarantees this latter condition and this is the assumption made here. However, the future discount rate is related to

$$\frac{E(X_2^i | X_1)}{P_{12}^i | X_1} = r_2 + \lambda_2 \frac{\text{cov}(X_2^i X_2^M | X_1)}{P_{12}^i | X_1},$$

which is clearly stochastic if $P_{12}^i | X_1$ is so. Fama is effectively excluding stochastic future prices, an extreme and unnecessary condition. It is far safer to base a multiperiod analysis on fundamental assumptions (such as joint normality) rather than to make arbitrary sufficient assumptions.

To summarize the problems that arise with applying to SLM model to multiperiod investments are: the extent to which the Fama [3] conditions fail to hold, the arbitrariness of the assumptions that have to be made regarding the market price of risk, the possible lack of normality of derived prices, and the lack of generality due to the simplifying assumptions made regarding the stochastic process generating cash flows. The model derived in the next section is designed to overcome these problems and provide an internally consistent valuation model.

2. Values and the market price of risk in a two-period model

In Stapleton and Subrahmanyam [16] we develop an n period model of the value of the firm assuming constant absolute risk aversion (CARA) utility functions and joint normality of the cash flows in the economy. These two assumptions are sufficient to guarantee that the future market price of risk was nonstochastic when derived endogenously, as assumed by the papers reviewed in § 1. These assumptions, together with no debt financing, no limited liability and known future interest rates, guarantee also that derived future stock prices are normally distributed as required for the mean-variance period by period model with nonquadratic utility. In this section we briefly describe a simplified version of the multiperiod theory assuming exponential utility for terminal wealth and a two period model, sufficient to appreciate the general n-period solution.

The investor's multiperiod problem is to choose proportions Z_{01}^k, Z_{02}^k at $t = 0$ in the cash flows X_1^k and X_2^k of firm h (we assume that it is possible to purchase shares in the individual cash returns of the firm at each point in time) and a revised set of proportions Z_{12}^k at $t = 1$. The investor's decision problem can be solved recursively used dynamic programming. At $t = 1$ the investor inherits a portfolio of shares in the X_2^k given by the vector Z_{02} and chooses a new portfolio Z_{12}. At $t = 1$ he maximizes the expected utility of terminal wealth

$$U(w_1|X_1) = \max_{Z_{12}} E[U(w_2)] = \max_{Z_{12}} E[-a \exp(-aw_2)] - \tag{4}$$

subject to

$$w_1 = Z_{12}'P_{12} + M_1$$

where

$$w_2 = M_1 r_2 + Z_{12}'X_2$$

where a is his coefficient of absolute risk aversion,
P_{12} is the vector of $t = 1$ prices of the X_2,
r_2 is one plus the interest rate over the second period and
M_1 is the amount of risk free lending at $t = 1$.

The solution to (4) is a vector of shares

$$Z_{12} = \frac{1}{a}\,\Omega_2^{-1}[E(X_2|X_1) - r_2 P_{12}|X_1] \tag{5}$$

where

$$\Omega_2 = \begin{bmatrix} \mathrm{var}(X_2^1|X_1) & \cdots & \mathrm{cov}(X_2^1 X_2^j|X_1) & \cdots \\ \vdots & \ddots & \mathrm{var}(X_2^j|X_1) & \cdots \\ & & & \ddots \end{bmatrix} \tag{6}$$

The variances and covariances are conditional on the vector X_1 of outcomes at $t = 1$. (5) implies SLM equilibrium prices

$$P_{12}|X_1 = \frac{1}{r_2}[E(X_2|X_1) - \lambda_2 \Omega_2 1] \tag{7}$$

where 1 is the unit vector and $\lambda_2 = 1/\Sigma_{i=1}^h(1/a_i)$ is the market price of risk.

Substituting the prices in (7) in the demand equation (5) and the resulting demands back in (4) yields the value of the maxima

$$U(w_1|X_1) = -a \exp(-a\{w_1 r_2 + A_2\}) \tag{8}$$

where

$$A_2 = \frac{\lambda_2^2}{2a} \, \mathbf{1}' \Omega_2 \mathbf{1}.$$

In (8) the utility of w_1 is dependent on $w_1 r_2$, the wealth at $t = 2$ if the whole of w_1 were reinvested in the risk free asset and A_2 the value of having the opportunity to invest in risk assets.

The investors' optimal contingent decisions at $t = 1$ and the resulting equilibrium prices have been derived. The method of dynamic programming can now be used to solve for optimal portfolios at $t = 0$ and the associated equilibrium prices. If r_2 and A_2 in (8) are constants, the derived utility of wealth function is a simple, nonstate dependent, exponential function of w_1. Possible state dependence arises through uncertainty of r_2, excluded by assumption, or uncertainty of λ_2 and of Ω_2. However, given exponential utility λ_2 is a known constant. This is the basic reason for assuming the constant absolute risk aversion utility function. [3] Secondly, given the assumption of joint normality of the X_t^h, the conditional covariance matrix Ω_2 is nonstochastic, i.e., not dependent on the vector X_1. Joint normality and exponential utility are hence sufficient conditions for avoiding state dependence of the derived utility function (8).

At $t = 0$ the investor faces the following maximization problem

$$\max_{\begin{bmatrix} Z_{01} \\ Z_{02} \end{bmatrix}} E[-a \exp(-a\{w_1 r_2 + A_2\})] \tag{9}$$

subject to

$$w_0 = Z'_{01} P_{02} + Z'_{02} P_{02} + M_0$$

where

$$w_1 = M_0 r_1 + Z'_{01} X_1 + Z'_{02} P_{12}$$

where the vector of shares is a vector of holdings in the cash flow X_1 and X_2, and the returns on these assets at $t = 1$ are cash flows X_i and prices of X_2, denoted by the vector P_{12}.

---

[3] Any other risk averse function would yield λ_2, a function of expected wealth which in general will be a function of X_1 and the state of the world at $t = 1$. (The logarithmic utility function is an exception.) For a discussion see Stapleton and Subrahmanyam [16].

Following the same procedure as before the optimal portfolio is

$$\begin{bmatrix} Z_{01} \\ Z_{02} \end{bmatrix} = \frac{1}{ar_2} \, \Omega^{-1} \begin{Bmatrix} \Omega_1^{-1}[E(X_1) - r_1 P_{01}] \\ \Omega_1^{-1}[E(P_{12}) - r_1 P_{02}] \end{Bmatrix} \qquad (10)$$

where Ω_1 is a variance-covariance matrix of cash flows X_1 and prices P_{12}, i.e.

$$\Omega_1 = \begin{bmatrix} F & G \\ G' & H \end{bmatrix},$$

$$F = [\text{cov}(X_1^j X_1^k)], \quad G = [\text{cov}(X_1^j P_{12}^k)], \quad H = (\text{cov}(P_{12}^j P_{12}^k)].$$

Equilibrium prices at $t = 0$ are hence

$$P_{01} = \frac{1}{r_1} [E(X_1) - \lambda_1 \Omega_1 1],$$

$$P_{02} = \frac{1}{r_1} [E(P_{12}) - \lambda_1 \Omega_1 1]. \qquad (11)$$

Again, prices are in the form assumed in (2).
The value of λ_1, the market price of risk, is now

$$\lambda_1 = 1 \Big/ \sum_{i=1}^{1} \frac{1}{a_i r_2}$$

or

$$\lambda_1 = \lambda_2 r_2.$$

The current market price of risk is equal to the future price compounded at the future risk free rate of interest.

3. Capital budgeting decision rules for multiperiod prospects

The prices in (7) and (11) can be used directly to derive decision rules for projects as in Fama [4] and Myers and Turnbull [13]. However, the relationship between λ_1 and λ_2 derived above leads to a far simpler approach to the problem. [4]

---

[4] The same relationship is shown to hold in Stapleton and Subrahmanyam [16] for the multiplicative separable exponential utility case. It is also a reasonably good approximation in the additive separable case.

Substituting the expected value of (7) in the expression for P_{02} in (11) we find

$$P_{02} = \frac{1}{r_1 r_2} [E(X_2) - \lambda_2 \Omega_2 1 - r_2 \lambda_1 \Omega_1 1]$$

$$= \frac{1}{r_1 r_2} [E(X_2) - \lambda_2 (\Omega_2 1 + r_2^2 \Omega_1 1)]. \tag{13}$$

Now for any particular cash flow X_2^j (13) is

$$P_{02}^j = \frac{1}{r_1 r_2} [E(X_2^j) - \lambda_2 \{\text{cov}(X_2^j X_2^M | X_1) + r_2^2 \text{cov}(P_{12}^j, P_{12}^M + X_1^M)\}]. \tag{14}$$

Again from (7)

$$\text{cov}(P_{12}^j P_{12}^M) = \frac{1}{r_2^2} \text{cov}(E(X_2^j | X_1) E(X_2^M | X_1))$$

and

$$\text{cov}(P_{12}^j X_1^M) = \frac{1}{r_2} \text{cov}(E(X_2^j | X_1) X_1^M)$$

and given joint normality

$$\text{cov}(E(X_2^j | X_1) E(X_2^M | X_1)) = \text{cov}(X_2^j X_2^M) - \text{cov}(X_2^j X_2^M | X_1)$$

and

$$\text{cov}(E(X_2^j | X_1) X_1^M) = \text{cov}(X_2^j X_1^M)$$

Substituting in (14)

$$P_{02}^j = \frac{1}{r_0 r_1} [E(X_2^j) - \lambda_2 \{\text{cov}(X_2^j X_2^M) + \text{cov}(X_2^j X_1^M r_2)\}]. \tag{15}$$

The certainty equivalent in (15) is the expected value of X_2^j less the future market price of risk times the sum of the covariances between the compounded cash flows.

An alternative version of (15) is

$$P_{02}^j = \frac{1}{r_1} \left[\frac{E(X_2^j)}{r_2} - \lambda_1 \left\{ \text{cov}\left(\frac{X_2^j}{r_2} \frac{X_2^M}{r_2}\right) + \text{cov}\left(\frac{X_2^j}{r_2} X_1^M\right) \right\} \right]. \tag{16}$$

In (16) the cash flows are first discounted to $t = 1$ and then evaluated at the period 1 market price of risk.

The alternative end of period one evaluation of X_2^j allows a simple comparison with the value of X_1^j.

From (11)

$$P_{01}^j = \frac{1}{r_i} [E(X_1^j) - \lambda_1 \{ cov(X_1^j, X_1^M + P_{12}^M) \}]$$

$$= \frac{1}{r_1} \left[E(X_1^j) - \lambda_1 \left\{ cov(X_1^j X_1^M) + \frac{1}{r_2} cov(X_1^j E(X_2^M | X_1)) \right\} \right]$$

$$= \frac{1}{r_1} \left[E(X_1^j) - \lambda_1 \left\{ cov(X_1^j X_1^M) + cov\left(X_1^j \frac{X_2^M}{r_2} \right) \right\} \right]. \tag{17}$$

This time the covariance terms are between X_1^j and X_1^M and between X_1^j and the discounted value of the market return at $t = 2$, X_2^M. Evaluation of a project j yielding X_1^j and X_2^j involves the comparison of $P_{01}^j + P_{02}^j$ with the cost of the project X_0^j.

From (16) and (17) the net present value of the project

$$P_{01}^j + P_{02}^j - X_0^j$$

$$= \frac{1}{r_1} \left[E\left(\frac{X_2^j}{r_2} + X_1^j \right) - \lambda_1 \left\{ cov\left(\frac{X_2^j}{r_2} + X_1^j, \frac{X_2^M}{r_2} + X_1^M \right) \right\} \right]. \tag{18}$$

The square bracket includes the expected value and covariances of the discounted value (to $t = 1$) of the cash flows. The covariances are with the discounted values of the cash flows in the economy. It should be emphasized that the covariances are between end of period 1 discounted (at the risk-free rate) *cash flows* in the economy and not between end of period 1 values. (18) gives an alternative and much simpler evaluation than the period by period application of (7) and (11). It is also general in the sense that no particular dependence structure of the cash flows is assumed.

4. The behaviour of β over time

The major problem with the capital budgeting fromulations of § 3 is that the risk measures involving covariances between cash flows, across time, are unfamiliar and empirically obscure. This is in spite of the fact that they represent simply a cross-time generalization of the standard single period measures. The normal observable empirical relationship is that between β and the expected rate of return on shares. β, however, involves covariances between prices rather than cash flows. The relationship between the usual β measure of risk and the risk measures required for analysis based on § 3 is complex and will be discussed after first looking at the determinants of β and its behaviour over time.

Myers and Turnbull [13] have discussed the determinants of β using their single index model. They show that its behaviour depends upon the relative predominance of later as opposed to earlier cash flows (growth) and on the pattern of resolution of uncertainty over time. The results of § 2 of this paper allow a rather more general analysis.

The β of a firm normally refers to the expression

$$\beta^j = \frac{\text{cov}(r^j r^M)}{\text{var}(r^M)} \tag{19}$$

where r^j and r^M are the rates of return on firm j's shares and on the market portfolio. In a multiperiod model β_t^j is [5]

$$\beta_t^j = \frac{\text{cov}(X_t^j + P_t^j, X_t^M + P_t^M | X_{t-1})}{\text{var}(X_t^M + P_t^M | X_{t-1})} \cdot \frac{P_{t-1}^M}{P_{t-1}^j} . \tag{20}$$

The determinants of β_t^j can be appreciated by looking at the β_1^j and β_2^j of the single cash flow X_2^j in the two period model

$$\beta_2^j = \frac{\text{cov}(X_2^j X_2^M | X_1)}{\text{var}(X_2^M | X_1)} \cdot \frac{P_1^M}{P_1^j} , \tag{21}$$

$$\beta_1^j = \frac{\text{cov}(P_1^j, X_1^M + P_1^M)}{\text{var}(X_1^M + P_1^M)} \cdot \frac{P_0^M}{P_0^j} . \tag{22}$$

Using the result of § 3

$$\text{cov}(P_1^j, X_1^M + P_1^M) = \text{cov}(P_1^j X_1^M) + \text{cov}(P_1^j P_1^M)$$

$$= \frac{1}{r_2} \text{cov}(X_2^j X_1^M) + \frac{1}{r_2^2} [\text{cov}(X_2^j X_2^M) - \text{cov}(X_2^j X_2^M | X_1)].$$

The numerator of (21) and hence the value of β_1^j depends upon the degree of risk resolved over the first period. There are two extreme cases: (1) independence of X_2^j and X_1 where no uncertainty is resolved over the first period; and (2) the case

---

[5] (20) assumes that the X_t^j and X_t^M are paid out as dividends. P_t^j refers to the value at t of all the future flows X_{t+1}^j, X_{t+2}^j, ... To be consistent with this notation, P_{12}^j used earlier to denote the value of X_2^j at $t = 1$ will now be written as P_1^j.

where all the risk of X_2^j is resolved over period 1.

(1) If X_2^j is independent of all the X_1^k and independent therefore of X_1^M, $\text{cov}(X_2^j X_1^M) = 0$ and also $\text{cov}(X_2^j X_2^M | X_1) = \text{cov}(X_2^j X_2^M)$. In this case $\beta_1^j = 0$.

(2) If all the uncertainty is resolved over period 1 $\text{cov}(X_2^j X_2^M | X_1) = 0$, hence $\beta_2^j = 0$ and

$$\beta_1^j = \frac{\left(\text{cov} \dfrac{X_2^j}{r_2} X_1^M\right) + \text{cov}\left(\dfrac{X_2^j}{r_2} \dfrac{X_2^M}{r_2}\right)}{\text{var}(X_1^M + P_1^M)} \cdot \frac{P_0^M}{P_0^j}. \tag{23}$$

In between these extremes the behaviour of β_1^j and β_2^j depends on the proportion of risk resolved over the period. The total risk of X_2^j is measured by $\text{cov}((X_2^j/r_2)X_1^M) + \text{cov}((X_2^j/r_2)(X_2^M/r_2))$. The higher is $\text{cov}(X_2^j X_1^M)$, the lower is the residual covariance $\text{cov}(X_2^j X_2^M | X_1)$ and the higher is β_1^j relative to β_2^j. It is of course possible (but unlikely) that the proportion of uncertainty over the period 1 will be such that β_1^j and β_2^j are equal.

The β of a series of cash flows, or of a firm, over a particular period is a weighted average of the βs of the individual cash flows. Since we would expect a greater amount of uncertainty resolution to take place in a given period for early flows than for later flows, other things being equal projects with predominantly later cash flows will have lower βs.

For the firm as a whole it is perhaps reasonable to expect the pattern of uncertainty resolution to be such that β stays fairly constant period by period. This is not likely, however, for a particular cash flow or for a project. As we have seen, for the β of X_2^j to be constant over time a very particular degree of uncertainty resolution must occur in each period. In fact, we would expect the β for a project to vary quite widely over time. There is no reason to expect β for a particular cash flow or project to be constant over time.

5. A new β for capital budgeting analysis

The behaviour of the normally defined β of a cash flow over time depends on the pattern of the resolution of uncertainty over time as well as the total covariance risk of the flow. Capital budgeting methods that rely on using constant risk adjusted discount rates over time (for example Fama [4]) are restrictive in that uncertainty resolution is *assumed* to be such as to yield constant βs and discount rates for individual cash flows and projects. They also run into well-known problems of risk over time (Robichek and Myers [14]). On the other hand, β is a common, well understood and empirically observable risk measure of the firm which should convey information useful in capital budgeting.

The capital budgeting method suggested in § 3 requires covariance between discounted cash flows rather than the covariances between stock price returns which determine β. However, an alternative beta can be defined in terms of covariances between discounted cash flows, and under reasonable assumptions it can be shown to relate closely to the normally defined β. In this way, the market risk information contained in β can be used as an input in capital budgeting without any restrictive assumption being made about the resolution of uncertainty over time.

In § 3 we showed for a two-period project that a risk adjustment could either be made at a future point in time (15), at the present time (16) or at the end of one period (18). Which form is used is a matter of taste. The first is in line with the certainty equivalent method whose advantages were shown in Robichek and Myers [14]. The second is consistent with one of the well-known methods in Hillier [6] and again is a form of certainty equivalent method. These two have operational advantages over the third which is on the face of it rather circuitous. However, we will pursue this third method because it can be developed as a risk adjusted discount rate approach (using a beta measure to estimate the discount rate) without the restrictive assumptions of the normal period by period risk adjusted discount rate approach. We define β^j for a project or firm as

$$\beta^j = \frac{\operatorname{cov}(X_1^j + X_2^j/r_2, \, X_1^M + X_2^M/r)}{\operatorname{var}(X_1^M + X_2^M/r_2)} \cdot \frac{P_0^M}{P_0^j}. \tag{24}$$

The rationale for this particular definition comes from the relationship between β and the appropriate risk adjusted discount rate. In the single period model the valuation relationship

$$P^j = \frac{1}{r} \left[E(X^j) - \lambda \operatorname{cov}(X^j X^M) \right] \tag{25}$$

implies the linear relationship

$$E(R^j) = r - 1 + \lambda' \beta^j$$

between the expected rate of return or cost of capital $E(R^j)$, and β^j, where $\lambda' = \lambda P^M \operatorname{var}(R^M)$. Firms can use $E(R^j)$ to discount expected cash flows to their market value, i.e.,

$$P^j = \frac{E(X^j)}{1 + E(R^j)}. \tag{26}$$

Similarly, in our multiperiod model the value of X_1^j and X_2^j in (18)

$$P_0^j = \frac{1}{r_1} \left[E\left(X_1^j + \frac{X_2^j}{r_2}\right) - \lambda_1 \operatorname{cov}\left(X_1^j + \frac{X_2^j}{r_2}, \, X_1^M + \frac{X_2^M}{r_2}\right) \right] \tag{27}$$

where

$$P_0^j = P_{01}^j + P_{02}^j$$

implies the linear relationship

$$E(R_1^j) = r_1 - 1 + \lambda' \hat{\beta}^j. \tag{28}$$

where $E(R_1^j)$ is the risk adjusted discount rate in

$$p_0^j = \frac{E(X_1^j + (X_2^j/r_2))}{1 + E(k_1^j)} \tag{29}$$

and R^M is defined analogously. Also

$$\lambda' = \lambda_1 P_0^M \, \text{var}(k_1^M) \, .$$

$\hat{\beta}_j$ in (24) is a timeless measure of the relative riskiness of the project. It aggregates risk in the two time periods and is not affected by timing of resolution of the uncertainty of X_2^j. [6] If $\hat{\beta}_j$ is estimated and the market parameter λ' is known, the appropirate discount rate can be applied to the expected end of period one discounted cash flows to value the project. The problem then is to estimate the risk measure $\hat{\beta}_j$.

6. The relationship of $\hat{\beta}^j$ to β^j

The typical capital project, which is in the same risk class as the existing assets of the firm, may be defined as one which has a $\hat{\beta}$ equal to that of the firm as a whole. This is the multiperiod analogue of the normal single period definition of risk class. [7] If we assume that the project is an equal risk project the problem is one of

---

[6] If $\hat{\beta}$ is the same for a new project as it is for the existing assets (cash flows) of the firm the project is a comparable risk project in the Modigliani and Miller [11] sense. It captures risk over all time periods whereas the period by period β does not. It can easily be shown that a project with a normally defined β equal to that of the firm is not an equal risk project in any real sense. In fact, two projects can have equal βs and be of entirely different risk. For example, a cash flow at $t = 2$ may have a total risk approximately twice that of a $t = 1$ cash flow, with equal risk resolved in periods 1 and 2. In this case it could have the same β as the $t = 1$ flow over the first period. Clearly the period by period β does not accurately reflect the total risk. $\hat{\beta}$, on the other hand, measures to total risk across time of the project.

[7] For $\hat{\beta}$ for a project to equal that of the firm, the ratio

$$\text{cov}\left(X_1^j + \frac{X_2^j}{r_2}, X_1^M + \frac{X_2^M}{r_2}\right) \bigg/ E\left(X_1^j + \frac{X_2^j}{r_2}\right)$$

must be the same. This is the normal concept of relative risk being equal, with risk now defined across both time periods.

estimating the $\hat{\beta}^j$ of the whole firm. We now show that $\hat{\beta}^j$ is closely related to the normal period by period β^j of the firm. In fact, under reasonable assumptions and for the firm with average expected growth $\hat{\beta}^j = \beta^j$.

Although it is quite unreasonable to assume that β is constant over time for an individual cash flow or stream of cash flows associated with a given project, it is reasonable to assume that the β of the firm as a whole is constant over time. Unless the type of business engaged in by the firm changes significantly or its growth prospects alter, there is little reason to expect the overall β to change. Assuming β is constant we have from (21) and (22), for the two period case,

$$\beta_1^j = \frac{\text{cov}(X_1^j + P_1^j, X_1^M + P_1^M)}{\text{var}(X_1^M + P_1^M)} \cdot \frac{P_0^M}{P_0^j} = \beta_2^j$$

$$= \frac{\text{cov}(X_2^j X_2^M | X_1)}{\text{var}(X_2^M | X_1)} \cdot \frac{P_1^M}{P_1^j}. \tag{30}$$

Substituting the relationships for covariances and variances of values from § 2 we have

$$\beta_1^j = \left\{ \left[\text{cov}(X_1^j X_1^M) + \text{cov}\left(X_1^j \frac{E(X_2^M | X_1)}{r_2} \right) + \text{cov}\left(\frac{E(X_2^j | X_1)}{r_2} X_1^M \right) \right.\right.$$

$$\left.\left. + \text{cov}\, \frac{E(X_2^j | X_1)}{r_2} \frac{E(X_2^M | X_1)}{r_2} \right) \right] \Big/ \text{var}\left(X_1^M + \frac{E(X_2^M | X_1)}{r_2} \right) \right\} \cdot \frac{P_0^M}{P_0^j}. \tag{31}$$

Now, if we divide the numerator and denominator of β_2^j in (30) by r_2^2 and assume that the ratio P_1^M / P_1^j is both nonstochastic and equal to P_0^M / P_0^j we find that the sum of the numerators in (30) equals the numerator of $\hat{\beta}^j$ in (24) (after using the statistical properties of joint normal X_t^j). [8] Also, the sum of the denominators equals the denominator in (24). It follows that $\hat{\beta}^j = \beta_1^j = \beta_2^j$ in this case.

The above equality relationship between $\hat{\beta}^j$ and the assumed equal β_t^j has been shown for the strict two period case. However, it can be shown to hold in a three period world where $\beta_1^j = \beta_2^j = \beta_3^j$ and indeed in the general n period case. [9] However, the estimate of $\hat{\beta}^j$ from the period by period observable βs will be accurate only if the ratio P_t^M / P_t^j is constant. The ratio of the total market value of securities to the value of the individual firm will remain constant as long as the growth rate of the firm (of its cash flows and value) is the same as that of the whole market.

If the ratio $(P_1^M / P_1^j) < (P_0^M / P_0^j)$ the value of j has grown faster than the average firm in the market. If the inequality is in the opposite direction the firm is of below

---

[8] For a detailed exposition refer to the Appendix in Stapleton and Subrahmanyam [16].

[9] The proof of the three period case is tedious, requiring successive substitutions for the P_2^j and P_1^j. It will be supplied by the authors on request. The period case can be established by induction.

average growth. For the above average growth firm, equality of the β_t^j in (30) implies that

$$\frac{\operatorname{cov}(X_1^j + P_1^j, X_1^M + P_1^M)}{\operatorname{var}(X_1^M + P_1^M)} < \frac{\operatorname{cov}(X_2^j X_2^M | X_1)}{\operatorname{var}(X_2^M | X_1)}. \tag{32}$$

Now since (31) implies that

$$\hat{\beta}_j = \frac{\operatorname{cov}(X_1^j + P_1^j, X_1^M + P_1^M) + r_2^2 \operatorname{cov}(X_2^j X_2^M | X_1)}{\operatorname{var}(X_1^M + P_1^M) + r_2^2 \operatorname{var}(X_2^M | X_1)} \cdot \frac{P_0^M}{P_0^j}, \tag{33}$$

(32) means that $\hat{\beta}^j > \beta_1^j = \beta_2^j$. For the above average growth firm the normally defined β understates the relative riskiness of the cash flows. Conversely, the below average growth firm has a normal β that overstates its true relative risk.

7. Conclusion

The implications of multiperiod equilibrium in capital markets are that the risk of an investment project can and should be measured on an intertemporal rather than period-by-period basis. Although it might well be true that risk is resolved in such a manner that the period-by-period beta of the firm as a whole stays constant, individual cash flows and streams of cash flows from projects have betas which vary with the particular timing of uncertainty resolution. Capital budgeting methods that rely on constant betas for projects are highly restrictive.

The intertemporal risk measure suggested by the exponential terminal wealth utility valuation model of § 2 is the covariance by discounted (at the risk-free rate) cash flows. The suggested capital budgeting method is closely related to the present value method in Hillier [6].

Although it relies on a particular utility function, the period-by-period prices derived in § 2 allow us to analyse the determinants of the behaviour over time of the normally defined beta of a firm, project or cash flow. The behaviour depends on the degree of uncertainty resolved over each time period.

The main problem with our proposed capital budgeting method is the unfamiliarity of the risk measure. Covariances between cash flows of firms in the market across time cannot be observed easily, whereas the normally defined beta can be observed from share price data. In the final section of the paper we show the relationship between this beta and a newly defined beta based on covariances between discounted cash flows. For an average growth firm with a constant period-by-period beta the new beta is the same as the normal one observable from price data. For above average growth firm the required risk measure is understated by the normally defined beta.

References

[1] H. Bierman and S. Smidt, The Capital Budgeting Decision (Collier Macmillan, New York, 1975).
[2] Marcus C. Bogue and Richard Roll, Capital budgeting for risky projects with 'imperfect' markets for physical capital, Journal of Finance 29 (May 1974).
[3] Eugene F. Fama, Multiperiod consumption–investment decisions, American Economic Review 60 (March 1970).
[4] Eugene F. Fama, Risk-adjusted discount rates and the cost-of-capital in a two-parameter world, Journal of Financial Economics 5 (August 1977).
[5] Robert Hamada, Multiperiod capital asset prices in an efficient and perfect market: a valuation of present value model under two parameter uncertainty, mimeo, University of Chicago (1974).
[6] Frederick S. Hillier, The derivation of probabilistic information for the evaluation of risky investments, Management Science 9 (April 1963).
[7] John Lintner, Optimum or maximum corporate growth under uncertainty, in The Corporate Economy: Growth, Competition and Innovative Potential, R. Marris and A. Wood eds. (Harvard, Cambridge, Mass, 1971).
[8] John Lintner, The valuation of risk assets and the selection of risky investments in stock portfolios and capital budgets, Review of Economics and Statistics 47 (February 1965).
[9] John Long, Stock prices, inflation and the term structure of interest rates, Journal of Financial Economics 1 (June 1974).
[10] Robert C. Merton, An intertemporal capital asset pricing model, Econometrica 41 (September 1973).
[11] Franco Modigliani and Merton H. Miller, The cost of capital, corporation finance and the theory of investment, American Economic Review 48 (June 1958).
[12] Jan Mossin, Equilibrium in a capital asset market, Econometrica 34 (October 1966).
[13] Stewart C. Myers and Stuart M. Turnbull, Capital budgeting and the capital asset pricing model: good news and bad news, Journal of Finance 32 (May 1977).
[14] Alexander A. Robichek and Stewart C. Myers, Conceptual problems in the use of risk-adjusted discount rates, Journal of Finance 21 (December 1966).
[15] William F. Sharpe, Capital asset prices: a theory of market equilibrium under conditions of risk, Journal of Finance 19 (September 1964).
[16] Richard C. Stapleton and Marti G. Subrahmanyam, A multiperiod equilibrium asset pricing model, Econometrica 42 (September 1978).
[17] Guy Stevens, On the impact of uncertainty on the value and investment of the neoclassical firm, American Economic Review 64 (June 1974).

TIMS Studies in the Management Sciences 11 (1979) 249–253
© North-Holland Publishing Company

NOTES ABOUT AUTHORS

Vijay S. Bawa ("Optimal Portfolio Choice and Equilibrium in Lognormal Securities Markets") is Supervisor, Economic and Financial Studies Group of Bell Laboratories, Murray Hill, New Jersey and Professor of Finance, Graduate School of Business Administration, New York University. He received B. Tech (Honors) in Mechanical Engineering from I.I.T., Bombay and Ph.D. in Operations Research from Cornell University. He has published extensively in several journals. He is co-author of a forthcoming book *Estimation Risk and Optimal Portfolio Choice* with Brown, S.J. and Klein, R.W. He is a Associate Editor of *Management Science*.

Menachem Brenner ("The Impact of Inflation Upon Portfolio Selection") is Lecturer of Finance at the Jerusalem School of Business Administration, Hebrew University and Visiting Assistant Professor at the University of California, Berkeley. He has served as visiting professor at New York University, University of California, Berkeley and University of Bergamo. He received his Ph.D. in finance and M.A. from Cornell University, and a B.A. in economics from Hebrew University. He is the author or co-author of numerous articles.

Abraham I. Brodt ("A Multi-Period Portfolio Theory Model for Commercial Bank Management") is Assistant Professor of Finance at the Faculty of Administration at the University of Ottawa, Ottawa, Canada K1N 9B5. He received his B.Sc. in Mathematics from McGill University and his M.B.A. and Ph.D. in Finance from the Graduate School of Business Administration, New York University. His current interests are financial institution balance sheet management and bond portfolio management. He is a member of AFA, ASAC, FMA, TIMS and WFA.

Willard T. Carleton ("A Note on the Use of the CAPM for Utility Rate of Return Determination") is the William R. Kenan, Jr., Professor of Business Administration, University of North Carolina, Chapel Hill. He received undergraduate and M.B.A. degrees from Dartmouth College, his M.A. and Ph.D. in economics from the University of Wisconsin. His current research is in the areas of utility regulation, the structure of interest rates, and dynamic corporate financial decision models.

Lewis M. Chakrin ("Optimal Portfolio Choice and Equilibrium in a Lognormal Securities Market") is Supervisor of the Operations Research Studies Group at Bell Laboratories, Holmdel, New Jersey 07733. He received his B.S. from New York University, his M.S. in Operations Research from Columbia University and his M.B.A. and Ph.D. in Finance and Quantitative Analysis from New York University's Graduate School of Business Administration. His current interests are in the application of Operations Research to Finance and Marketing problems.

Kalman J. Cohen ("On the Existence of Serial Correlation in an Efficient Securities Market") received a B.A. from Reed College, a B.Litt. from Oxford University, and an M.S. and Ph.D. from Carnegie Institute of Technology. He has been Distinguished Bank Research Professor at Duke University's Graduate School of Business Administration since 1974. Prior to that, he served for two years as Distinguished Professor of Finance and Economics and as the first Director of the Salomon Brothers Center for the Study of Financial Institutions at New York University. He also spent 14 years on the faculty of Carnegie-Mellon University's Graduate School of Industrial Administration. He has written five books and more than 60 articles in the areas of banking and finance, strategic planning, management science, and computer simulation. He has pioneered in the applications of management science techniques in banking.

Edwin J. Elton ("Simple Criteria for Optimal Portfolio Selection: The Multi-Index Case") is Professor of Finance at New York Univeristy. He has published 5 books and over 45 articles in areas of portfolio theory, corporate finance and investment. He is associate editor of *Management Science* and *Journal of Finance.*

George M. Frankfurter ("Measuring Risk and Expectation Bias in Well Diversified Portfolios") is Professor of Finance at the School of Management, Syracuse University. He received a B.A. from the Hebrew University in Jerusalem, and an M.B.A. and Ph.D. in Business Administration from SUNY at Buffalo. He has authored several articles which appeared in this joural, *The Journal of Finance, The Journal of Financial Management, The Review of Economics and Statistics, The Accounting Review, Decision Sciences* and others.

Martin J. Gruber ("Simple Criteria for Optimal Portfolio Selection: The Multi Index Case") is Professor of Finance at the Graduate School of Business of New York University. He holds a S.B. from MIT and a Ph.D. from Columbia University. He is the author of 7 books and over 40 journal articles dealing with various topics in corporate finance, investments and general equilibrium theory. He is currently co-department editor of finance for *Management Science.*

Myron J. Gordon ("Optimal Dynamic Consumption and Portfolio Planning in a Welfare State") is Professor of Finance at the Faculty of Management Studies, University of Toronto. He received his Ph.D. in economics from Harvard University, an M.A. in economics from Harvard University and a B.A. in economics from the University of Wisconsin. He is author or co-author of three books and more than 50 journal articles. In 1975 he was president of the American Finance Association. His major research interests are in the area of investment financing and valuation of the firm.

Nils H. Hakansson ("A Characterization of Optimal Multi Period Portfolio Policies") is Sylvan C. Coleman Professor of Finance and Accounting at the University of California, Berkeley. He received a B.S. in business administration from the University of Oregon, an M.B.A. in accounting and a Ph.D. in quantitative methods, both from University of California, Los Angeles. In the past Professor Hakansson held academic positions at Yale University and UCLA. Professor Hakansson has published a variety of articles in the economics, finance, accounting, and management science literature. His present fields of research interest include investment theory, financial markets, and accounting theory. He is a member of ORSA, TIMS, American Accounting Association, American Institute of Certified Public Accountants, American Economic Association, Econometric Society, American Finance Association, and American Statistical Association.

Brian Ingham ("Optimal Dynamic Consumption and Portfolio Planning in a Welfare State") graduated with the Bachelor of Applied Science degree in Industrial Engineering in 1973 and the M.B.A. degree in 1974 from University of Toronto. Since then, he has been working as the Product Coordinator in the Data Center Division of IBM Canada in Toronto.

Haim Levy ("Does Diversification Always Pay?") is a Professor of Finance in the Jerusalem School of Business Administration, Hebrew University, Israel. Over the past few years he has been interested in decision making under condition of uncertainty, equilibrium in the capital market, and the relationship between the mean-variance rules and stochastic dominance rules. He also investigated the impact of changes in the assumptions underlined the Capital Asset Pricing Model (e.g., transaction cost, investment horizons, etc.) on the equilibrium relationship.

Eric B. Lindenberg ("Capital Market Equilibrium with Price Affecting Institutional Investors") is Supervisor, Antitrust Studies American Telephone and Telegraph Company. He received his Ph.D. in Economics from New York University. His current interests include Stochastic Dominance, Capital Market and Portfolio Theory and related areas of Financial Economics.

Robert Litzenberger ("On Distributional Restrictions for Two Fund Separation") is a Professor of Finance at the Graduate School of Business, Stanford University. He holds an M.B.A. degree from the University of Pennsylvania (1966) and a Ph.D. degree from the University of North Carolina at Chapel Hill (1969), and has taught at Carnegie-Mellon University (1969–70) and Columbia University (Fall 1975). He has authored more than 30 articles on valuation under uncertainty, corporation finance and investments.

Steven F. Maier ("On the Existence of Serial Correlation in an Efficient Securities Market") received a B.S. from Cornell University and an M.S. and Ph.D. from Stanford University. He is currently an Associate Professor at the Graduate School of Business Administration, Duke University. He is a member of TIMS, ORSA, The American Finance Association and several other societies. His articles have appeared in several journals, including *Management Science, The Journal of Finance, The Journal of Bank Research, The Journal of Financial and Quantitative Analysis, Financial Management,* and *The Journal of Banking and Finance.*

Manfred W. Padberg ("Simple Criteria for Optimal Portfolio Selection: The Multi-Index Case") is Professor of Quantitative Analysis at the Graduate School of Business Administration, New York University. Prior to joining NYU, he was affiliated with the International Institute of Management in West Berlin and with Mannheim University in Mannheim, Germany. In addition, Dr. Padberg has held visiting appointments at the T.J. Watson Research Center (IBM Research Division, Yorktown Heights) and the University of Bonn and short-term appointments at Carnegie-Mellon University, the University of Münster of Waterloo. He holds an M.S. in Mathematics from the University of Münster (Germany), and an M.S. and Ph.D., both in Industrial Administration from Carnegie-Mellon University in Pittsburgh. Dr. Padberg has written more than 35 articles which have appeared in journals such as *Applied Statistics, Journal of Finance, Journal of Financial and Quantitative Analysis, Mathematical Programming, Management Science, Naval Research Logistics Quarterly, Operations Research* and others. His current research interests are in the areas of mathematical programming (with a particular emphasis on combinatorial and integer programming) and financial theory (with a particular emphasis on portfolio selection). Dr. Padberg is a member of the Mathematical Programming Society and the Operations Research Society of America. He also is a member of the editorial board of the journals *Mathematical Programming* and *Mathematical Programming Studies.*

Herbert Phillips ("Measuring Risk and Expectation Bias in Well Diversified Portfolios") is Professor of Finance at Temple University. He received his Ph.D. in Business Administration from the University of Washington in 1968. His recent papers appear in the *Journal of Financial and Quantitative Analysis, The Reviews of Economics and Statistics,* and *Financial Management.* He is co-author of the soon to be released text, *Investment Analysis and Portfolio Selection: An Integrated Approach,* by South-Western.

Krishna Ramaswamy ("On Distribution Restrictions for Two Fund Separation") is a member of the Technical Staff at Bell Laboratories at Murray Hill, New Jersey. He received a bachelors degree in Electrical Engineering from the Indian Institute of Technology in 1971, the M.B.A. from Duke University in 1973, and the Ph.D. from Stanford University in 1978. He is currently engaged in research in finance.

Scott F. Richard ("A Generalized Capital Asset Pricing Model") is Associate Professor of Industrial Administration at Carnegie-Mellon University. He received his doctorate in Decision and Control from Harvard University. His current research interests are the term structure of interest rates and the growth of government. He has published in the *Journal of Financial Economics, Management Science, Operations Research* and the *SIAM Journal on Control and Optimization.*

Richard Roll ("Testing a Portfolio for Ex Ante Mean/Variance Efficiency") is professor of Finance in the Graduate School of Management at UCLA. He received a Ph.D. in 1968 from the University of Chicago. His research has involved various subjects in finance, including capital markets, corporate decision-making, and monetary phenomena. He has published several articles on these subjects.

Barr Rosenberg ("Realistic Portfolio Optimization") is Professor of Business Administration at the University of California, Berkeley. He received a B.A. from the University of California, Berkeley, a M.Sc. from the London School of Economics, and a Ph.D. from Harvard, all in economics. He is the author of more than thirty articles and is a member of the Econometric Society, ASA, and WFA.

Andrew Rudd ("Realistic Portfolio Optimization") is Assistant Professor of Finance and Operations Research at the Graduate School of Business and Public Administration, Cornell University. He received the B.S.C. (Honors) in Mathematics from the University of Sussex, England and the M.B.A. in finance, M.S. and Ph.D. in Operations Research, all from the University of California at Berkeley. His current research interests include the application of normative models to investment decision making.

Marshall Sarnat ("The Impact of Inflation upon Portfolio Selection") is Professor of Finance at the Jerusalem School of Business Administration, Hebrew University and Senior Research Fellow at the International Institute of Management, Berlin. He has served as visiting professor at New York University, University of California, Berkeley and the University of Toronto. He received his Ph.D. in finance and M.B.A. from Northwestern University, and an A.B. in economics from Hebrew University. He is the author or co-author of eight books and 50 journal articles. His most recent books are *Inflation and Capital Markets* and *Capital Investment and Financial Decisions.*

Robert A. Schwartz ("On the Existence of Serial Correlation in an Efficient Securities Market") is Professor of Economics at the Graduate School of Business Administration, New York University. His papers have dealt with various aspects of microeconomic theory, corporate finance, and investments. Currently, his research is largely focused on securities markets microstructure and architecture.

Suresh P. Sethi ("Optimal Dynamic Consumption and Portfolio Planning in a Welfare State") was born in Ladnun, Rajasthan, India, on July 8, 1945. He received the B.Tech. degree in mechanical engineering from the Indian Institute of Technology, Bombay, India, the M.B.A. degree from Washington State University, Pullman, and the M.S. and Ph.D. degrees in industrial administration and operations research from Carnegie-Mellon University in 1971. In 1972 he was a Visiting Research Associate at the Department of Operations Research at Stanford University, and during 1972–1973 he was a Visiting Assistant Professor at Rice University. Since 1973, he has been at the University of Toronto, where he is currently a Professor of Management Science in the Faculty of Management Studies. He visited Carnegie-Mellon during December 1977–July 1978. His papers have appeared in several journals, including *Operations*

Research, Journal of Optimization Theory and Applications, SIAM Review, Biometrics, Journal of Financial and Quantitative Analysis, and *Annals of Economic and Social Measurement.* Dr. Sethi is a member of The Institute of Management Sciences, Operations Research Society of America, and several other societies.

Richard C. Stapleton ("Multiperiod Equilibrium: Some Implications for Capital Budgeting") is National Westminster Bank Professor of Business Finance at Manchester Business School. He received his B.A. in Economics and Ph.D. in Finance from Sheffield University. He is Associate Editor of *Journal of Banking and Finance* and *Journal of Business Finance and Accounting.* His research interests are in Corporate Finance and Capital Market Theory.

Marti G. Subrahmanyam ("Multiperiod Equilibrium: Some Implications for Capital Budgeting") teaches at Indian Institute of Management, Ahmedabad and New York University. He received a B. Tech. in Mechanical Engineering from Indian Institute of Technology, Madras, a Post Graduate Diploma in Management from Indian Institute of Management, Ahmedabad and a Ph.D. in Finance and Economics from Massachusetts Institute of Technology. He is Associate Editor of *Journal of Banking and Finance* and *Management Science.* His research interests are in Corporate Finance, Capital Market Market Theory and Public Economics.

David K. Whitcomb ("On the Existence of the Serial Correlation in an Efficient Securities Market") recieved a B.S.B.A. Columbia University, Graduate Faculties. He has been Associate Professor of Finance at Rutgers University's Graduate School of Business Administration since 1975. Prior to that, he served on the faculties of the Graduate Schools of Business Administration of Baruch College (CUNY) and New York University, and as Economist at the Rand Corporation. He has written a book and about 20 articles in the areas of economic theory, security market microstructure and efficiency, and credit markets.

AUTHORS' ADDRESSES

Vijay S. Bawa
Bell Laboratories, Homdell, New Jersey 07733, U.S.A.

Menachem Brenner
Jerusalem School of Business Administration, Hewbrew University, Jerusalem, Israel

Abraham Brodt
Faculty of Administration, University of Ottawa, Ottawa, Ontario K1N 6N5, Canada

Willard T. Carleton
University of North Carolina, Chapel Hill, North Carolina 27514 U.S.A.

Lewis M. Chakrin
Bell Laboratories, Holmdel, New Jersey 07733, U.S.A.

Kalman J. Cohen
Graduate School of Business Administration, Duke University, Durham, North Carolina 27706, U.S.A.

Edwin J. Elton
Graduate School of Business Administration, New York University, New York, New York 10006, U.S.A.

George Frankfurter
Syracuse University, Syracuse, New York 13210, U.S.A.

M.J. Gordon
Faculty of Management Science, University of Toronto, Toronto, Ontario M5S 1A4, Canada

Martin J. Gruber
Graduate School of Business Administration, New York University, New York, New York 10006, U.S.A.

Nils H. Hakansson
University of California, Berkeley, California 94720, U.S.A.

B. Ingham
IBM of Canada, Toronto, Ontario, Canada

Haim Levy
Jerusalem School of Business Administration, Hebrew University, Jerusalem, Israel

Eric Lindenberg
Supervisor, Antitrust Studies American Telephone and Telegraph Company, 195, Broadway, New York, New York 10007, U.S.A.

Robert Litzenberger
Stanford University, Stanford, California 94305, U.S.A.

Steven F. Maier
Graduate School of Business Administration, Duke University, Durham, North Carolina 27706, U.S.A.

Manfred Padberg
Graduate School of Business Administration, New York University, New York, New York 10006, U.S.A.

Herbert Phillips
Temple University, Philadelphia, Pennsylvania 19122, U.S.A.

Krishna Ramaswany
Stanford University, Stanford, California 94305, U.S.A.

Scott F. Richard
Carnegie-Mellon University, Pittsburgh, Pennsylvania 15213, U.S.A.

Richard Roll
Graduate School of Management, University of California, Los Angeles, California 90024, U.S.A.

Barr Rosenberg
Schools of Business Administration, University of California, Berkeley, California 94720, U.S.A.

Andrew Rudd
Graduate School of Business and Public Administration, Cornell University, Ithaca, New York 14853, U.S.A.

Marshall Sarnat,
Jerusalem School of Business Administration, Hebrew University, Jerusalem, Israel

Robert A. Schwartz
Graduate School of Business Administration, New York University, New York, New York 10006, U.S.A.

S.P. Sethi
Faculty of Management Studies, University of Toronto, Toronto, Ontario M5S 1A4, Canada

R.C. Stapleton
New York University, New York 10006, U.S.A.

M.G. Subrahmanyam
Graduate School of Business Administration, New York University, 100, Trinity Place, New York, New York 10006, U.S.A.

David K. Whitcomb
Graduate School of Business Administration, Rutgers University, New Brunswick, New Jersey 08903, U.S.A.